This book fills a crucial missing piece in today's dialogue about international education in the United States – the value of community colleges. As we witness a fundamental shift in higher education due to the COVID-19 pandemic, the global potential for community college education is immense. For ESL professionals, the book also brings to life student experiences, including their successes and challenges with language learning. A must read for community college international education and ESL educators.

–**Vinicio J. López,**
Dean, Mission Campus/PDSO,
City College of San Francisco, USA

America's community colleges have become attractive options for international students for several reasons. They are the largest single segment of American higher education; they enroll a diverse student body; they are affordable; they provide curricula that are focused on skill building; and they offer a pathway to a baccalaureate or higher degree. International students also contribute significantly to the community colleges they attend, both financially and through their interactions with American students. The knowledgeable authors of *International Students at US Community Colleges: Opportunities, Challenges, and Successes* provide a valuable resource for college leaders who are interested in internationalizing their campuses and serving their international students.

–**George R. Boggs,**
Superintendent/President Emeritus, Palomar College,
President and CEO Emeritus, American Association of
Community Colleges, USA

From their inception, community colleges have played a critical role in furthering our nation's historic mission of educating for democracy. This book offers invaluable insights into how faculty and administrators can fulfill a 21st-century equity mandate by ensuring community colleges are places of welcome and belonging for international students, while positioning this growing student population for success in a global knowledge economy.

–**Lynn Pasquerella,**
President, Association of American Colleges and
Universities, USA

Malveaux and Bista bring together on and off-campus professionals invested in international students at community colleges. Their perspectives showcase strategies and challenges students face in diverse US and Canadian community colleges and advance the way international student experiences are framed in light of transfer and immigration policies, social justice, stress, and other key issues. This text will be useful to administrators, teachers, and international students, alike.

–**Marilyn Amey,**
Professor, Department of Educational Administration,
Michigan State University, USA

This is a must-read for community college leaders, faculty, and students who are advocating for their international footprints as this book offers an overview of international initiatives and its advantages to our students and faculty members.

–**Terry O'Banion,**
Senior Professor of Practice, Kansas State University and
President Emeritus, League for Innovation in the
Community College, USA

In *International Students at US Community Colleges: Opportunities, Challenges, and Successes,* the editors hit upon the real crux of what keeps international education from reaching its much-needed full potential: issues of access and mobility. Just as the COVID-19 pandemic laid bare the fragility and inequalities of education, the related closing of borders laid equally bare international education and exposed significant barriers hiding in plain sight. The editors' call – and thought-provoking action plan – to "provide broader access and opportunity for student mobility at an accelerated pace," is not only timely but a signpost to a better world.

–**James E. Callaghan,**
Assistant Vice-President for International Education and
Director of the International Education Center,
Georgia College & State University, USA

This timely book speaks directly to how to rebuild study abroad to make it more accessible, equitable, and aligned with inclusive social and economic mobility outcomes. Informed by the diverse perspectives of authors who have worked in a variety of national, cultural and institutional contexts, this book points to a way forward for a field that needs bold thinking and fresh ideas to guide it into the future. This is a must read for all involved with developing, managing and assessing study abroad programming.

–**Brian Whalen**
Executive Director, American International Recruitment Council;
University at Albany, USA

International student advisers, administrators, and higher education leaders can celebrate *International Students at US Community Colleges: Opportunities, Challenges, and Successes*, a new, essential resource for understanding the policies and trials; successes and impacts; and rightful voice of international students in the American and global community college system of higher education. This timely work brings needed scholarly erudition amidst record declining enrollment numbers triggered by global campus closures caused by the Covid-19 pandemic. This book's trailblazing research shows that US community colleges are the right model to lead in advancements with American higher education through evolving curriculum and workforce approaches for catapulting international, and higher education students on a whole, to new heights of success for the future.

–**Henry Stoever,**
President and CEO, The Association of Governing Boards of Universities and Colleges, USA

Malveaux and Bista have highlighted what makes International students in community colleges successful as higher education competitors. Articles on physical and cultural support systems, on the concepts of promotion and diversity and the potential of oppression, and on issues arising from the global pandemic are included in this much needed new text on international students.Theories of social justice and cultural integration concepts undergird the research foci.

–**Rosemary Gillett-Karam,**
Associate Professor, Morgan State University; Former President of Louisburg College, Louisburg, USA

From the pandemic to global social justice, this collection of essays provides engaging, insightful, and courageous dialogues that bring to surface the challenges international education faces during the unprecedented time, while providing practical approaches to best support international students. The most significant impact of this collection is its emphasis on the key roles Community Colleges play in advancing international education in North America. The evidence-based studies presented in this volume bring the much-deserved attention to the Community College system, that is at the core of diversity, equity, and inclusiveness efforts across the US and Canadian campuses. It's a must-read for Community College faculty and administrators.

–**Jia-Yi Cheng-Levine,**
Dean, International Affairs & Global Engagement, College of the Canyons, USA

The essays in this collection lay bare the stark challenges facing US higher education in the wake of decreased international student enrollments, the global pandemic, and a range of restrictions, including prohibitive visa processes, increasingly high tuition costs, and a political climate that has left many international students feeling "unwelcome." Despite this bleak outlook, the editors and the authors highlight the successes of international students and internationalization efforts at community colleges as inventive pathways forward in the post-pandemic global landscape. *International Students at US Community Colleges: Opportunities, Challenges, and Successes* will be of special interest and great value to higher education thought leaders among international education administrators, SIOs, international student advisors, faculty, researchers, and study abroad coordinators for its cogent presentation and analysis of the current state of the field.

–**Richard F. Johnson,**
Director, Office of International Education,
Harper College, Palatine, IL, USA

Malveaux and Bista have provided us with a comprehensive portrait of international students at community colleges in the US and Canada. This book will significantly contribute to a better understanding of international students' experiences, challenges, and opportunities for a wide array of audiences.

–**Yi Leaf Zhang,**
Associate Professor,
The University of Texas at Arlington, USA

International Students at US Community Colleges: Opportunities, Challenges, and Successes, provides important and overdue recognition to the research and understanding concerning the growing population of international students at the nation's community colleges. A vital contribution to the research on the most diverse and inclusive sector of higher education.

–**Larry Galizio,**
President/CEO,
Community College League of California, USA

Given the dearth of literature on international education at community colleges, this book is a much-needed resource, providing invaluable information and insights from practitioners and other relevant sources. As international educators emerge from what has been an extremely challenging landscape these past few years, it could not have come at a better time!

–**Samira Pardanani,**
Executive Director, International Education,
Shoreline Community College, USA

International Students at US Community Colleges: Opportunities, Challenges, and Successes is a timely practical and intellectual guide for international educators at community colleges seeking to navigate the challenges of the past few years and support international students on their campus. Look no further for help in understanding how we move forward!

–**Stephanie M. Kelly,**
Executive Director,
Community Colleges for International Development,
USA

International Students at US Community Colleges

This volume documents the experiences of international students and recent international initiatives at US community colleges to better understand how to support and nurture students' potential. Offering a range of case studies, empirical and conceptual chapters, the collection showcases the unique curricula and diverse opportunities for career development that colleges can offer international students.

International Students at US Community Colleges addresses issues of student access, enrolment barriers, college choice, and challenges relating to integration in academic and professional networks. Ultimately, the book unpacks institutional factors which inhibit or promote the success of international students at US community colleges to inform faculty, student affairs, administration, and institutional policy. With international students' declining enrollment, this book considers the measures being taken by community college officials to bring continued access and equity to international students.

Offering insights from a range of international scholars as well as on-the-ground case studies, this text will benefit researchers, academics, and educators with an interest in multicultural education, international and comparative education, and higher education management. Those specifically interested in educational policy and the sociology of education will also benefit from this book.

Gregory F. Malveaux is Professor in the Department of English and Literature and is the College-wide Coordinator of Study Abroad and International Education at Montgomery College, Maryland, USA.

Krishna Bista is Professor in the Department of Advanced Studies, Leadership and Policy at Morgan State University, Maryland, USA.

Routledge Studies in Global Student Mobility
Series Editors: Krishna Bista and Christopher Glass

Routledge Studies in Global Student Mobility offers a scholarly forum for original and innovative research which explores, explains, and increases understanding of issues and opportunities relating to international student mobility in K-12, higher education, and beyond. Consisting in peer-reviewed authored and edited volumes, the series advances theoretical understanding and identifies best practices for educators and professionals involved in study abroad.

As an interdisciplinary scholarly venue, the series showcases new ideas and fresh perspectives relating to international student mobility, study abroad, exchange programs, student affairs from the US and around the world, and from a wide range of academic fields, including student affairs, international education, and cultural studies.

This series is produced in collaboration with the CIES SIG Study Abroad & International Students, STAR Scholars Network, and Open Journals in Education (OJED).

Books in this series include:

Critical Perspectives on Equity and Social Mobility in Study Abroad
Interrogating Issues of Unequal Access and Outcomes
Edited by Chris R. Glass and Peggy Gesing

The Experiences of International Faculty in Institutions of Higher Education
Enhancing Recruitment, Retention, and Integration of International Talent
Edited by Chris R. Glass, Krishna Bista, and Xi Lin

Online Teaching and Learning in Higher Education during COVID-19
International Perspectives and Experiences
Edited by Roy Y. Chan, Krishna Bista, and Ryan M. Allen

For more information about this series, please visit: https://www.routledge.com/go/routledge-studies-in-global-student-mobility

International Students at US Community Colleges

Opportunities, Challenges, and Successes

Edited by
Gregory F. Malveaux and
Krishna Bista

NEW YORK AND LONDON

First published 2022
by Routledge
605 Third Avenue, New York, NY 10158

and by Routledge
2 Park Square, Milton Park, Abingdon, Oxon, OX14 4RN

*Routledge is an imprint of the Taylor & Francis Group, an
informa business*

© 2022 selection and editorial matter, Gregory F. Malveaux and
Krishna Bista; individual chapters, the contributors

The right of Gregory F. Malveaux and Krishna Bista to be
identified as the authors of the editorial material, and of the
authors for their individual chapters, has been asserted in
accordance with sections 77 and 78 of the Copyright, Designs
and Patents Act 1988.

All rights reserved. No part of this book may be reprinted
or reproduced or utilised in any form or by any electronic,
mechanical, or other means, now known or hereafter invented,
including photocopying and recording, or in any information
storage or retrieval system, without permission in writing from
the publishers.

Trademark notice: Product or corporate names may be
trademarks or registered trademarks, and are used only for
identification and explanation without intent to infringe.

Library of Congress Cataloging-in-Publication Data
A catalog record for this title has been requested

ISBN: 978-0-367-64064-4 (hbk)
ISBN: 978-0-367-64070-5 (pbk)
ISBN: 978-1-003-12197-8 (ebk)

Typeset in Sabon
by KnowledgeWorks Global Ltd.

Contents

List of Figures	xiv
List of Tables	xv
About the Editors	xvii
Foreword by Linda Serra Hagedorn	xviii
Acknowledgments	xx

PART I
Reimagining International Student Mobility in Community Colleges   1

1   Reimagining the Field: International Students in American Community Colleges   3
GREGORY F. MALVEAUX AND KRISHNA BISTA

2   Community College International Student Research: A Critical Time Series Analysis   15
ROSALIND LATINER RABY

3   Characteristics and Patterns of International Students at Community Colleges: Lessons from the *Open Doors* Data   37
JULIE BAER

4   International Students at Canadian Community Colleges: Origins, Evolution, and Current Trends   55
OLEG LEGUSOV AND HAYFA F. JAFAR

5   Community College Finances and International Student Enrollment   71
JI YEON BAE AND MANUEL S. GONZÁLEZ CANCHÉ

xii *Contents*

PART II
Understanding Support System and Challenges of International Students at Community Colleges 87

6 International Students' Career Development Preparation at the American Community College 89

HANNAH RAPP, YI-JUNG WU, RAN LIU, AND XIAOLI JING

7 Latinx ESL Students' Successful English Language Transition at Community Colleges 104

DuEWA M. FRAZIER

8 Assessing Acculturative Stress of International Students at a US Community College 118

HARDAYE R. HANSEN, YULIYA SHNEYDERMAN, GLORIA S. McNAMARA, AND LISA GRACE

9 Frontline Advising for International Students at American Community Colleges: Understanding the Challenges and Policy Issues during the COVID-19 Crisis 133

GREGORY F. MALVEAUX AND MARLON VALLEJO

PART III
Promoting Diversity and International Education at Community Colleges 153

10 Community College as a Gateway to Baccalaureate Success for International Students 155

VERONIKA ROZHENKOVA AND ELIZABETH S. PARK

11 From Oppression to Global Social Justice: Practitioners' Responsibility to International Students in the US Community College 173

TIFFANY VIGGIANO, EVELYN VÁZQUEZ, AND ARIADNA I. LÓPEZ DAMIÁN

12 International Education and the Global Pandemic in the Community College: Reflections and Best Practices 187

MARC THOMAS

13 Trends in International Student Enrollments in Canadian Community Colleges 203

ELIZABETH BUCKNER, SARAH MORALES, TAIYA BROWN, AND SCOTT CLERK

Contents xiii

14 Global Begins from Local: International Students and International Programs at Historically Black Community Colleges and Tribal Community Colleges 215

KRISHNA BISTA

15 Epilogue: Voices and Perspectives on International Student Mobility: Where Are Community Colleges? 228

KRISHNA BISTA AND GREGORY F. MALVEAUX

Index 240

List of Figures

2.1	Community College International Student Cartography	18
3.1	International Students at Community Colleges, 1970/1971–2019/2020	38
3.2	International Students at Community Colleges as a Percent of Total International Students, 1999/2000–2019/2020	39
3.3	International Students at Community Colleges by Institutional Type, 2019/2020	40
3.4	International Students at Community Colleges as a Percent of Total International Students by Selected States, 2019/2020	42
3.5	Top Ten Places of Origin of International Students at Community Colleges, 2019/2020	43
3.6	Top Six Places of Origin for International Students at Community Colleges, 2005/2006–2019/2020	44
3.7	Gender of International Students at Community Colleges and International Undergraduates at All Institution Types, 2019/2020 and Gender of U.S. Students at Community Colleges, 2015/2016 (U.S. Department of Education, 2018a)	46
3.8	*Open Doors* Data Usage of Carnegie Classifications	52
4.1	International Postsecondary Students in Canada	62
5.1	Line Trend Plot of Foreign Student Enrollment	80
5.2	Trends in Fiscal Variables	81
11.1	Reproduction of Hegemony and Oppressive Conditions	176

List of Tables

2.1	Type of Publications over Time	21
2.2	Frequency of Published Authors over Time	22
2.3	Authorship over Time	22
2.4	Geographical Institutional Connections	23
2.5	Primary Topics Found in Journal and Dissertation Publications	24
2.6	Most Mentioned Keywords over Time	25
2.7	Most Mentioned Themes Overtime	27
3.1	Top 25 Community Colleges Hosting International Students, 2019/2020	41
3.2	Fields of Study of International Students at Community Colleges and Undergraduates and All Institutions, 2019/2020 and Fields of Study of US Students at Community Colleges, 2015/2016 (US Department of Education, 2018d)	49
4.1	International College Students by Province, 2017–2018	59
5.1	Descriptive Statistics	77
5.2	Regression Results	79
7.1	Participant Information	108
8.1	Regression Results (Showing Significant Associations Only)	125
10.1	Demographic Breakdown by Transfer and Traditional International Students	162
10.2	Visa Status by Transfer and Traditional International Students	163
10.3	Switch Out Patterns by Initial Major among Transfer and Traditional International Students, Row Percentages	164
10.4	Proportion of International Students that Graduated within Each Time Frame	167
12.1	Crosswalk between Chickering's Principles and Tran's International Student Framework	197

xvi *List of Tables*

13.1	International Students as a Percentage of Total Enrollments, by Year and Sector	207
13.2	Enrollments of International Students from India, by Year and Sector	208
13.3	International Students in the College Sector, by Province (2018)	209
14.1	Selected 2-Year Black Community Colleges and Online Information for International Students	217
14.2	Selected 2-Year Tribal Community Colleges and Online Information for International Students	223

About the Editors

Gregory F. Malveaux, PhD, is a Professor in the Department of English and Literature and has been the College-wide Coordinator of Study Abroad and International Education at Montgomery College, Maryland. His previous books include *Study Abroad Opportunities for Community College Students and Strategies for Global Learning,* w/Raby (IGI Global, 2019); and *Look Before Leaping: Risks, Liabilities, and Repair of Study Abroad in Higher Education* (Rowman & Littlefield, 2016).

Krishna Bista, EdD, is a Professor of Higher Education in the Department of Advanced Studies, Leadership and Policy at Morgan State University, Maryland. Dr. Bista is the founding editor of the *Journal of International Students,* a quarterly publication in international education. He is also the founding chair of the Study Abroad and International Students SIG at the Comparative and International Education Society. His latest books are *Inequalities in Study Abroad and Student Mobility,* w/Kommers, (Routledge, 2021), *Higher Education in Nepal,* w/Sharma and Raby (Routledge, 2020), and *Global Perspectives on International Experiences in Higher Education* (Routledge, 2019).

Foreword

Although my research agenda has always included the unlikely mix of community colleges and international students, I have long lamented the dearth of research and information aimed at the intersection of these topics. I welcome and invite you to *International Students at US Community Colleges: Opportunities, Challenges, and Successes* as a most welcomed resource to cover the overlooked landscape.

The research literature has systematically ignored international community college students because US community colleges were never designed for international students. Rather, they were created to meet the business and economic needs of their local geographic areas and the Americans who abide there.

This book boldly states the truth; International students continue to increasingly attend US community colleges; bringing with them many advantages and resources not only to themselves but also for their campuses and the American students who they study alongside them.

Divided into three parts, this book examines the landscape of issues affecting international students and the community colleges they attend. Part I provides the ideal introduction beginning in Chapter 1, with Malveaux and Bista's general overview of the topic. Using sophisticated time-series analyses, Raby in Chapter 2 argues that the extant research on the topic has been marginalized. Baer, in Chapter 3 examines the respected Institute of International Education's Open Doors data source to provide a profile of international students. We then head north where Legusov and Jafar provide information on this topic within Canada. The final chapter in Part I, by Bae and Gonzalez Canche, examines the important topic of institutional finance.

The chapters in Part II of the book are dedicated to understanding the support and challenges that international students meet. From career development (Chapter 6 by Wu et al.) to acculturative stress (Chapter 8 by Hansen et al.), we learn how international students must adapt to these institutions that were never designed for their attendance. However, in Chapter 9, Malveaux and Vallejo address the frontline of student services, advisors, and how they can assist international students

Foreword xix

to be successful. Also, in this section, Frazier (Chapter 7) uses Hispanic students to address language transition, and how colleges can support international students.

In Part III, the important issue of diversity becomes the focus. At the time of publication, 2021, the United States is embroiled in a crisis of issues including severe political unrest, division, travel bans, pockets of xenophobia, as well as a Covid-19 pandemic. Suitably, Chapter 11 by Viggiano lays bare the oppressive conditions that international community college students may face. While Thomas, in Chapter 12, studies the global pandemic and its effects. Park and Rozhenkova examine the important path through transfer from community colleges to US universities for international students. Finally, Buckner et al., bring us back north to Canada to finish the book with a critical look at internationalizations strategy and discourse.

Welcome to this volume dedicated to international students who **chose** to attend one of the American community colleges. Community colleges can and do provide quality education worthy of traveling across the globe to receive.

Linda Serra Hagedorn, PhD
Professor Emeritus—Iowa State University

Acknowledgments

We are most grateful to Elsbeth Wright, our acquisitions editor at Routledge Publishing for her encouragement, coordination, and support through the project. Special thanks to Dr. Chris Glass and colleagues in the *Routledge Student Mobility Series* as well as at the STAR Scholars Network. We also appreciate the support of colleagues whom we worked with over the years at the Open Journals in Education, a consortium of the professional journals, the Comparative and International Education Society's Study Abroad and International Students SIG, and the *Journal of International Students*.

We would also like to acknowledge the help of all the scholars who were involved in this project and, more specifically, to the authors and reviewers that took part in the review process. Without their support, this book would not have become a reality. At Morgan State University, I, Dr. Krishna Bista, would like to thank my colleagues from the Community College Leadership Program including Dr. Gaulee, Dr. Parsons, Dr. Davis, Dr. Dorsey, Dr. Gillett-Karam, Dr. Hollis, Dr. Linck, Dr. Roberts, Dr. Said, and Prof. Hicks for their encouragement and support including graduate students and graduate assistants in the Department of Advanced Studies, Leadership, and Policy. At Montgomery College, I, Dr. Gregory Malveaux, appreciate the shared experiences of International student advisers at community colleges throughout the country, including my colleague, Heidi Russell-Kalkofen.

Special thanks to the following reviewers who assisted us in reviewing manuscripts received for this book, *International Students at US Community Colleges: Opportunities, Challenges, and Successes*. It could not be possible to finalize the selected chapters without their evaluations and constructive feedback.

The time, support, and love provided by our families to take on the joyous rigors involved with this book project are not forgotten. Thank you.

Acknowledgments xxi

Chapter Reviewers: Special thanks to all of the following reviewers who contributed quality reviews to improve the chapters considered in this book.

Abid Yahya | Benjamin H. Nam | Crystal London | Elizabeth Park | Gregory H. Maddox | Hannah Rapp | Kim Manturuk | Hannah Covert | Ran Liu | Elizabeth Buckner | Yi-Jung Wu | Veronica Rozhenkova | Scott Cleark | Rita Berger | Ruchi Permvattana

We would like to thank the following colleagues for their feedback on the early draft of this book as well for their endorsements:

- *Brian Whalen*, PhD., Executive Director, American International Recruitment Council; International Education Leadership Fellow, University at Albany, USA
- *George R. Boggs*, PhD., Superintendent/President Emeritus, Palomar College, President and CEO Emeritus, American Association of Community Colleges, USA
- *Henry Stoever*, President and CEO, The Association of Governing Boards of Universities and Colleges, USA
- *James E. Callaghan*, PhD., Assistant Vice-President for International Education and Director of the International Education Center, Georgia College & State University, USA
- *Jia-Yi Cheng-Levine,* PhD., Dean, International Affairs & Global Engagement, College of the Canyons, USA
- *Lynn Pasquerella*, PhD, President, Association of American Colleges and Universities, USA
- *Marilyn Amey*, Professor, Department of Educational Administration, Michigan State University, USA
- *Richard F. Johnson,* PhD, Director, Office of International Education, Harper College, Palatine, IL, USA
- *Rosemary Gillett-Karam*, PhD, Associate Professor, Morgan State University; Former President of Louisburg College, Louisburg, USA
- *Terry O'Banion*, Senior Professor of Practice, Kansas State University and President Emeritus, League for Innovation in the Community College, USA
- *Vinicio J. López*, EdD, Dean, Mission Campus/PDSO, City College of San Francisco, USA

Part I

Reimagining International Student Mobility in Community Colleges

1 Reimagining the Field

International Students in American Community Colleges

Gregory F. Malveaux and Krishna Bista

Introduction

American community colleges are special institutions of higher education with about 13 million students studying in a wide range of "open enrollment" programs and disciplines. In the last few decades, these innovative institutions have rapidly transformed their educational programs and international exposure by increasing their study abroad programs, faculty, student exchange programs, international student enrollments, and institutional agreements in the United States and beyond (Raby & Valeau, 2016). These institutions provide workforce education and college transfer academic programs, including certificates, diplomas, and associate degrees. Among the 1,462 American community colleges, several contain large enrollment such as 174,000 students at Miami Dade College in Florida; 90,000 at Lone Star College in Texas; 76,000 at Northern Virginia Community College in Virginia; 67,258 at Broward College in Florida; and 63,015 at Houston Community College in Texas (AACC, 2020). With their open enrollment processes, which means that students with a high school diploma or general education diploma (GED) can enroll in courses, English as a Second Language (ESL) programs, affordable fee structure, and workforce focused certificates and degree programs; today American community colleges are global institutions as their faculty, staff, and students represent many diverse languages, countries, cultures, and educational courses (Bista, 2016; Hagedorn, 2020). Not only domestic students but international students choose to pursue their education in community colleges to advance their career paths, to engage in lifelong education, and/or to transfer to a four-year institution. This chapter outlines international student trends at American community colleges and their contribution to campus diversity, internationalization initiatives, and national revenues in the United States. It also discusses the current and future educational approaches that directly impact international students at American community colleges.

4 Gregory F. Malveaux and Krishna Bista

American community colleges provide low-cost, workforce/technical, and lower-division college instruction particularly to support and prepare nontraditional students of color, veterans, working students, students with low socio-economic status, student-parents, individuals with circumstances preventing them to attend four-year institutions, or those who choose to forgo attending a four-year college or university in a globally competitive world (Hagedorn, 2020; Levin, 2017). Of 1,462 community colleges, 941 are public, 148 private, and 32 tribal (US Department of Education, 2020). There are a number of Historically Black Colleges and Universities (HBCU) community colleges (two-year institutions) with locations in Alabama (Bishop State Community College), Mississippi (Coahoma Community College), Washington DC (University of the District of Columbia Community College), South Carolina (Denmark Technical College), Arkansas (Shorter College), Texas (Southwestern Christian College), and Alabama (Trenholm State Community College) which are popular for the HBCU experience. Community college tuition is free in some states including Delaware, Mississippi, Missouri, Indiana, Louisiana, and Tennessee. Because of the recent declines in enrollment patterns across the country in the last few decades, American community colleges started actively attracting and recruiting more international students. In the 2017–2018 academic year, 1,094,792 international students in all types of institutions contributed more than $39 billion to the US economy and have supported in excess of 455,000 jobs (NAFSA, 2019). At least 96,562 of them are enrolled at American community colleges. Again, community colleges are popular destinations for many international students and their families to pursue overseas education because of the low tuition costs and a wide range of technical and vocational degrees and certificates of interest. Some international students consider community colleges as an easy pathway to universities because of the open admission processes and ESL support. This is especially germane because the English language proficiency requirement for admissions is sought before pursuing academic programs (Hagedorn, 2020).

Globally, colleges and universities have had to evolve, implementing remote or virtual classroom instruction in response to restrictions provoked by the COVID-19 pandemic; this has driven the approach for an alternative, online educational curricula, as well as new innovative technological possibilities for learning. In the context of the pandemic, online learning software, including Mango, Collaborative Online International Learning (COIL), and other course management platforms (e.g. Blackboard, Canvas, Moodle), have been embraced by community college faculty and staff in an effort to increase student global awareness to their campuses. In addition, many international students take classes in different time zones because they were unable to return to their campuses, which were closed as a precautionary measure in response to the pandemic. Faculty are incorporating Mango content, accessing instructor guides, adding teacher lesson plans, and providing student workbooks to sync with curricula. Also, the emergence of COIL has helped community college leaders to meet the important objective to "encourage and support the development of courses incorporating international collaborations which have a significant online component" (SUNY COIL Center, 2020). For example, Tompkins-Cortland Community College, a small (3,000 enrollment), rural college in upstate New York, has become a national model for using virtual technologies to expand academic programs for both domestic and international students, in collaboration with SUNY COIL.

International Student Trends and Impacts in the US Community College System

It is well documented that international student enrollment, for decades, has been prevalent within the community college sector of higher education. According to the Institute of International Education (IIE), around 94,562 international students studied at American community colleges during the 2017–2018 academic year which decreased to 79,187 in 2019/2020 (Open Doors, 2020). Although international students account for little more than 1 percent of the entire community college population, almost 10 percent of the nearly 1.1 million international students in the United States study at community colleges; when graduate students are excluded from the total number, community college students make up approximately 17 percent of all international undergraduates (West, 2018). The most popular states for international student attendance are California, Florida, New York, Texas, and Washington (Open Doors, 2020). The largest number of students who study in American higher education are from China and India; 33.7 percent come from China and 18.4 percent come from India (Open Doors, 2020).

Economic and Financial Influence

American colleges and universities immensely benefit, economically, from the enrollment of international students. In fact, for every 200 international students enrolled, a college can expect as much as $1.2 million in tuition (Lu, 2020). Throughout the 2018/2019 school year, international students contributed $41 billion to the US economy; this measure of economic value is based on student tuition and living expense data (Open Doors, 2020). By drawing from a pool of the world's most talented, the US economy is fueled with great advancements and gains. An impressive 23 percent of billion-dollar startup companies in the United States were founded or co-founded by an international student (Lu, 2020). As Bista (2020) listed in his essay, about 25 percent of the most innovative American companies, such as Intel (Andy Grove, Hungary), eBay (Pierre Omidyar, France), Yahoo! (Jerry Yang, Taiwan), and Google (Sergey Brin, Russia), were started by former international students who graduated from American colleges and universities. Community college officials are well aware of the impacts and benefits that international students bring. For example, the vice president of international programs at Green River Community College in Washington, Wendy Lee Stewart, disclosed that 10 percent of the college's current local and state operating budget is funded by international tuition revenue (Gobel, 2012). International student tuition helps fund the college's general operations, as well as its capital projects (Gobel, 2012). In this national context, for instance, Miami Dade Community College—graduates more Hispanic and African American students than any other institutions—offers a unique study abroad program called "Diasporic Knowledge Remittance" to its students. The program allows its students to engage with their heritage countries and cultures in the Caribbean and Latin America, particularly within the health-related field. To strengthen STEM education and workforce needs, Madison Area Technical College's Community College Sustainable Development Network has offered specialized study abroad programs for faculty members from 24 US community colleges in Central America and beyond. As the American Association of Community Colleges (2020) relates, community colleges are "essential and uniquely situated to ensure America's future economic prosperity" (p. 1).

Enrollment Trends and Evolving Community Colleges

During the 2018/2019 academic year, new international student enrollment was down to 269,383; and since 2001, the share of international students in America has fallen from 28 to 21 percent (Lu, 2020). Community college officials are taking measures to offset lower enrollment numbers by offering courses in foreign countries. For example, enrollment at Hudson Valley Community College (HVCC) in upstate New York decreased by nearly 3,000 students from the previous year with 11,000 enrolled in 2010 (Smith, 2019). The college's administrators started offering programs and courses to students in Trinidad and Costa Rica. Such programs are mutually beneficial for both sides involved; the desire is to help the countries build up the skills and English proficiency of their workforce, and the countries help the US colleges grow their student bodies (Smith, 2019). Pima Community College has started the "Mexico Project" to expand educational programs for its students in Mexico. Other community colleges have started similar programs; for example, Broward College in Florida (total enrollment 67,000) has developed several education centers in Ecuador, Peru, Spain, Sri Lanka, and Vietnam to increase enrollment by bringing the community college to the students' home region; in addition, the college provides study abroad programs in Spain, Germany, Italy, England, and India that allow students to complete coursework for college credits and gain cross-cultural experiences. Nearly 9,000 international students at Broward's international centers pursue American associate degrees without leaving their home countries.

Despite bringing new challenges and global chaos, the pandemic has helped college leaders and faculty explore the potential of online teaching and virtual communication. They have attempted to successfully run the classes, communicate with their students, and effectively operate despite many major impediments. Students and faculty across the institutions of higher education became aware of global issues, programs, and initiatives for a common goal and stronger community during the pandemic. The coronavirus has severely impacted broader internationalization efforts at community colleges including the US Fulbright Program, exchange programs, branch campuses, and other professional development programs for community college faculty and students.

Pandemic and Immigration Difficulties

Because of the COVID-19 pandemic, similar to their counterpart four-year institutions, community colleges have been forced to close their campuses and move classes online to remote learning. The National Student Clearinghouse data indicated that college enrollment has decreased by 11.2 percent among international students, 7.7 percent among Native American students, and 6.3 percent among both Black and White students which has been the hardest hit to all community colleges (Hess, 2020). Many international students were unable to arrive in the United States because American embassies and consulates were not conducting visa interviews and our borders were still mostly closed. At the beginning of the pandemic, Daiya (2020, para 2) writes, "as their American peers swiftly left campus for homes across the country, many of these international students, along with Deferred Action for Childhood Arrivals (DACA) students, have become newly and swiftly invisible for their college administrators. Many campuses allowed their international students already living in the dorms to remain there safely when domestic students were sent home midsemester."

With being isolated and far from home, there have been several strict immigration changes for international students under the Trump administration (2016–2020) including the barring of students from travel to predominantly Muslim countries, strict limits placed on a program completion timeline, obstructing online class enrollment, and hindering post-study work permits or eligibility for H1B work visas (Fischer, 2020a; Fischer, 2020b;). President Trump's punitive immigration policies, according to Wallace and Zepeda-Millán (2020), were deeply linked to citizens who "feel culturally threatened by" growing immigrants and "who fear a future in which the United States will be a majority-minority country." Trump's harsh immigration policies drew world-wide attention, creating negativism and fear of deportation not only for current international students who were currently studying at American colleges and universities, but also for those prospective students who were dreaming of an American education. Fischer (2020) writes in the *Chronicle of Higher Education*,

> Isolation isn't the only issue facing international students. The first cases of COVID-19 were in the Chinese city of Wuhan, leading to a rise in anti-Asian sentiment worldwide. The group Stop AAPI Hate has tracked more than 2,500 reports of anti-Asian discrimination nationwide since the start of the pandemic, while an analysis of Twitter and other online message boards has shown a surge in Sinophobic slurs.

The Trump administration imposed new restrictions on asylum seekers, attacked the diversity visa program, imposed a "wealth test" for immigrants with legal status, created obstacles with Optional Practical Training (OPT) and H1B visa workers, slowed applications for green cards, attacked DACA and temporary protected status, increased the cost of immigration fees and services, changed the structure of student and exchange visitor visa, imposed restrictions to online and remote learning, and limited other policies which directly and indirectly impacted international students and their families (Ibe, 2020).

Shifting Characteristics with Community Colleges and Their Global Expansion

International students have become increasingly aware of community colleges as a unique and valuable resource for higher education. These host colleges have been evolving to improve campus offerings for international students. Senior director of international enrollment management and international student and scholar services at NAFSA Educators, Joann Ng Hartmann, mirrors the sentiment that there is both an increased awareness of the US community college system abroad, and colleges have become more sophisticated in their recruitment (West, 2018).

American community colleges are under constant pressure to produce globally competitive workforce-ready graduates with different associate degrees and certificates who can interact and work easily in a culturally diverse world (Raby & Valeau, 2016). The leaders of these community colleges, including presidents, provosts, and deans, have already noticed the power of international education, as well as the significant positive impacts of having international students on their campuses. These international students serve as ambassadors for their own countries, and in turn, represent US colleges. After graduating, they bring back to their home country cross-cultural competence and diversity, as well as new trades and skills for workforce development.

Along with diverse student enrollment in American community colleges, the same holds true for faculty and staff at these colleges. Foreign-born faculty and staff members working at community colleges have been gradually increasing in the last three decades (Bista, 2016). Earlier studies suggest this particular faculty/staff population contributes to foster global and international perspectives in academic discourses and teaching or developing international programs for all students (Bista, 2016; Kisker, 2019; Mamiseishvili, 2011). Currently, there is a large portion of foreign-born faculty members, many of them are former international students, teaching in the community colleges (Bista, 2020).

College leadership is essential to develop the programs and initiatives that expand international student recruitment, exchange programs for domestic students, and support resources for all students. The coronavirus pandemic has already resulted in a greater economic depression across the country, yet the international student population remains a strong component for bolstering enrollment and academic programs at American community colleges. As the pandemic has taught a big lesson to all, it is high time for all college presidents to seriously update their college mission statement to make references to globally informed citizens. Historically, it has been "infrequent for a community college to have a mission statement with language promoting global outreach" (Malveaux, 2019, p. 269). These institutions should include "a reference to serving international students" (Hagedorn, 2020, p. 2). As Hagedorn suggested, the financial benefits of having international students are quite high; for instance, Santa Monica College in California receives at least $105.60 million from international student enrollment as the college fee for international students is approximately eight times higher than the fee for in-state students.

The community college model has been globally embraced, and these schools are expanding overseas. For example, major community college growth resulted when Indira Gandhi's National Open University established a large community college system that included more than 540 colleges (Panwar, 2013). In addition, to gain workforce development, students from India pursue degrees from technical schools as opposed to the typical university. There are more than 3,200 polytechnics and equivalent technical institutions that can give vocational skills to millions of youths (Panwar, 2013). Canada is another example with a 125 community college system that is attracting a large international student population (Institutes in Canada, 2020). Canada is already recognized for its diversity and quality of education, and it is swiftly becoming an attractive destination for international students. The country offers expedited visa processing for qualified individuals, as well as a three-year work visa for graduates (Lu, 2020). Canada's first country-wide internationalization strategy which occurred in 2014 has targeted having 450,000 international students enrolled by 2022 (Foreign Affairs, Trade and Development Canada, 2013). Both India and Canada exemplify the ongoing expansion of community colleges on a global scale.

Overall, this book provides data, findings, and practical advice for international student Advisors, Principal Designated School Officials, International Education Directors, community college faculty and administrators, and parents of international students. The chapters chart the pathways, obstacles, program opportunities, higher education access, matriculation directions, and other important facets relating to international students at community colleges in the United States and around the world. Their enrollment at community colleges has grown over the decades, yet enrollment numbers, for the first time, have been on the decline for the last few years. This work, through various lenses, addresses the reason for both occurrences. It examines not only the path of these students at US community colleges, but also among community colleges on a global scale, with Canada serving as a model. In addition, the book explores the reasons why students from certain countries are flooding the US community college school system, with the greatest influx of students coming from India. New governmental policies and increased regulations for various types of international students, including F-1 visa holders, are provided to give these students' counselors and advocates tools for proper advising. Often COVID-19 impacts are in the backdrop of writings, and a couple of the chapters are exclusively dedicated to chronicling the community college response to the pandemic in 2020. The chapters reaffirm that international students choose community colleges for career and workforce development, but takes research further by examining the economic benefits that host institutions attain from high international student enrollment. The book dispels international student stereotypes, including the notion that they make up an economically privileged class. In addition, the publication history surrounding international students from 1950 to 2020 illuminates that such publications have existed for multiple decades and yet are marginalized in the field. With language being a major barrier for some of these students, the book examines the successful English language transition of Latinx ESL students who matriculated to college English. These institutions furnish international students with essential college access, degree completion, and workforce development. These foci, and many more, bring new theories and research findings that further enrich understanding of international students at community colleges, and best practices necessary to serve their needs.

Moving Forward

The importance of international education at American community colleges has been increasingly acknowledged in recent years as a foundation to "ensure a civil society in a nation of rapidly changing demographics, to transform everyday Americans into competent global citizens who can successfully navigate an increasingly interconnected world, and to provide American businesses with a globally competent—as well as globally competitive—workforce that can ensure the nation's future economic prosperity" (p. 1). International students and foreign investments have the potential to leverage the economic development of the rural areas and their community colleges as the rural areas experienced the largest growth of immigrant populations (AACC, 2020). For example, there are at least 26.8 million US immigrants who are 16 years or older. In the United States, the largest percentage of international students (19 percent of them are from China alone) are enrolled at community colleges, and California is the most popular destination for all international students.

There are certainly new challenges for American community colleges to strengthen international programs and campus internationalizations, during and post-COVID, due to the greater economic impact of closed campuses that forced remote teaching and learning. Therein, meanwhile, these institutions, similar to their four-year counterparts, have learned about the technological transformation and positive potential of distance and virtual learning. More than ever, community college officials are eager to explore and establish new exchange programs, international collaborations, and international student recruitment. International student enrollment is a multi-billion-dollar industry that brings a number of positive changes in socio-cultural diversity by enriching classroom practices, bilateral research, and publications. As editors of this book project, we strongly believe that American community colleges are very promising destinations for international students. These colleges are also rapidly expanding their overseas exchange programs for domestic students to study overseas. Once we are at the post-pandemic period, student mobility will be revived with an exceptional growth of two-way traffic with students leaving for study abroad and international students entering into American community colleges. Internationalization and international initiatives will remain integral to American community colleges and international students will aggressively transcend geographical boundaries to expand their professional fields. We are optimistic that community college senior leadership will put international students and study abroad programs as their top priority; develop systematic

12 Gregory F. Malveaux and Krishna Bista

recruitment plans in partnership with local and international four-year institutions; support services and resources for both domestic and international students; develop a globalized curriculum; and create campus internationalization strategies for inclusive campus communities.

References

American Association of Community Colleges [AACC]. (2020). The importance of global education. https://www.aacc.nche.edu/wp-content/uploads/2020/01/Importance-of-Global_Education_2020.pdf

All India Council for Technical Education. (2017). Community colleges. https://www.aicte-india.org/education/community-colleges

Bista, K. (2020). Let us stand with Julia! International students and immigrant workers in the United States. *Journal of International Students, 10*(3), v–viii. DOI: 10.32674/jis.v10i3.2401

Bista, K. (2016). Faculty international experience and internationalization efforts at community colleges in the United States. In R. L. Raby & E. J. Valeau (Eds.), *International education at community colleges* (pp. 23–37). Palgrave.

Daiya, K. (2020, June 16). The current plight of international students. *Inside Higher Ed.* https://www.insidehighered.com/views/2020/06/16/colleges-need-help-international-students-now-opinion

Foreign Affairs, Trade and Development Canada. (2013). Harnessing our knowledge advantage to drive innovation and prosperity. *Canada's International Education Strategy* (2014–2018).

Gobel, R. (2012, October 4). Why international students should consider community colleges. https://www.usnews.com/education/best-colleges/articles/2012/10/04/why-international-students-should-consider-community-colleges

Hagedorn, L. S. (2020). *International students in community colleges: An unplanned diversity*. American Council on Education.

Hess, A. (2020, October 1). College enrollment is down because of the pandemic. *CNBC.* https://www.cnbc.com/2020/10/01/how-the-coronavirus-pandemic-has-impacted-college-enrollment.html

Ibe, P. (2020, April 23). Trump's attacks on the legal immigration system explained. Retrieved from https://www.afsc.org/blogs/news-and-commentary/trumps-attacks-legal-immigration-system-explained

Institutes in Canada. (2020). Our Canada college list. http://www.institutesincanada.com/canadian-colleges/canada-college-list/

Fischer, K. (2020a, October 20). Where are most international students? https://www.chronicle.com/article/where-are-most-international-students-stranded-here-needing-colleges-help

Fischer, K. (2020b, October 21). DHS arrests international students https://www.chronicle.com/article/department-of-homeland-security-arrests-international-students-in-work-program-investigation?cid=gen_sign_in

Kisker, C. B. (2019). *Enabling faculty-led student success efforts at community colleges*. American Council on Education.

Levin, J. S. (2017). *Community colleges and new universities: Organizational change and stability*. Palgrave.

Lu, M. (2020, February 24). The impact of international students on the US economy. https://www.visualcapitalist.com/international-students-impact-u-s-economy/

Malveaux, G. F. (2019). How to survive and thrive as a community college consortium: A case study of the Maryland Community College International Education Consortium. *Study abroad opportunities for community college students and strategies for global learning*. IGI-Global.

Mamiseishvili, K. (2011). Academic and social integration and persistence of international students at US two-year institutions. *Community College Journal of Research and Practice, 36*(1), 15–27.

NAFSA. (2019). National Association of International Educator. *International students contribute $39 billion to the US economy.* https://www.nafsa.org/about/about-nafsa/new-nafsa-data-international-students-contribute-39-billion-us-economy

Open Doors. (2020). Home—annual release. *Institute of International Education.* http://opendoorsiie.wpengine.com/annual-release/

Panwar, B. S. (2013). The U.S. community college as a model for global higher education system. In N. Jha (Ed.), *In the U.S. community college model: Potential for applications in India* (pp. 14–16). Institute of International Education.

Raby, R. L., & Valeau, E. J. (2016). *Introduction. International education at community colleges* (1–6). Springer.

Smith, A. (2019). Community college expands internationally to grow enrollment. *Inside Higher Ed.* https://www.insidehighered.com/news/2019/05/08/community-colleges-go-international-enrollment

SUNY COIL Center. (2020). COIL Center: Collaborative Online International Learning. http://devcoil.suny.edu/page/brief-history-suny-coil-center

U.S. Department of Education. (2020). Community colleges facts at a glance. https://www2.ed.gov/about/offices/list/ovae/pi/cclo/ccfacts.html

Wallace, S. J., & Zepeda-Millán, C. (2020). *Walls, cages, and family separation: Race and immigration policy in the Trump era.* Cambridge University Press.

West, C. (2018). International students are keeping community colleges afloat. *Pacific Standard.* https://psmag.com/education/international-students-are-keeping-community-colleges-afloat

Author Bios

Gregory F. Malveaux, PhD, is a Professor in the Department of English and Literature and has been the College-wide Coordinator of Study Abroad and International Education at Montgomery College, Maryland. His previous books include: *Study Abroad Opportunities for Community College Students and Strategies for Global Learning,* w/Raby (IGI Global, 2019); and *Look Before Leaping: Risks, Liabilities, and Repair of Study Abroad in Higher Education* (Rowman & Littlefield, 2016).

Krishna Bista, EdD, is a Professor of Higher Education in the Department of Advanced Studies, Leadership and Policy at Morgan

State University, Maryland. Dr. Bista is the founding editor of the *Journal of International Students,* a quarterly publication in international education. He is also the founding chair of the Study Abroad and International Students SIG at the Comparative and International Education Society. His latest books are *Inequalities in Study Abroad and Student Mobility,* w/Kommers (Routledge, 2021), *Higher Education in Nepal,* w/Sharma and Raby (Routledge, 2020), and *Global Perspectives on International Experiences in Higher Education* (Routledge, 2019).

2 Community College International Student Research

A Critical Time Series Analysis

Rosalind Latiner Raby

Introduction

Almost every publication that discusses (United States) community college international students begins with the premise that there is a dearth of literature in the field. I have also been guilty of promoting such a view (Raby, 1993; Raby, 2012; Raby & Valeau, 2007). The reality, however, shows a much different picture. There is a deep and varied history of US community college international student research that defines a distinctive field of study, including 305 forms of scholarship published from 1950 to 2020. Although the book, *Community Colleges and Global Counterparts Worldwide* documented research on international student programs, this chapter focuses only on the ones in the United States It is important for practitioners and researchers to know about historical and current research because it enables them to understand of what has been done, shows that some dialogues have remained constant for over 70 years, and shows that other discourses are new and represent the times in which they are situated. This chapter unpacks this scholarship and is guided by three research questions: how are themes on community college international student research presented in higher education journals, chapters, dissertations, and other forms of publications?; what themes predominate in these publications?; and do these themes change over time?

This chapter uses a time series analysis to capture thematic changes, trends, and patterns in the literature over time. In that, knowledge is socially constructed and is influenced by political, historical, cultural, and economic factors. Time then becomes a significant influencer that denotes how knowledge is processed by key stakeholders. This includes a critical focus on who is publishing, when they are publishing, and what thematic discourses exist within the publications on community college international students.

16   *Rosalind L. Raby*

Theoretical Constructs

This chapter uses Raby and Zhang's (2019) *International Student Social Cartography* to situate the literature found on community college international students. Social cartography was utilized by Paulston (1999) to make sense of the changing theoretical constructs in the field of comparative and international education. Stein (2019) used cartography to map the field for international student research. Raby and Zhang (2019) used cartography to map theories used in academic studies on international students and to chart patterns of knowledge production that reinforce or challenge dominant narratives. Jing et al. (2020) used cartography to map the quantity of citations as a way to define dominant narratives in the field. In each of these cartographies, published literature shows how knowledge is influenced by political, cultural, economic, geographic, and time factors. This chapter uses cartography to see how power differences are addressed in terms of what is published and what is not published (Raby, 2008; Raby & Zhang, 2019) in "an area of study that problematizes the overwhelmingly positive and depoliticized approaches to international higher education" (Stein, 2019, p. 1).

Research Method

I use critical discourse analysis, which focuses on language as "social practice" (Fairclough & Wodak, 1997, as cited in Wodak, 2007, p. 209) and that targets issues of power, ideology, domination, and control (Wodak, 2007). In particular, I use critical analysis to assess in the literature the ways in which issues are framed, how publications influence change, whose scholarship matters (Kincheloe & McLaren, 2000), and if the scholarship supports or counters dominant knowledge dissemination (van Dijk, 2008). Time series analysis is used to chart patterns by arranging data in chronological order (Vogt, 2005) and by examining how periods of time capture change (Yin, 2012). These methods help to unpack how knowledge is reproduced through various forms of scholarship that are often not value-neutral (Mwangi et al., 2018; Raby, 2008).

Data Collection

I conducted a literature search from 1950 to 2020 in EBSCOhost, PROQUEST, Google, ERIC Database, and the IDP Database of Research on International Education. 1950 marks the earliest publications in the field. Scholarship was chosen based on the process defined by the

Comparative Education Review Bibliography (Raby, 2008), in which the title had to reference students who come from another country to study in the United States by including one or more of the following keywords that are typically used in studies on student mobility: "international students," "mobility," "exchange," "cross-border," "internationalization," or "international education." The title also had to reference the US institutional type that is the focus of this article by including "community college," "junior college," "2-year college," "associate degree," "career education," "vocational education," or "technical education." Each abstract was then read to determine if the focus conformed to the data collection criteria (Ritchie & Spencer, 2002). It must be noted that publications that only listed "international education" without a sub-focus on international students were not included. If aligned, each manuscript was then read in its entirety for content, focus, and purpose. At each stage, sources that did not meet the criteria were eliminated. From 1950 to August 2020, I found 97 monographs/reports, 87 journal articles, 56 dissertations, 24 chapters, 12 books, 24 conference presentations, and 5 newsletter articles.

Data Analysis

Multiple steps were taken to place the data into meaningful patterns with the purpose of allowing multiple perspectives to emerge and the interrelationships between data sets to become evident. Using a titles approach, I sorted publications into types (e.g. reports, dissertations, etc.) and then used a key-word search to build categorization of themes that were then used to define cartography families (Raby & Zhang, 2019).

In reading the full manuscripts, preliminary coding and analysis were done in an iterative manner (Creswell, 2014) to break the text down into chunks. I used a literature review mapping approach (Hovater, 2000) to place each publication into groups, organized by year of publication, and then coded for publication source, author, key terms that aligned with the literature, and perspective in terms of dominant knowledge dissemination. Finally, specific codes were applied based on research questions (Ravitch & Carl, 2016). Throughout the data analysis, I assessed how data describes contexts that are shifting and fluid (Creswell, 2014). Triangulation of recurring narrative themes helped to process different interpretations of the literature and to build a content analysis approach. Being aware that analysis is filtered through a research lens (Merriam, 1998), I take ownership of my biases as a researcher in the field for more than 35 years. This helped to maintain the integrity of data collection, analysis, and interpretations.

18 Rosalind L. Raby

Findings

Building a Community College International Student Cartography

A community college international student cartography is represented in Figure 2.1 and shows an inner circle with four broad themes that intersect with four specified time periods that are grounded in the literature.

Pre-2001

Raby and Valeau (2007) defined four periods of community college international education. In the *Recognition Phrase* (1967–1984), scholarship defined international students as a benefit for the college based on the belief that they bring new perspectives to the classroom and contribute to the intercultural development of domestic students. In the *Expansion and Publication Phase* (1980–1990), scholarship charted the growth of the number of international student programs. In the *Augmentation Phase* (1990–2000), scholarship showed the conflict of public good in which international students helped to build friendships across borders vs. private good in which college profit margin increased as a result of international student tuition/fees. In the final phase, *Institutionalization*

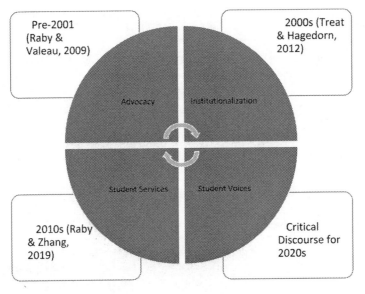

Figure 2.1 Community College International Student Cartography

Phase (2000–2007), scholarship advocated for international students to be included in mission & vision statements and in general budgets.

2000s

Treat and Hagedorn (2013) defined three stages of international education. In the *Prepass/11 world stage* (the term is given to the years prior to 9/11), educational change was "spiky" or uncertain as it responded to globalization. In the *Post-9/11 world*, change was "flat" or stable and was influenced by the global economy and global terrorism. In the final stage, *Post-Flat World* (post-2013), predictions were made that the opening of global trade and communication would make education important for employability and that it would support an emerging middle class throughout the world. In each of these stages, scholarship responded by focusing on the economic benefits of international students with a particular focus on recruitment efforts.

2010s

I call the 2010s the *Global Economic Events* decade which had three stages. In the first stage, the *Great Recession (2008–2012)*, scholarship documented the catastrophic effects that resulted from a sharp decline in state budgets combined with lowered international student enrollments (Raby, 2012). Scholarship advocated that community colleges adopt comprehensive internationalization to counter the economic crisis. The *Economic Gain Years (2013–2018)* saw dramatic enrollment increases for international students. Scholarship used a neoliberal lens to link international student enrollment to profit (NAFSA Economic Tool, 2019). As a bookend to the decade, the final stage, the *COVID-19 Global Pandemic and World Recession (2019–2020)* once again is showing how intricately connected international student enrollment is to institutional funding.

2020s

I call the 2020s the *Criticality Decade*. Reflections on the history of US community college international students show areas of neglect, institutional racism, and prejudice. The inequities caused and sustained by COVID-19 is already a focus of future publications. Unique to this decade will be scholarship that focuses on student voices and uses a post-colonial lens. Three criticality themes that have been repeated in publications over multiple time periods will be increasingly important for future scholarship: (a) critiques on the purposeful dismissal of the community college as a contributing institution for internationalization; (b) critiques on labeling international students as a homogenous population;

20 *Rosalind L. Raby*

and (c) critiques on barrier narratives and adoption of anti-barrier narratives to advance social justice and equity.

Quantitative Time-Series Findings

Findings chart over time, the frequency of the type and years of publications, specific authors published over time, authorship affiliations, regional focus of study, and keywords over time. The pictorial presentations of data were inspired by Jing et al. (2020) whose use of visuals fits well with the cartography schema.

Types of Scholarship

Table 2.1 lists the type of publications and the decades in which the scholarship was published. The most populous form of scholarship is the article (87), followed by dissertation (56), Institute for International Education (IIE) Open Doors Reports (31), and Book Chapters (24). Three journals had the most publications: *New Directions in Community Colleges* (17), *Community College Journal of Research and Practice* (16), and *Journal on International Students* (16). Most scholarship was published in the 2010s (122), followed by the 2000s (88), and the 1990s (56). Graph 1 shows the frequency of publications over time.

Authorship Frequency

Table 2.2 shows the frequency in which authors published over time—158 authors published only once from 1950 to 2020 and 33 of these authors did not publish beyond their dissertations. The limits of a singular publication minimize the overall influence of that publication. Fifteen authors published in more than one time period while eight authors, Ayers, Franco, Frost, King, Levin, Maniseivili, Serban, and Tsunoda, published in three or four different decades and helped to frame many of the discussions in the field. Finally, Hagedorn, Raby, and Zhang, all published five or more times over four decades and whose publications had notably influenced other scholarship as they are frequently cited.

Authorship Positions and Authority

Table 2.3 examines authorship affiliations to gain insight into their authority on knowledge about international community college students. From 1960 to 1980, 13 of the 28 authors were community college presidents who wrote about their own institutions. Authority came

Table 2.1 Type of Publications over Time

Publication Type		60s–70s	80s	90s	00s	10s	20s	Total
Dissertation				5	35	14	2	56
Journal								
	New Directions	7		2	1	7	0	17
	CCJRP	1		2	1	11	1	16
	Community College Week					2		2
	College and University			1				1
	Community College Review		2		3	4	0	9
	Community College Journal	1				2		3
	Journal of International Students					15	1	16
	Journal of Comparative and International Higher Education	0	0	0	0	1	1	2
	Chronicle			1	2	1	0	4
	Other Journals	1		1	4	10	1	17
Newsletter Articles			1	3		1		5
Reports and Monographs								
	AACC			4	4	1		9
	AACC/ACCT				2			2
	ACE				3			3
	CCIE		4	10	10	3	0	27
	CCID	1	2	3		2		8
	College Based			2	1	1	0	4
	IIE	1			10	20	0	31
	NAFSA	2		1		4	0	7
	other			3	1	2	0	6
Book		1	2	6	3			12
Chapters			1	4	7	11	0	24
Presentation		2	3	8	1	10	0	24
TOTAL		17	15	56	88	122	6	305

22   Rosalind L. Raby

Table 2.2 Frequency of Published Authors over Time

Mentioned 1 X	Total: 158 Authors	
Mentioned 2 X	Published in One Time Period	Anayah (10s); Blair (00s); Copeland (15s); Elsner, Tsunoda & Korbel (90s); Green (00s); Harder (10s); Koh (00s); Martorana (70s); Raby & Zhang (15s); Chen, Y. (15s);
	Published in Two Time Periods	Bohman (10s & 15s); Diener (70s & 80s); Raby & Valeau (00; 15s);
Mentioned 3 X	Published in One Time Period	Farrugia & Bhandari (15s); Fersch (80s); Garza, T., & Garcia, H. (15s); Hayward & Siaya (00s);
	Published in Two Time Periods	Franco (90s; 00s); Frost (00s; 10s); King (70s & 90s); Maniseivili; (00s; 10s); Serban (10s; 15s); Tsunoda (90s; 00s)
	Published in Three Time Periods	Breuder (70s & 90s; & 10s);
Mentioned 4 X	Published in Two Time Periods	Ayers (00s & 15s); Levin (00s & 15s)
Mentioned 5 X	Published in Two Time Periods	Zhang & Hagedorn (00s & 10s)
Mentioned 12 X	Published in Three Time Periods	Hagedorn (00s, 10s; & 15); Zhang (00s; 10s; 15)
Mentioned 14 X	Published in Four Time Periods	Raby (99; 00; 10; 15)

Table 2.3 Authorship over Time

	60s/70s	80s	90s	00s	10–15	16–20
President	12	1	2	2	2	2
Senior Administrator	1	2	4	4	1	1
President / Practitioner Team	1	2	5	1	2	1
Association Administrator	2	4	18	22	6	2
Practitioner	0	1	9	7	3	1
University Professor	0	0	4	7	15	19
Doctoral Student	0	0	3	36	13	12
Professor-Doctoral Student Team	0	0	0	1	1	14

from their position as presidents. In the 1990s, 18, almost half of the authors, were American Association of Community College administrators whose authority came from their high-level positions. Many of these authors' professional status also demonstrates the changing levels of support for international students in US community colleges. Nine other authors were practitioners who wrote about their own institutions and whose authority came from their daily work with international students. In the 2010s, most authors were university professors (35) and doctoral students (25) who conducted research about community college international students. Authority was grounded in the resulting empirical research.

Geographical Focus

Table 2.4 lists the geographic focus of the research over time. In the 1970s, scholarship mostly focused on community colleges in Florida where early leaders on community college internationalization resided. In the 1990s, the focus was mostly on California which was emerging as a destination of choice for international students, and in the 2010s, the focus shifted to the Mid-West and Texas where many doctoral programs were supporting research on international students. Across time, the states with the most focus were California, Florida, Hawaii, Iowa, and Texas. In this century, the "Midwest" is often mentioned in scholarship that does not identify participants. Finally, in each decade, there were annual comparative reports and national publications, most of which came from the Institute for International Education Open Doors reports (Institute for International Education, 2019).

Table 2.4 Geographical Institutional Connections

Focus of Study	60s/70s	80s	90s	00s	10s	20s
National	11	5	13	25	22	1
Comparative	10	5	5	10	10	0
Arizona	0	0	0	1	0	1
California	1	5	17	18	15	1
Canada	0	0	1	3	1	0
Florida	3	3	5	0	4	0
Hawaii	0	0	7	1	0	0
Illinois	0	0	0	4	0	0
Iowa	0	0	0	1	6	0
Mid-West	0	0	0	12	14	2
New York/Tri-State	0	1	0	0	0	1
Texas	0	0	0	4	18	0
Virginia	0	0	0	1	0	0
Washington	0	0	0	1	5	0

24   *Rosalind L. Raby*

Table 2.5 Primary Topics Found in Journal and Dissertation Publications

	50s–70s	80s	90s	00s	10s	20s
Journal						
Survey	0	0	0	0	0	0
Advocacy	4	0	6	4	6	1
Admission/ Marketing	0	0	1	5	11	0
How To	2	0	2	1	3	0
Institutional Report	1	0	1	2	5	0
Problem	2	0	0	1	6	0
Achievement	0	0	0	0	4	0
Dissertation						
Survey	0	0	0	0	0	0
Advocacy	0	0	0	0	0	0
Admission/ Marketing	0	0	0	4	3	0
How To	0	0	1	6	2	0
Institutional Report	0	0	0	11	3	0
Problem	0	0	1	5	1	1
Achievement	0	0	2	10	2	1

Primary Topics from Leading Journals and Dissertations

Table 2.5 lists the primary topics found in journal articles and dissertations. Findings show that in journals, prior to the 90s, the most mentioned topic was "advocacy." In the 2000s and 2010s, the most mentioned topic in journals was "admission/marketing." The journal publications in the 2010s also favored the topics of "advocacy," "student problems," and "institutionalization practices." The most mentioned dissertation topic in the 1990s was "student achievement," in the 2000s, it was "student problems" and "student achievement," and in the 2010s, it was "institutionalization practices" and "admission/marketing." Many of the terms coincide with the cartography eras previously defined.

Keywords over Time

Figure 2.1 provides a word-map of the most mentioned keywords over time, and Table 2.6 details those keywords. Comparatively, some keywords, such as "adjustment concerns" were only important in the 90s and 00s, while "rationale" was important in all time periods. The number of keywords found in the publications grew from four in the 1950s/1960s, to 18 in the 1970s/1980s, 24 in the 1990s, 83 in the 2000s, and 54 in the 2010s. A reason for the decline in the 2010s is that many publications began using the same keywords thereby indicating their dominance in

International Student Research   25

Table 2.6 Most Mentioned Keywords over Time

	50s–60s	70s	80s	90s	00s	10s	20s	TOTAL
4–6 Mentions								
Acculturation & Adaptation	0	0	0	0	4	0	0	4
Adjustment Concerns	0	0	0	1	3	0	1	5
Stress & Alcohol Use	0	0	0	0	4	1	0	5
Orientation	0	1	1	0	0	3	0	5
Academic Needs	0	2	0	0	4	0	0	6
Special Support (racial/region, gender)	0	0	0	1	5	0	0	6
7–10 Mentions								
Decision to Enroll	0	0	0	0	2	6	0	8
Engagement & Sense of Belonging	0	0	0	0	3	5	0	8
Interaction with Domestic Students	0	0	0	0	2	7	0	9
Admissions / Enrollment	1	1	0	0	1	6	0	9
Social Needs	0	1	0	1	3	4	0	10
Voices: Students, Service Professionals & Agents	0	0	0	0	6	4	0	10
11–25 Mentions								
Comparative Institutional Studies	0	4	0	1	4	2	0	11
Campus Stakeholders, Environment, Politics	0	0	0	0	6	6	0	12
College-Based Strategic Play & Policy	0	0	0	0	1	11	1	13
Institutional Responsibility & Quality Assurance	0	0	0	1	1	11	0	13
Supportive Environment	0	0	0	2	0	10	1	13
College Support Services	3	7	3	0	0	5	0	18

(*Continued*)

26 *Rosalind L. Raby*

Table 2.6 (Continued)

	50s–60s	70s	80s	90s	00s	10s	20s	TOTAL
Recruitment & Marketing & Tuition Policy	0	2	1	2	7	9	0	21
Academic Success	1	0	0	1	6	8	1	23
Over 25 Mentions								
Guide / How To / Best Practices	2	2	1	18	6	1	0	30
Advocacy Specific to Community College	3	3	0	0	23	1	0	31
State-Wide Reports	0	0	6	15	9	3	0	33
Case Study of 1 College	2	4	1	20	27	7	1	62
Rational - Why Important	0	8	1	25	28	32	1	96
National State of Field Reports	6	5	7	8	38	30	6	100

the field. Three keywords were mentioned in five eras, "implementation guides," "recruitment marketing," and "rationale," while six keywords were mentioned in four different eras, "social needs," "comparative institutional studies," "college support services," "academic success," "advocacy specific to community colleges," and "state-wide reports."

Cartography Themes

The four themes in the Figure 2.1 cartography were chosen because they are present in each decade, and Table 2.7 compares them over time. The theme "student services" had 2 keywords found in 23 publications that were evenly published across the decades. The theme of "advocacy" included 6 keywords found in 272 publications that were published mainly in the 2000s. The themes "institutionalization" and "student voices each included nine keywords published mostly in the 2010s. "Institutionalization" was found in 183 publications and "student voices" in 84 publications.

Advocacy

Pre-1995, publications used advocacy to explain how international students benefited the community college (Elsner et al., 1994), while in the 2000s and 2010s, advocacy detailed why colleges should enhance

International Student Research 27

Table 2.7 Most Mentioned Themes Overtime

	50s–60s	70s	80s	90s	00s	10s	20s	TOTAL
Advocacy								
Interaction with Domestic Students	0	0	0	0	2	7	0	9
Advocacy Specific to Community College	3	3	0	0	23	0	1	31
State-Wide Reports	0	0	6	15	9	2	1	33
Rational - Why Important	0	8	1	25	28	32	1	95
National State of Field Reports	6	5	7	8	38	30	6	100
Institutionalization								
Admissions / Enrollment	1	1	0	0	1	6	0	9
Comparative Institutional Studies	0	4	0	1	4	2	0	11
Campus Stakeholders, Environment, Politics	0	0	0	0	6	6	0	12
College-Based Strategic Policy	0	0	0	0	1	11	1	13
Institutional Responsibility & Quality Assurance	0	0	0	1	1	11	0	13
Supportive Environment	0	0	0	2	0	10	1	13
Recruitment & Marketing & Tuition Policy	0	2	1	2	7	9	0	21
Guide / How To / Best Practices	2	2	1	18	6	0	1	30
Case Study of 1 College	2	4	1	20	27	7	1	61
Student Services								
Orientation	0	1	1	0	0	3	0	5
College Support Services	3	7	3	0	0	5	0	18

(*Continued*)

28 Rosalind L. Raby

Table 2.7 (Continued)

	50s–60s	70s	80s	90s	00s	10s	20s	TOTAL
Student Voices								
Stress & Alcohol Use	0	0	0	0	4	1	0	5
Academic Needs	0	2	0	0	4	0	0	6
Special Support (racial/region, gender)	0	0	0	1	5	0	0	6
Acculturation & Adaptation	0	0	0	1	7	0	0	8
Decision to Enroll	0	0	0	0	2	6	0	8
Engagement & Sense of Belonging	0	0	0	0	3	5	0	8
Social Needs	0	1	0	1	3	4	0	10
Voices: Students, Service Professionals & Agents	0	0	0	0	6	4.	0	10
Academic Success	1	0	0	1	6	8	1	23

recruitment efforts (Bohman, 2014; Brennan & Dellow, 2013). Advocacy targeted the roles of CEOs, Senior Administrators, and Trustees to inform that internationalization was part of the community college mission (Ayers, 2005; Budd et al., 2016; Levin, 2010; Raby, 2016).

Institutionalization

Pre-1995, associations detailed best-practices to help community colleges build their own international student programs (ACCIE/Stanley Foundation 1994; AACJC/NLCFSA, 1977) and detailed institutional responsibilities to better serve international students (Diener & Keer, 1979). In the 2010s, colleges adopted frameworks to apply the principles of comprehensive internationalization (Bissonette & Woodin, 2013; Copeland et al., 2017). This century, scholarship detailed marketing strategies to generate profit that were supported by practitioners (Ardalan & Sevanthinathan, 2015; Frost, 2002) but were critiqued by academics (Ayers, 2005; Raby & Zhang, 2019).

Student Services

In all time periods, publications explored why international students enroll in US community colleges and how college student personnel designed programs and services to deal with the challenges that these students face. Publications pre-1995 examined the need to enhance admissions policies (Elliott, 1969), student social needs (Hagey & Hagey, 1972), and advising practices (Fujikawa, 1995). In the 2000s, publications detailed types of student services (Colondres, 2005) and the cost of those services (Fitzer, 2007). Finally, in the 2010s, the quality of those services became a focus (Bennani, 2018) with discussions of how weak services negatively influenced student success (Zhang, 2016).

Student Voices

Pre-1995, few publications targeted student voices. Those that did, focused on student financial problems (Giammarella, 1986), adjustment concerns (Hagey & Hagey, 1972), and student academic success (Moore, 1995). In the 2000s, publications detailed student experiences (Zeszotarski, 2003), alcohol use (Koyama, 2005), and the degree of engagement (Riley, 2007). Publications, over time, mostly defined international students as a heterogenous population. Yet, some studies focused on students from Latin America (Kidder, 2000); from China (Chen, 2003); and male students from the Middle East (Burnett, 2009).

The 2010s focused on student voices that shared their personal stressors including: (a) stress of adapting to a new culture (Anayah & Kuk, 2015); (b) stress from dealing with cultural conflict (Zhang, 2016); (c) stress from using a new language in the classroom (Hansen et al., 2018); (d) stress in forming new friendships due to language issues (Bennani, 2018); (e) stress from receiving incorrect information from poorly trained counselors which negatively impacts on-time graduation (Zhang, 2017); (f) stress from being marginalized as a result of prejudice and discrimination (Hansen et al., 2018); and (g) stress from being labeled as a privileged group which skews services that they receive (Viggiano et al., 2018). At the end of the decade, publications began to build counter-barrier profiles and began to identify student success markers, including: (a) academic success resulting from engagement (Slantcheva-Durst & Knaggs, 2017; Zhou & Cole, 2017); (b) success from family and peer support (Bennani, 2018); (c) success from high academic aspirations (Friedman, 2018); and (d) from high degree aspirations (Chen, 2014).

Discussion

In critically reviewing the field of US community college international student research, analysis targets patterns of inequities that reside within the publishing field. This is done to assess if scholarship supports or counters dominant knowledge dissemination. It is essential to

30 *Rosalind L. Raby*

understand these inequities to forecast changes in the post-COVID-19 era to impact change in the next decade of the 2020s.

Absence of Themes

In each decade, noted themes were excluded from the literature. First, international publications mostly focus on universities with a noted absence of community colleges (King & Breuder, 1979; Veerasamy, 2020). Likewise, community college publications mostly ignore issues of internationalization (Adams, 1979; Raby & Valeau, 2007), the absence of which, is believed to have led to chronic under-funding and minimal institutional support (Elsner et al., 1994; Raby & Valeau, 2019). Second, there is a near exclusion on the heterogeneity of international students. Aside from IIE Open Doors that quantifies where international students come from (IIE, 2019), few dissertations have profiled diverse student populations and only newer publications are now detailing students from specific countries (Zhang, 2016), social classes (Lynch, 2020), and those who have been minoritized within their home country (Kim, 2018; Viggiano et al., 2018). The final absent theme is an anti-barrier approach to dismiss barrier stereotypes as an explanation of international student behavior and instead is documenting how institutional practices limit success (Ghazzawi et al., 2019) or build positive practices grounded in equity (Viggiano et al., 2018) and global justice (Ayers & Palmadessa, 2015).

Low Occurrence of Themes

While Jing et al. (2020) suggest that keywords with low occurrences are "trending," I suggest that due to the lack of attention in published works on community college international students, the low occurrence themes are mostly linked to a specific time period and thus have minimal influence on future publications and the direction in which scholarship influences practice. In the 1950s–1980s, 18 keywords were mentioned once, like "housing" or "support for black students." If these themes were "trending" they would have been repeated in other time periods or at least used to inform new themes. Similarly, many of the 123 keywords mentioned only once in the 2000s were not being repeated in the 2010s. I proposed that it is likely that the low occurrence of themes indicates that some themes are more applicable in certain time frames than others. For example, "national security" in the early 2000s was a post- 9/11 response while "glocalization" in the 2010s was a response to an association conference theme. In the end, "it just may be that these pivotal and defining themes for our field, that were so prevalent in the 1970s, 1980s, and 1990s are just no longer of relevance for today's audiences" (Raby, 2008, p. 468).

International Student Research   31

Hegemonic Practices of Publishing

One of the findings of this literature review is the hegemonic practices of publishing in which the broader theme of community college internationalization is not evenly found in traditional higher education sources. For example, in 2019–2020, the mainstream journals *Compare*; *Comparative Education*; *International Journal of Higher Education*; *Journal of Comparative and International Higher Education*; and *Journal of Studies in International Education* combined published only six articles on international students in US community colleges. Some suggest the reason for the void is that "there has been scant research on the role of community colleges and technical vocational and education and technology (TVET) colleges in advancing international education" (Varghese & Püttmann, 2011, p. 28). Yet, as evidenced by this chapter, there is a varied scholarship. That being said, most publications continue to be found in only seven journals, five of which focus exclusively on community colleges. The absence of publications in mainstream higher education journals and particularly in international focused journals is problematic because it silences discourse in the field and mandates that those conducting literature reviews need to go outside mainstream journals to seek other venues, such as chapters and dissertations, that are publishing pertinent scholarship.

Conclusion

This chapter, while documenting the depth of community college international students' publications, also illuminates hegemonic practices of the publishing world that contribute to a marginalized field of study. Publications are the way in which knowledge is disseminated. Absent themes of heterogeneity of international students and anti-barrier focus need to be corrected. Imbalances in the publishing world self-perpetuate the belief that the low occurrence of research on community college internationalization is connected to the belief that so few community colleges are engaged in international education. More avenues are needed for publications on community college international students, especially those that show the uniqueness of community college institutional practices, the uniqueness of community college students, and the uniqueness of the community college mission in meeting the needs of international students.

In moving forward, it is important for practitioners and researchers to understand the existing wealth of publications on community college international students. For practitioners, it is important to understand what others have done to avoid duplicating problematic policies and practices as well as to see where modifications can best serve their own institutions. For researchers, it is important to understand the narratives

32   Rosalind L. Raby

that exist, the narratives that are biased, and the narratives that are simply missing. In this context, it is important to be aware of the sense-making of the publishing process itself. In conclusion, it is likely that because so many of the publications on community college international students were not read, their messages could not then influence change in the field.

References

Adams, H. (1979). A rationale for international education. In M. C. King, & R. I. Breuder (Eds.), (pp. 1–11). New Directions for Community Colleges. No. 26. Jossey-Bass.

ACIIE/Stanley Foundation. (1994). Airlie I retreat 'building the global community': The next step. Stanley Foundation Publications.

American Associations of Community and Junior Colleges and the National Liaison Committee of Foreign Student Admission. (1977). The foreign student in the United States Community and Junior Colleges: A colloquium [held at Wingspread, Racine, Wisconsin. October 18–20]. ERIC: ED 154 858.

Anayah, B., & Kuk, L. (2015). The growth of international student enrollment at community colleges and implications. *Community College Journal of Research and Practice*, *39*, 1099–1110. DOI: 10.1080/10668926.2014.934409

Ardalan, S., & Sevanthinathan, N. (2015). Community colleges: The perfect enterprise for the 21st century. In P. Bradley (Ed.), *A collection of community college week's POVs: Opinions, issues, solutions* (pp. 28–30). Autumn Publishing Enterprises, Inc.

Ayers, D. F. (2005). Neoliberal ideology in community college mission statements: A critical discourse analysis. *The Review of Higher Education*, *28*, 527–549.

Ayers, D. F., & Palmadessa, A. C. (2015). The community college and a rising global imaginary: An analysis of practical reasoning, 1950–2013. *The Journal of Higher Education*. *86*(6), 865–892. https://doi.org/10.1353/jhe.2015.0032

Bennani, W.. (2018). Perspectives on improving BA transfer for international community college students. [unpublished doctoral dissertation]. San Francisco State University.

Bissonette, B., & Woodin, S. (2013). Building support for internationalization through institutional assessment and leadership engagement. In T. Treat & L. S. Hagedorn (Eds.), *The community college in a global context* (pp. 11–26). New Directions for Community Colleges, no. 161(Spring). https://doi.org/10.1002/cc.20045

Bohman, E. (2014). Attracting the world: Institutional initiatives' effects on international students' decision to enroll. In P. Eddy (Eds.), Special issue: Community colleges and their internationalization efforts. *Community College Journal of Research and Practice*, *38*(8), 710–720. https://doi.org/10.1080/10668926.2014.897081

Brennan, M., & Dellow, D. A. (2013). International students as a resource for achieving comprehensive internationalization. In T. Treat & L. S. Hagedorn (Eds.), *The community college in a global context* (pp. 27–37). New Directions for Community Colleges No. 161. Jossey-Bass. https://doi.org/10.1002/cc

Budd, D., Serban, A., Van Hook, D. G., & Raby, R. L. (2016). Addressing myths about international students. In R. L. Raby & E. J. Valeau (Eds.), *International education at community colleges: Themes, practices, research, and case studies* (pp. 215–222). Palgrave McMillan.

Burnett, E. II. (2009). Three international student services professionals' perceptions of Middle Eastern male students at a Texas community college following September 11, 2001. [unpublished doctoral dissertation]. Sam Houston State University.

Chen, P. (2003). Factors influencing academic success of Chinese international students in Los Angeles community colleges. [unpublished doctoral dissertation]. University of Southern California.

Chen, Y. (2014). The influence of self-efficacy on degree aspiration among domestic and international community college students. [unpublished doctoral dissertation]. Iowa State University.

Colondres, D. M. W. (2005). International student support services: A model for United States community colleges. [unpublished doctoral dissertation]. Pepperdine University.

Copeland, J. M., McCrink, C. L., & Starratt, G. K. (2017). Development of the community college internationalization index. *Journal of Studies in International Education, 21*(4), 349–374.

Creswell, J. W. (2014). *Designing and conducting mixed methods research* (4th ed.). Sage.

Diener, T. J., & Keer, L. (1979). Institutional responsibilities to foreign students. In M. C. King & R. I. Breuder (Eds.), *Advancing international education* (pp. 49–57). New Directions in Community Colleges. No. 26. Jossey-Bass.

Elliott, F. G. (1969). The dilemma of foreign student admissions. *Junior College Journal, 40*(10), 2–10.

Elsner, P. A., Tsunoda, J. S., & Korbel, L. A. (1994). *Building the global community: The next step*. Points of Departure for the American Council on International Intercultural Education/Stanley Foundation Leadership Retreat, (November 28–30, 1994). Stanley Foundation Press.

Fairclough, N., & Wodak, R. (1997). Critical discourse analysis. In T. A. van Dijk (Ed.), *Discourse as social interaction. Discourse studies: A multidisciplinary introduction* (Vol. 2, pp. 258–284). Sage.

Fitzer, J. K. (2007). Foreign students at California community colleges: Benefits, costs, and institutional responsibility. [unpublished doctoral dissertation]. State University of New York.

Friedman, J. Z. (2018). A horse of a different color? Re-examining international students at community colleges in the U.S. and Canada. In R. L. Raby & E. J. Valeau (Eds.), *Handbook on comparative issues of community colleges and global counterparts* (pp. 523–51). Springer. ISBN 978-3-319-50910-5.

Frost, R. A. (2002). International enrollment management: Attracting international students to the community college. In R. M. Romano (Ed.), *Internationalizing the community college* (pp. 13–31). Community College Press.

Fujikawa, R. (1995). Creating an international campus through student advising. In R. W. Franco & J. Shimabukuro (Eds.), *Beyond the classroom: International education and the community college: Internationalizing the campus environment* (Vol. 2, pp. 42–46). University of Hawaii Press.

34 *Rosalind L. Raby*

Ghazzawi, D., McKinney, L., Horn, C. L., Carales, V., & Burridge, A. (2019). The road to the baccalaureate: Assessing the viability of community colleges as transfer pathways for international students. *Journal of International Students, 10*(2), 420–442. https://doi.org/10.32674/jis.v10i2.339

Giammarella, M. (1986). A profile of the foreign student at a public two-year college: The borough of Manhattan community college response to the financial problems of foreign students. *Community Review, 7*(1), 6–13.

Hagey, A. R., & Hagey, J. (1972). The international student and the junior college: Academic and social need. *Journal of College Student Personnel, 13*(1), 140–144.

Hansen, H. R., Shneyderman, Y., McNamara, G. S., & Grace, L. (2018). Acculturative stress and native and U.S. culture immersion of international students at a community college. *Journal of International Students, 8*(1), 215–232. https://doi.org/10.5281/1134293

Hovater, S. E. (2000). Preparing culturally responsive teachers through preservice teaching programs. [unpublished doctoral dissertation]. University of Nebrasks – Lincoln.

Institute for International Education. (2019). Open doors community colleges web-page. http://opendoors.iienetwork.org/?p=25122

Jing, X., Ghosh, R., Sun, Z., & Liu, Q. (2020). Mapping global research related to international students: A scientometric review. *Higher Education*. Online first. January, 2020 https://doi.org/10.1007/s10734-019-00489-y

Kidder, N. L. (2000). Border crossing: The experience of international students from Latin America in a California community college. [unpublished doctoral dissertation]. University of Southern California.

Kim, S. (2018). Voluntarily exiled? Korean state's cultural politics of young adults' social belonging and Korean students' exile to a US community college. *Higher Education, 76*(2), 353–367. https://doi.org/10.1007/s10734-017-0212-3

Kincheloe, J. L., & McLaren, P. (2000). Rethinking critical theory and qualitative research. In .K. Denzin & Y. S. Lincoln (Eds.), *Handbook of qualitative research* (2nd ed., pp. 279–313). Sage.

King, M. C., & Breuder, R. L. (Eds.). (1979). *Advancing international education.* New Directions for Community Colleges. No. 26. Jossey-Bass.

Koyama, C. (2005). Acculturation stress and alcohol use among international college students in a United States community college setting. [unpublished doctoral dissertation]. Virginia Polytechnic Institute and State University.

Levin, J. S. (2010). Global culture and the community college. *Community College Journal of Research and Practice, 26*(2), 121–145. DOI: 10.1080/106689202753385474

Lynch, A. (2020). Community college internationalization: The intentional integration of cultural perspectives into the student experience. [unpublished doctoral dissertation]. University of Pennsylvania.

Merriam, S. B. (1998). *Qualitative research and case study applications in education.* Jossey-Bass.

Moore, S. K. (1995). Indicators of academic success and the student characteristics of international students at Santa Monica college. [unpublished doctoral dissertation]. Pepperdine University.

Mwangi, C. G., Latafat, S., Hammond, S., Kommers, S., Hanni, S., Berger, J., & Blanco- Ramirez, G. (2018). Criticality in international higher education research: A critical discourse analysis of higher education journals. *Higher Education*, 76(6), 1091–1107. DOI: 10.1007/s10734-018-0259-9

NAFSA: Association of International Educators. (2019). NAFSA international student economic value tool. http://www.nafsa.org/Policy_and_Advocacy/Policy_Resources/Policy_Trends_and_Data/NAFSA_International_Student_Economic_Value_Tool/eis2019/pdf

Paulston, R. G. (1999). Mapping comparative education after postmodernity. *Comparative Education Review*, 43(4), 438–463.

Raby, R. L. (1993). Implementation of international education at California community colleges. The News Community College League of California (September 1993).

Raby, R. L. (2008). The globalization of journals. *Comparative Education Review*, 51(3), 461–475.

Raby, R. L. (2012). Re-imagining international education at community colleges. *Audem: International Journal of Higher Education and Democracy*, 3, 81–99.

Raby, R. L. (2016). Global is not the opposite of local: Advocacy for community college international education. In Raby, R. L. & Valeau, E. J. (Eds.), *International education at Community colleges: Themes, practices, research, and case studies*. (Vol. 2016, pp. 9–23). Palgrave Macmillian Publishers.

Raby, R. L., & Valeau, E. J. (2007). Community college international education: Looking back to forecast the future. In R. L. Raby & E. J. Valeau (Eds.), *International reform efforts and challenges in community colleges* (pp. 5–14). New Directions for Community Colleges 138 (Summer). Jossey-Bass.

Raby, R. L., & Valeau, E. J. (2019). Position training and succession planning for community college international education leaders. *Community College Journal of Research and Practice*. Online First. July 26, 2019. https://doi.org/1 0.1080/10668926.2019.1645055

Raby, R. L., & Zhang, L. (2019). Changing theoretical perspectives on transnational mobility: A review of the literature. In G. Uttan (Ed.), *Rethinking education across borders* (pp. 19–46). Springer Nature. https://doi.org/10.1007/978-981-15-2399-1_2

Ravitch, S. M., & Carl, N. M. (2016). *Qualitative research: Bridging the conceptual, theoretical, and methodological*. Sage.

Riley, R. (2007). Student engagement and intercultural competence in the North Harris Montgomery community college district. [unpublished doctoral dissertation]. Minnesota State University.

Ritchie, J., & Spencer, L. (2002). Qualitative data analysis for applied policy research. In A. M. Huberman & M. B. Miles (Eds.), *The qualitative researcher's companion*. Sage.

Slantcheva-Durst, S., & Knaggs, C. K. (2017). Community college international students and their campus involvement. *Community College Journal of Research and Practice*, 43(2), 81–93.

Stein, S. (2019). Contested imaginaries of global justice in the internationalization of higher education. [unpublished doctoral dissertation]. University of British Columbia.

36 Rosalind L. Raby

Treat, T., & Hagedorn, L. S. (Eds.) (2013). *Resituating the community college in a global context*. New Directions for Community Colleges. Jossey-Bass.

Van Dijk, T. A. (2008). Critical discourse analysis and nominalization: problem or pseudo-problem? *Discourse and Society, 19*(6), 821–828. https://doi.org/10.1177/0957926508095897

Varghese, N. V., & Püttmann, V. (2011). *Trends in diversification of postsecondary education*. UNESCO IIEP. https://unesdoc.unesco.org/ark:/48223/pf0000191585.locale=en

Veerasamy, Y. P. S. (2020). U.S. national higher education internationalization policy: A historical analysis of policy development between 2000 and 2019. [unpublished doctoral Dissertation]. University of Toledo.

Viggiano, T., López Damián, A. I., Morales Vázquez, E., & Levin, J. S. (2018). The others: Equitable access, international students, and the community college. *Journal of Studies in International Education, 22*(1), 71–85.

Vogt, W. P. (2005). Time-series data. In W. P. Vogt (Ed.), *Dictionary of statistics and methodology* (3rd ed., pp. 325–335). Sage.

Wodak, R. (2007). Pragmatics and critical discourse analysis: A cross-disciplinary enquiry. *Pragmatics and Cognition, 15*(1), 203–225.

Yin, R. K. (2012). *Applications of case study research* (3rd ed.). Sage.

Zeszotarksi, P. (2003). Expectations and experiences of international students in an American community college in the context of globalization. [unpublished dissertation]. University of California at Los Angeles.

Zhang, Y. L. (2016). An overlooked population in community college: International students' (in)validation experiences with academic advising. *Community College Review, 44*(2), 153–170. DOI: 10.1177/0091552116633293

Zhang, Y. L. (2017). International students in transition: International community college transfer students in a Texas research university. *New Directions for Institutional Research, 170*, 35–48.

Zhou, J., & Cole, D. (2017). Comparing international and American students: Involvement in college life and overall satisfaction. *Higher Education, 73*(3), 655–672.

Author Bio

Rosalind Latiner Raby, PhD, teaches at California State University, Northridge in the Educational Leadership and Policy Studies Department and is the Director of California Colleges for International Education, a nonprofit consortium of California community colleges. Dr. Raby received her PhD in Comparative and International Education from the University of California, Los Angeles (UCLA) and since 1984, has worked with community college faculty and administrators to help them internationalize their campuses. Dr. Raby has been publishing in the field of community college internationalization since 1985.

3 Characteristics and Patterns of International Students at Community Colleges

Lessons from the *Open Doors* Data

Julie Baer

International Students and Community Colleges

Over the past 50 years, the number of international students at community colleges grew from just over 15,000 in 1971 to 79,187 in 2019/2020 according to the *Open Doors® Report on International Educational Exchange,* an annual report sponsored by the US Department of State with funding provided by the US government and published by the Institute of International Education (IIE, 1948/1949–2019/2020). This upward trajectory followed the general trend for overall international students, which showed immense growth over the past five decades.

Unlike the trend line for overall international students in the United States, which steadily increased, the number of international students at community colleges experienced periods of both growth and decline (Figure 3.1). The number of students at community colleges climbed until the late 1970s. However, in the early 1980s, international students attending community colleges fell by 30 percent in the 5-year period between 1980/1981 and 1985/1986. The falling number of international students from Iran, the number one place of origin in the late 1970s and early 1980s, may have partially caused this steep decline. Over the next 30 years, the international student total at community colleges fluctuated, often increasing for several years, followed by smaller declines.

The number of international students at community colleges peaked at 96,472 in 2016/2017 and has fallen for the past 3 years. This decline in international students at community colleges is likely due to decreases in new enrollments over the past 4 years. As community colleges often enroll international students for only one to two years, the falling number of new international students quickly impacted the overall total of international community college students. In contrast, despite declines in new enrollment since 2016/17, the overall number of international students in the United States declined for the first time in 2019/2020. This time lag in the national number is partly because the larger student cohorts from 4 years ago began to complete their studies in 2019/2020.

38 *Julie Baer*

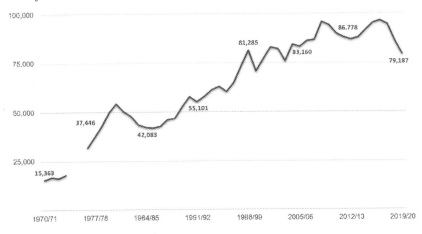

Figure 3.1 International Students at Community Colleges, 1970/1971–2019/2020

Note: Data not reported in 1974/1975 and 1975/1976. Refugees were counted from 1975/1976 to 1990/1991

The number of students attending community colleges as a proportion of all international students in the United States also fell over the past 20 years (Figure 3.2). International students at community colleges comprised approximately 14 percent of the total international student population in 1999/2000. In comparison, community college students made up around 7 percent of all international students in 2019/2020, which is the smallest proportion of total since *Open Doors* began tracking this information. While the decline in enrollment over the past 3 years contributed to the smaller share, the principal reason for this trend was the considerable growth in the number of international students attending other institutional types. In the 20 years from 1999/2000, the number of international students at community colleges increased by approximately 8,500 students, while all other institutional types increased by over 552,000 international students.

Despite the downward trend, many US community colleges continue to support internationalization. Additionally, the US Department of State has reiterated their support by encouraging international students to attend community colleges and promoting the benefits of the "2+2 model" where international students can attend their first 2 years of studies at community colleges before finishing their last two years at a 4-year institution. As noted by Marie Royce, Assistant Secretary of State for Educational and Cultural Affairs:

> The State Department is promoting the 2+2 model, which really is a wonderful way of promoting higher education by reducing the cost for the student. There are so many benefits. One is that you can live

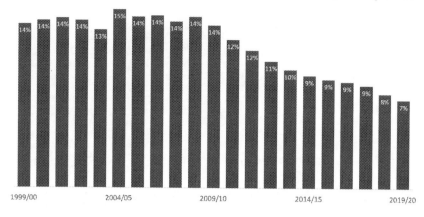

Figure 3.2 International Students at Community Colleges as a Percent of Total International Students, 1999/2000–2019/2020

in two places in the US, and if your English proficiency is not high you can go to a community college and start off there before going to university.

And then, of course, the cost. We hear from so many people that the number one concern for international students is the cost of higher education, so the 2+2 really helps. And I know a lot of people that have started out in community college and gone on to a doctorate.

(Civinini, 2019)

At What Types of Community Colleges Do International Students Study?

International students studied in a wide array of community colleges across the United States to include different Carnegie Classifications. Carnegie's program mix categorization classifies community colleges as either high transfer, mixed transfer/career-technical, or high career-technical (The Carnegie Classification of Institutions in Higher Education, 2020). International students studied at all types of community colleges in 2019/2020, with the largest numbers of students studying at high transfer associate's colleges (38,397) or at baccalaureate/associates colleges (21,801) (Figure 3.3). Together, 76 percent of international students attended community colleges within these two institutional classifications. This high proportion reflects the fact that many community colleges have articulation agreements that allow students to continue their studies at 4-year institutions after completing 2 years, sometimes referred to as the 2+2 model. As such, community colleges

40 *Julie Baer*

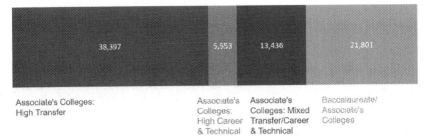

Figure 3.3 International Students at Community Colleges by Institutional Type, 2019/2020

offer an important pathway for international students to pursue further education in the United States. As of fall 2020, 44 percent of US institutions cite that they are actively recruiting international students at community colleges (Baer & Martel, 2020).

Where Do International Students at Community Colleges Study in the United States?

International students attended community colleges across all 50 US states in 2019/2020. The top four states hosting international students at community colleges were California (22,825), Texas (13,291), Washington (8,849), and Florida (6,082). Each of these top four states has large higher education sectors with robust community college systems that have the capacity to host many students.

The number of international students was highly concentrated among the top 25 community colleges (Table 3.1). These leading institutions accounted for 45 percent of all reported international students at community colleges in 2019/2020. In comparison, the top 25 institutions across all institution types host 24 percent of all international students.

Houston Community College System has been the number one host of international students at community colleges since 2002/2003. Since the early 1990s, Northern Virginia Community College and Santa Monica College have also held the top rank among community colleges. Also, of note is Miami-Dade College, which was the number one host of international students at community colleges and nationally for nearly every year from 1970/1971 through 1990/1991, a period of time when *Open Doors* counted refugees as international students.

The analysis of the proportion of international students at community colleges relative to all international students is another important way to understand the distribution of international students across states. Figure 3.4 illustrates the thirteen states that host a higher proportion

International Students at Community Colleges 41

Table 3.1 Top 25 Community Colleges Hosting International Students, 2019/2020

Institution	City	State	Total International Students
Houston Community College System	Houston	TX	4,723
Lone Star College System	The Woodlands	TX	3,097
Santa Monica College	Santa Monica	CA	2,714
De Anza College	Cupertino	CA	2,352
Montgomery College	Rockville	MD	1,759
Valencia College	Orlando	FL	1,667
Northern Virginia Community College	Annandale	VA	1,457
Orange Coast College	Costa Mesa	CA	1,400
Green River College	Auburn	WA	1,295
Miami-Dade College	Miami	FL	1,260
Edmonds Community College	Lynnwood	WA	1,176
Seattle Central College	Seattle	WA	1,147
Foothill College	Los Altos Hills	CA	1,108
Bellevue College	Bellevue	WA	1,007
San Mateo County Community College	San Mateo	CA	983
Diablo Valley College	Pleasant Hill	CA	955
Shoreline Community College	Shoreline	WA	928
Richland College	Dallas	TX	922
Santa Barbara City College	Santa Barbara	CA	883
Irvine Valley College	Irvine	CA	838
Pasadena City College	Pasadena	CA	822
CUNY Borough of Manhattan Community College	New York	NY	813
Bunker Hill Community College	Boston	MA	784
City College of San Francisco	San Francisco	CA	694
Broward College	Fort Lauderdale	FL	690

of international students at community colleges than the national average of 7.4 percent. Over one-third of all international students in Washington State attended community colleges in 2019/2020. This statistic has remained relatively consistent since this analysis was first conducted in 1977/1978 when 32 percent of international students in Washington attended 2-year institutions. Hawaii, Texas, Wyoming, and Nevada all reported that over 15 percent of their international students studied at community colleges in 2019/2020.

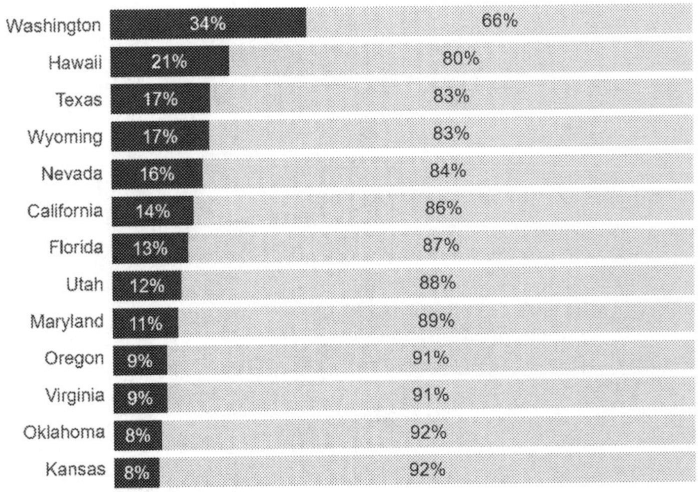

42 *Julie Baer*

State	Community College %	Other %
Washington	34%	66%
Hawaii	21%	80%
Texas	17%	83%
Wyoming	17%	83%
Nevada	16%	84%
California	14%	86%
Florida	13%	87%
Utah	12%	88%
Maryland	11%	89%
Oregon	9%	91%
Virginia	9%	91%
Oklahoma	8%	92%
Kansas	8%	92%

Figure 3.4 International Students at Community Colleges as a Percent of Total International Students by Selected States, 2019/2020

Note: Percent distributions may not sum to 100.0 because of rounding

What Is the Distribution of International Students across Academic Levels at Community Colleges?

International students at community colleges are often enrolled students (96 percent), which include students studying intensive English and pursuing an associate degree or certificate. The vast majority of students studied at the associate's level, with over 67,500 students pursuing associate degrees.

Of the approximately 7,200 students enrolled at the nondegree level, more than 3,900 students studied intensive English. Notably, the proportion of international students pursuing intensive English at community colleges (5 percent) was higher than the percentage of intensive English students nationally (2 percent). This higher proportion reflects how intensive English programs at community colleges may serve as an affordable way for international students to improve their speaking, writing, and understanding of English before accessing further academic study at the undergraduate level. An additional 3,200 students pursued other nondegree options, such as certificate programs.

Additionally, approximately 4 percent of the international student population at community colleges pursued post-completion Optional Practical Training (OPT) in 2019/2020. OPT allows international students at community colleges to pursue work opportunities in their field of study for up to 12 months. Approximately 3,400 students availed themselves of this opportunity to gain experience in their field of study in 2019/2020.

However, the proportion of international students pursuing post-completion OPT at community colleges was much lower than the national rate. In comparison, 21 percent of all international students nationally, over 223,500 recent graduates, took advantage of OPT as of 2019/2020.

What Places of Origin Do International Students at Community Colleges Come from?

Studying at a US community college holds global appeal, with international students traveling from across the world to pursue educational opportunities at US community colleges. As of 2019/2020, international students came from 205 places of origin, which has grown considerably from the 135 places of origin reported in 1971.

In comparison to national statistics, community colleges have a diverse international student body. The top ten places of origin represent 59 percent of all international students at community colleges, while the top ten places of origin comprise 71 percent of all international students nationally. In 2019/2020, the top ten places of origin for international students at community colleges were China, Vietnam, Japan, South Korea, Brazil, Mexico, Venezuela, India, Taiwan, and Nepal (Figure 3.5).

China was the leading place of origin for international students at community colleges in 2019/2020, a position it has held since 2011/2012

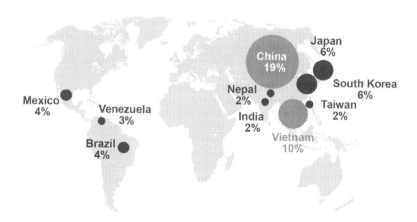

Figure 3.5 Top Ten Places of Origin of International Students at Community Colleges, 2019/2020

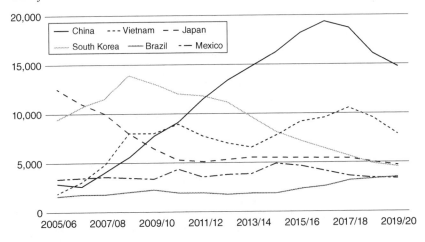

Figure 3.6 Top Six Places of Origin for International Students at Community Colleges, 2005/2006–2019/2020

when it overtook South Korea (Figure 3.6). Approximately 19 percent of international students at community colleges came from China in 2019/2020, reflecting more than 14,700 students. The number of students at community colleges from China fell for the past 3 years, aligning with the national trend of declines in international students at community colleges. However, despite the decrease, the number of Chinese international students at community colleges remains significantly higher in 2019/2020 compared to a decade ago.

Vietnam ranked second for the number of international students at community colleges in 2019/2020. Despite declines over the past 2 years, the number of international students from Vietnam has increased seven-fold over the past two decades. Twenty years ago, Vietnam ranked 14th, with approximately 1,100 students, reflecting less than 2 percent of international students at community colleges. As of 2019/2020, 11 percent of international students at community colleges were from Vietnam. This swift growth has likely been due to Vietnam's rapid economic growth and emerging middle class as well as limited higher education capacity (Trines, 2017).

Japan was the leading place of origin from 1998/1999 (when *Open Doors* began closely tracking international community college students by place of origin) through 2007/2008. In 1998/1999, there were over 16,000 international students at community colleges from Japan, and this number steadily fell until 2010/2011. Since then, the number of international students from Japan at community colleges has remained stable at around 5,000 students. In 2019/2020, approximately 4,700 Japanese students studied at US community colleges.

The number of international students studying in the United States from South Korea has fallen steadily since 2008/2009, which parallels the trend observed nationally among all international students studying from South Korea. Several factors have driven this downward trend. The first is the shifting demographics within South Korea, which has a smaller college-aged population than in the past. Additionally, South Korea has built its own higher education capacity, meaning that there are more opportunities for students to pursue higher education at home.

Brazil and Mexico rounded out the top places of origin for international students at community colleges in 2019/2020. Brazilian international students at community colleges have steadily increased over the past 5 years. Brazil (+3 percent) was the only place of origin within the top ten that experienced growth in 2019/2020, which pushed Brazil into the fifth leading place of origin, surpassing Mexico. This was the first time Brazil has ranked within the top five places of origin for international students at community colleges. The number of international students from Mexico has been relatively stable over the past 15 years and declined by 3 percent to approximately 3,300 students in 2019/2020.

What Is the Profile of International Students at US Community Colleges?

Gender

Community colleges were the only institutional type in 2019/2020 with gender parity among inbound international students. In 2019/2020, women comprised 49.9 percent of international students at community colleges, only 0.2 percentage points less than the percent of male international students who attended community colleges (50.1 percent) (Figure 3.7). Comparatively, women made up 45 percent of international undergraduate students at all institutions, and men comprised 55 percent.

This gender parity difference may be due to the differences among the leading places of origin of international students studying at community colleges. According to *Women on the Move*, men and women from China study in the United States at approximately the same rates (49 percent women and 51 percent men), and women made up the majority of students coming from Vietnam (54 percent women and 46 percent men) (Bhandari, 2017). In comparison, India, the second leading place of origin nationally, had a much wider gender disparity, as only 32 percent of Indian international students were women as of 2015/2016.

Historically, *Open Doors* has noted a narrowing of the gender gap among international students at community colleges. In 1970/1971,

46 *Julie Baer*

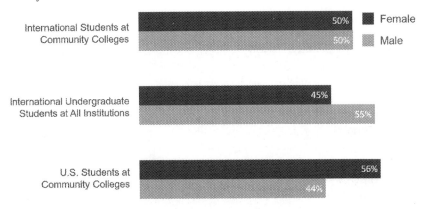

Figure 3.7 Gender of International Students at Community Colleges and International Undergraduates at All Institution Types, 2019/2020 and Gender of U.S. Students at Community Colleges, 2015/2016 (U.S. Department of Education, 2018a)

only 32 percent of international students at community colleges were women. This trend persisted for the following 10 years, with women comprising only one-third of international students at community colleges in 1980/1981. However, beginning in the 1990s, the gender gap began to narrow, with approximately 56 percent of international students being men and 44 percent women. As the gap continued to shrink, there have been years over the past decade when more female than male international students attended community colleges, which is in line with the national trends among all students attending community colleges. According to the US Department of Education, women comprised 56 percent of all undergraduate students at community colleges (US Department of Education, 2018a).

Marital Status

Throughout the history of *Open Doors* reporting, the majority of international students in the United States have been single. This trend continues to hold true among international students at community colleges, with 93 percent reported as single and 7 percent as married in 2019/2020. While there were slightly higher statistics of married students in the 1980s and the early 1990s ranging from 9 to 13 percent, this statistic has been relatively stable around 7 percent over the past decade.

However, variations exist when comparing the ratio of single to married students to other national metrics. *Open Doors* reported a slightly higher rate of 97 percent single students among all undergraduate students in the United States across all institutional types in 2019/2020.

Community college students' overall profile may influence the slightly higher rate of married international students at community colleges. National data from the National Postsecondary Student Aid Study indicates that only 80 percent of students at community colleges were single (US Department of Education, 2018b).

Enrollment Status

A similar phenomenon exists when examining international students by full- and part-time status. In 2019/2020, 90 percent of international students at community colleges studied full-time. This was a lower percentage than what was reported by international students among all institutional types (95 percent) and all international undergraduates (96 percent). However, this picture significantly differs from the national profile of US community college students where the majority (64 percent) of US students at community colleges pursued part-time studies (US Department of Education, 2018c).

These data points indicate that international students at community colleges often have a different profile than US students at community colleges overall. Understanding international students' characteristics and how they differ from US students at community colleges or the overall international student population can help community colleges better align outreach and on-campus supports for their international student body.

How Do International Students Fund Their Studies at Community Colleges?

To understand the economic impact of international students at community colleges, *Open Doors* collects data on the primary source of funding. While many students may use multiple funding types to pay for their studies, this data reflects the source that students principally rely on to pay for their studies. Since international students are not eligible for federal aid, the overwhelming majority of international students at community colleges paid for their education via personal and family funds (90 percent) in 2019/2020. This far exceeds the percentage of students relying on personal and family funding at the national level (56 percent) and the undergraduate academic level (84 percent).

Because most international students at community colleges rely on personal funding (89 percent), they represent an external infusion of financial capital into the local area, contributing economically to the colleges and communities where they study. According to NAFSA (2020), international students at community colleges contributed $2.3 billion and supported over 12,100 jobs in local communities across the United States in 2019/2020.

48 *Julie Baer*

Aside from personal funds, an additional 4.6 percent of international students at community colleges funded their studies with current employment in 2019/2020. This percentage was principally due to the 4.3 percent of international students who pursued post-completion OPT. Furthermore, only two percent of community college students depended on funding from their US college, which is a much lower share than among all international students.

What Do International Students Study at Community Colleges?

International students come from across the world to study the wide variety of fields offered at community colleges. Over the past 5 years, the top majors for international students at community colleges have remained relatively consistent. The leading three fields have been science, technology, engineering, and mathematics (STEM) majors, Liberal Arts or General Studies, and Business and Management (Table 3.2). Notably, these three fields are the same leading areas of study for US students at community colleges. However, the distribution of students across these fields varies significantly between international and US students at community colleges.

In 2019/2020, 28 percent of international students at community colleges studied within the STEM fields. In *Open Doors*, STEM majors include math and computer science, engineering, physical sciences, health professions, and agriculture. Overall, the proportion of international students majoring within the STEM fields is significantly lower than their US counterparts enrolled at community colleges (39 percent) as well as in comparison to the international student undergraduate population overall (39 percent) (US Department of Education, 2018d).

The leading STEM field of study in 2019/2020 was math and computer science (10 percent). Interest in this field has steadily grown over the past 10 years, likely due to increasing job opportunities within the computer science field. In contrast, only 5 percent of US students at community college studied math and computer science. Part of this stronger interest may be due to math and computer science's popularity among all international students. Nationally, 14 percent of international undergraduate students study math and computer science.

Engineering was the second most popular STEM major for international students at community colleges. While only comprising 7 percent of international students at community colleges, this was the leading STEM major among all international undergraduate students in the United States (15 percent). Approximately 5 percent of international students at community colleges major in the health professions and the physical and life sciences. Particularly notable is that the proportion

Table 3.2 Fields of Study of International Students at Community Colleges and Undergraduates at All Institutions, 2019/2020 and Fields of Study of US Students at Community Colleges, 2015/2016 (US Department of Education, 2018d)

Major Field of Study	International Students at Community Colleges (%)	International Undergraduate Students at All Institutional Types (%)	US Students at Community Colleges (%)
Science, Technology, Engineering, & Math Fields (STEM)	28.1	38.9	39.4
Math & Computer Science	10.0	14.1	5.1
Engineering	7.4	14.5	9.3
Physical & Life Sciences	5.3	6.7	2.5
Health Professions	5.1	2.7	21.4
Agriculture	0.3	1.0	1.1
Business & Management	23.1	20.8	13.1
Liberal Arts & Sciences & General Studies	21.7	8.4	18.1
Intensive English	5.8	0.3	-
Fine & Applied Arts	5.1	7.7	3.4
Social Sciences	3.9	10.3	5.1
Communications & Journalism	1.6	3.1	1.3
Education	1.4	0.9	4.2
Humanities	1.1	1.2	0.9
Legal Studies & Law Enforcement	0.8	0.5	6.0
Other Fields of Study	5.6	4.4	4.6
Undeclared	1.8	3.5	3.8

of international students studying in the health professions is significantly lower than that of US students at community colleges (21 percent) (US Department of Education, 2018d).

When comparing all fields of study individually (with the STEM fields disaggregated), business and management was the single largest field of study for international students at community colleges in 2019/2020, with approximately 23 percent of international students majoring in this field. In comparison, only 13 percent of US community college students studied in the business and management fields (US Department of Education, 2018d).

The higher concentration of business and management students is likely due to the interests of international students from the leading places of origin. In particular, 17 percent of students from China and Japan and 29 percent of Vietnamese students studied in the business and management fields in 2019/2020 according to national data.

50 *Julie Baer*

Additionally, 22 percent of international students at community colleges studied within the liberal arts and sciences or general studies classification in 2019/2020, which closely mirrors the percentage of US students studying within this area at community colleges (18 percent) (US Department of Education, 2018d). This is a much higher rate than among international students studying at the undergraduate level (8 percent). It is likely that many of these students, both international and US students, are taking general coursework with the intention of transferring the credits to a 4-year institution.

International Students at Community Colleges in 2020

Traditionally, the overall trends that we see in the *Open Doors* data remain steady year over year, often with incremental changes over time. However, 2020 is an unprecedented year due to the COVID-19 pandemic, which has caused travel restrictions, Embassy and Consulate closures worldwide, the rapid scaling of online learning, and college faculty and staff layoffs (Lederman, 2020; US Department of State, 2020). The data from the *Open Doors 2021 Report* will record the impact of this year's pandemic, and there will undoubtedly be significant impacts on international student mobility at institutions throughout the United States.

However, IIE, with nine higher education association partners, has collected preliminary data through the Fall 2020 International Student Enrollment Snapshot (Baer & Martel, 2020). This annual report presented data from over 700 US higher education institutions on current international student enrollment patterns. The focus of the 2020 report was on how the COVID-19 pandemic affected the US higher education sector and global student mobility to the United States. While this data is reflective of all institutions throughout the United States, the lessons learned from this report may also be insightful for community colleges.

This preliminary data indicated that many community colleges quickly adapted to the realities of COVID-19. Approximately 99 percent of responding institutions held classes online or implemented a hybrid model as of fall 2020. Along with allowing classwork to resume safely, online options were crucial for international students unable to travel to the United States as it allowed them to continue studies remotely. Initial indicators showed that international students took advantage of this option, with one in five international students reported as studying online from abroad in fall 2020. All responding institutions with students on campus cited establishing protocols to support students' safety, such as restricting campus events and social areas, publishing safety guidelines, requiring face coverings, and reducing class sizes.

While institutions quickly responded to COVID-19, the limitations on the ability to travel affected international student mobility to the United States. As a result, the total international students at higher education institutions in the United States and studying online outside the United States decreased by 16 percent in fall 2020. This decline was partially due to a 43 percent drop in new international student enrollment in the United States and online outside the United States. While the numbers fell considerably, the overwhelming majority of institutions (90 percent) indicated that approximately 40,000 students had deferred their studies to a future term. While this initial data provides an overall look at the national landscape, the *Open Doors 2021 Report* will record the full extent of the COVID-19 impacts on international student mobility at community colleges.

Despite the declines in fall 2020, US higher education institutions affirmed their commitment to international student outreach and recruitment. Over half of the responding institutions (64 percent) indicated a continuation of funding for outreach and recruitment at the same levels or higher than previously. To continue engaging with prospective international students, 82 percent of institutions reported increasing their virtual outreach through activities, such as online recruitment events (74 percent) and virtual campus visits (54 percent). Furthermore, colleges and universities cited working with current international students (68 percent), engaging on social media (56 percent), leveraging *EducationUSA* (53 percent), and utilizing international partnerships (53 percent) to promote their institution to future international students.

These preliminary findings indicate that while there are barriers to internationalization that US higher education faces as a result of COVID-19, many institutions throughout the United States, including community colleges, are adapting and remain committed to internationalization.

Conclusion

Over the past 50 years, community colleges have held open the doors and welcomed international students. As a result, over 79,000 international students availed themselves of this opportunity in 2019/2020. However, as the number of international students has fallen over the past several years, it is now more important than ever to understand the national profile of international students at community colleges. The *Open Doors* data and analysis highlights how community colleges attract a unique international student body different from national data on US students at community colleges and the national data on international students in the United States. By understanding the overview of the landscape of international students at community colleges, institutions can leverage this information to benchmark and develop internationalization strategies, create enrollment management roadmaps, target recruitment, and advocate for internationalization on campus. While there may be challenges ahead, community colleges have long showcased a commitment to internationalization and an ability to innovate, highlighting the benefits for all students on campus while adapting international recruitment to meet the needs of the future. This has resulted in international students from across the world coming through the open doors that community colleges offer.

Open Doors Methodology

The *Open Doors Report on International Educational Exchange* is an annual report published by the IIE and conducted in partnership with the US Department of State's Bureau of Educational and Cultural Affairs since 1972. The report provides information from US higher education institutions about international students and scholars as well as US study abroad. Unless otherwise cited, the statistics throughout this chapter come from the compendium of statistics from the *Open Doors* historical reports or special analyses of the data.

IIE has tracked international students attending community colleges since the *Open Doors* print publication began in 1948/1949. While early reports included data on junior colleges and vocational institutes, *Open Doors* began conducting an aggregate analysis of international students at community colleges starting in 1971. IIE first studied this information by analyzing the *Open Doors* data at 2-year colleges and published statistics on this classification until *Open Doors* 1993.

Since *Open Doors* 1994, the data has been analyzed using the Carnegie Classification of Institutions in Higher Education. The Carnegie classifications are periodically updated, and variations may occur on which institutions were classified as community colleges (Figure 3.8). Additionally, *Open Doors* includes both associate's and baccalaureate/associate's colleges in the community college analysis. While the category of baccalaureate/associate's includes 4-year colleges with at least one baccalaureate degree program, *Open Doors* incorporates these institutions into the community college analysis

Figure 3.8 Open Doors Data Usage of Carnegie Classifications

because the majority of degrees conferred were at the associate's level (The Carnegie Classification of Institutions in Higher Education, 2020).

References

Baer, J., & Martel, M. (2020). *Fall 2020 international student enrollment snapshot.* https://www.iie.org/en/Research-and-Insights/Publications/Fall-2020-International-Student-Enrollment-Snapshot

Bhandari, R. (2017). *Women on the move: The gender dimensions of academic mobility.* Institute of International Education. https://www.iie.org/Research-and-Insights/Publications/Women-on-the-Move-The-Gender-Dimensions-of-Academic-Mobility

Civinini, C. (2019). *Sitting down with The PIE during NAFSA, assistant secretary Marie Royce spoke about the department's efforts to promote inbound and outbound mobility and its support for the #youarewelcomehere campaign.* The PIE News. https://thepienews.com/pie-chat/marie-royce/

Institute of International Education (IIE). (1948/1989–2019/2020). *Open Doors report on international educational exchange, 1948/89–2019/20* [Data set]. Institute of International Education.

Lederman, D. (2020, July 10). *COVID-19's forceful financial hit: A survey of business officers.* Inside Higher Ed. https://www.insidehighered.com/news/survey/covid-19s-forceful-financial-hit-survey-business-officers

NAFSA. (2020). *NAFSA International Student Economic Value Tool: International students at U.S. community colleges.* https://www.nafsa.org/policy-and-advocacy/policy-resources/nafsa-international-student-economic-value-tool-v2

The Carnegie Classification of Institutions in Higher Education. (2020). *Basic classification description.* https://carnegieclassifications.iu.edu/classification_descriptions/basic.php

Trines, S. (2017). *Education in Vietnam.* World Education News + Reviews. https://wenr.wes.org/2017/11/education-in-vietnam

U.S. Department of Education, National Center for Education Statistics. (2018a). *2015–16 National postsecondary student aid study (NPSAS 16): Gender (GENDER) by citizenship (CITIZEN2) filtered by the 2015 Carnegie classification (CC2015B)* [Computation by NCES PowerStats Version 1.0 on 11/25/2020]. https://nces.ed.gov/datalab/index.aspx

U.S. Department of Education, National Center for Education Statistics. (2018b). *2015–16 National postsecondary student aid study (NPSAS 16): Marital status (SMARITAL) by citizenship (CITIZEN2) filtered by the 2015 Carnegie classification (CC2015B)* [Computation by NCES PowerStats Version 1.0 on 11/25/2020]. https://nces.ed.gov/datalab/index.aspx

U.S. Department of Education, National Center for Education Statistics. (2018c). *2015–16 National postsecondary student aid study (NPSAS 16): Enrollment status (ENRSTAT) by citizenship (CITIZEN2) filtered by the 2015 Carnegie classification (CC2015B)* [Computation by NCES PowerStats Version 1.0 on 11/25/2020]. https://nces.ed.gov/datalab/index.aspx

U.S. Department of Education, National Center for Education Statistics. (2018d). *2015–16 National postsecondary student aid study (NPSAS 16): Field of study (MAJORS) by citizenship (CITIZEN2) filtered by the 2015 Carnegie* classification (CC2015B) [Computation by NCES PowerStats Version 1.0 on 11/25/2020]. https://nces.ed.gov/datalab/index.aspx

U.S. Department of State. (2020). *Suspension of routine visa services*. https://travel.state.gov/content/travel/en/News/visas-news/suspension-of-routine-visa-services.html

Author Bio

Julie Baer is a Research Specialist at the Institute of International Education (IIE), where she manages the data collection and analysis for *Open Doors* and conducts specialized research for IIE program teams on strategic program design and planning. Her areas of expertise include analyzing trends in international academic mobility in US higher education across sectors and using geospatial analysis to highlight trends in educational access. Ms. Baer holds an EdM in International Education Policy from the Harvard Graduate School of Education and a BS from Centre College. She was a Fulbright English Teaching Assistant to Malaysia in 2012.

4 International Students at Canadian Community Colleges

Origins, Evolution, and Current Trends

Oleg Legusov and Hayfa F. Jafar

Introduction

International student mobility has increased steadily in recent decades. In 2017, international students numbered more than 5.3 million worldwide, up from 2 million in 2000 (UNESCO, 2019). Moreover, the Organization for Economic Co-operation and Development (OECD) forecasts that global demand for international higher education will grow to 6.4 million students in 2025 (Chakma et al., 2012). Most of the growth is expected to come from developing countries where the middle class is expanding amid recognition that an educated, intercultural population drives economic development and social progress (Ortiz et al., 2015). Research shows that various push and pull factors, such as immigration policies, government support, and growing capacity in sending countries, have increased international student mobility (Altbach, 1998; Mazzarol & Soutar, 2008; Wilkins & Huisman, 2011). The developed English-speaking countries, such as the United States, the United Kingdom, Australia, and Canada have traditionally been the most popular study-abroad destinations.

Even though research on international students is increasing, most of the studies focus on universities; thus there is a dearth of research on other postsecondary institutions, particularly community colleges (Hagedorn & Lee, 2005; Zhang, 2016). But, with the rising numbers of international students at community colleges in the United States (Garcia & De Lourdes Villarreal, 2014), the United Kingdom (Fisher & Saunders, 2017), Australia (Robertson, 2011), Canada (Usher, 2019), and other countries, more research on all aspects of this new development is needed (Zhang, 2016). This study, therefore, explores those factors that have historically driven the number of international students attending community colleges in Canada and identifies current trends in the internationalization of college education. Canada, which comprises ten provinces and three territories, each with a distinct educational system, has one of the world's fastest-growing populations of international community college students and thus presents an ideal setting for such

56 *Oleg Legusov and Hayfa F. Jafar*

a study, given that the trends taking place in Canada are likely to occur in other jurisdictions with large numbers of international community college students.

Context: Canadian Colleges and International Students

Canadian Community Colleges

The vast majority of Canada's public postsecondary educational institutions fall into one of two categories: universities or community colleges. Most Canadian community colleges were founded in the 1960s in response to an incipient and unprecedented increase in demand for postsecondary education (Sheffield, 1962) and the view that Canada's well-being would increasingly depend on the technical education of its workforce (Gallagher & Dennison, 1995).

Canadian colleges have differed significantly from one province to the next since inception. Canada's ten provinces and three territories each have distinct cultural and socioeconomic characteristics. As Gallagher and Dennison (1995, p. 383) pointed out, "The sociopolitical contexts and economic opportunities of the provinces were so different ... that a nationwide approach was soon seen as unrealistic." As a result, five distinct community college models emerged from 1965 to 1975 (Dennison & Gallagher, 1986). Ontario created vocationally oriented colleges of applied arts and technology. British Columbia and Alberta opted for locally governed comprehensive colleges with university transfer; Saskatchewan developed its so-called colleges without walls; Quebec's colleges of general and vocational education incorporated tuition-free technical and pre-university streams; and Newfoundland, Manitoba, New Brunswick, the Yukon Territory, and the Northwest Territories established technical colleges with a strong accent on short-term work-entry training (Gallagher & Dennison, 1995).

The colleges' ability to attract international students also differs significantly from one province to another. Colleges in Newfoundland and New Brunswick have very few international students, in sharp contrast to Ontario. As Legusov (2017) observed, "The role of Ontario's colleges of applied arts and technology (CAATs), most of which were founded in the late 1960s, has changed substantially over the years. From institutions that primarily trained skilled workers and tradespeople for local communities, they have evolved into complex educational organizations that fulfill multiple functions, with the education and training of international students quickly becoming one of the most important" (p. 2).

International Students at Canadian Colleges

The literature on the origins of international students at Canadian community colleges is scant. Most Canadian community colleges were founded with a mandate to provide education to growing numbers of young people requiring postsecondary credentials and to serve the economic needs of local communities. Internationalization was not part of their original mandate. Hurabielle (1998) observed that only 10 percent of all Canadian higher education institutions had international students before the 1980s. But, as Dennison and Gallagher pointed out, "From the very start, a few colleges had made it a practice to bring to Canada groups of foreign students during the summer months for language training" (1986, p. 160).

In a seminal paper, Dennison and Gallagher (1986) argued that, in the late 1970s, two main reasons prompted Canadian colleges to internationalize and to start accepting international students on a regular basis. The first reason derived from the colleges' mission to provide a diverse range of educational opportunities. To fulfill this objective, the colleges kept expanding the scope of their operations: they began providing a broader range of academic experiences for an increasing number of Canadians; they began developing more "educational links with business and industry in the communities they served"; and eventually they began internationalizing their practices (Dennison & Gallagher, 1986, p. 160). The second reason was that, as government funding became less generous, colleges welcomed international students, whose higher tuition fees covered all costs associated with their education and, in some cases, generated modest profits. By the mid-1980s, international education was a major growth area for several colleges and one of their favored ways of expanding entrepreneurially into new areas and generating revenues (Dennison & Gallagher, 1986). By the late 1990s, every community college in Ontario, Canada's largest province, had international students on campus (Galway, 2000).

Various factors have been driving the spectacular growth of international student enrolment at Canadian colleges. Knight (2006) observed that the top three reasons that institutions of higher education recruit international students are to promote their brand and profile internationally, to enhance the quality of education by bringing diverse perspectives to the local student body and to generate revenues. That said, Usher (2018, p. 18) thinks that, even though international students are appreciated because they add diversity to classrooms and to a lesser extent because "their presence burnishes institutions' standings in world rankings..., they are mainly prized because they pay much higher tuition fees than domestic students and are thus seen as a way of offsetting stagnant government funding." Demographic trends are another

58 *Oleg Legusov and Hayfa F. Jafar*

reason that colleges and other institutions of higher education are under pressure to admit more international students. Statistics Canada (2018) forecasts that the number of potential students (those aged 20–24) in Canada will increase slightly until about 2030, only to plateau until 2039, and then begin to drop. If this trend is not reversed, colleges will see lower revenues from tuition and other fees, wasted resources, including empty seats and program closures, and ultimately layoffs of college staff (Drea, 2004).

Current Trends

The literature on the subject is concerned primarily with such matters as international students' motivations for studying abroad (Chen, 2008; Perez-Encinas et al., 2020); their choice of destination (Bohman, 2010; Jafar & Legusov, 2020); their use of recruitment agents (Legusov, 2017); and their experiences in host countries (Mamiseishvili, 2012).

The COVID-19 pandemic has had a severe impact on all students, but especially on international students, whose ability to study in Canada depends on travel restrictions adopted not only by Canada but also by their own countries, in addition to Canadian immigration rules and regulations. Despite these difficulties, international students value the foreign educational experience highly. A survey of more than 40,000 prospective international students conducted by Consultants Ernst & Young (EY) revealed that only 5 percent of them were planning to abandon their international studies because of the pandemic (Ross, 2020). Moreover, Canada is expected to increase its share of the global international education market by 6 percent, at the expense of the United States, whose handling of the pandemic is regarded as poor (para.13).

Methodology

The study used the selection and analysis of relevant documents as its methodological approach. The documents include literature from provincial education departments; manuals, policy documents, and press releases from Immigration, Refugees and Citizenship Canada (IRCC) and Quebec's immigration department; college mission statements, strategies, reports, newsletters, and program proposals; and various other public records. The document-analysis process developed by O'Leary (2014) was used to analyze the documents. The process includes planning for all contingencies; gathering relevant documents; reviewing their credibility; interrogating their witting and unwitting evidence; reflecting on and refining the process; and analyzing the data. According to O'Leary, the two major techniques for analyzing documents are content analysis and the interview technique, which is used in this study. In the interview

Canadian Community Colleges 59

approach, the document is treated as an informant that provides pertinent information (O'Leary, 2014). As with an interview involving human subjects, a researcher needs to determine the information sought and whether the examined documents can provide relevant data. The researcher poses questions and then highlights the answers within the text. Such an approach is well suited to this study because the information sought in the documents is known.

Findings

This study highlights and discusses a number of trends in community college education as they pertain to international students. Some of the trends are not new while others are emerging, but all are likely to have a strong impact on the internationalization of the Canadian college system.

Trend One: Educational Destination

The number of international college students in Canada rose from about 2,000 in the year 2000 to almost 100,000 in 2017. The increase was gradual at first, then rapid from 2009 onward (Usher, 2018), but it did not affect all Canadian provinces and territories equally. Table 4.1 shows the distribution of international college students in the ten Canadian provinces in the 2007–2008 and 2017–2018 academic years.

As can be seen from Table 4.1, in the 2017–2018 academic year, more than two-thirds of Canada's international college students were

Table 4.1 International College Students by Province, 2017–2018

	2007–2008		2017–2018		10-year trend (%)
	Students	%	Students	%	
Ontario	17,394	57.1	68,037	68.1	291
British Columbia	7,350	24.1	17,409	17.4	137
Quebec	2,328	7.6	5,682	5.7	144
Alberta	2,703	8.9	5,067	5.1	87
Manitoba	84	0.3	2,148	2.1	2,457
Saskatchewan	27	0.1	723	0.7	2,578
New Brunswick	90	0.3	600	0.6	567
Prince Edward Island	393	1.3	180	0.2	–54
Newfoundland and Labrador	63	0.2	60	0.1	–5
Nova Scotia	45	0.1	3	0.0	–93
Canada	30,477	100.0	99,909	100.0	228

Source: Statistics Canada (2020)

in Ontario (68.1 percent), followed by British Columbia (17.4 percent), Quebec (5.7 percent), and Alberta (5.1 percent). Together, these four provinces accounted for 96.3 percent of the international college students in Canada. However, only Ontario made substantial gains over 10 years, increasing its market share from 57.1 percent in 2007–2008 to 68.1 percent in 2017–2018, while British Columbia, Quebec, and Alberta saw their shares fall significantly. Such an outcome is due to the attractiveness of Ontario, which was perceived as an excellent place to seek career employment, owing to its vibrant economy. It is noteworthy that Manitoba, Saskatchewan, and New Brunswick also recorded large increases in the number of their international college students over the past decade, partly because these provinces introduced programs facilitating international students' transition from temporary to permanent residency (Government of Manitoba, n.d.; Government of New Brunswick, 2020; Government of Saskatchewan, n.d.a). They have also offered financial incentives, such as a tuition-fee rebate of up to $20,000 for international students who stay on and work in Saskatchewan after graduation (Government of Saskatchewan, n.d.b). But, as Scott et al. (2015) point out, because of its appeal for international students, Ontario shapes and defines international education across Canada to a large extent.

That being said, the distribution of international students among Ontario's 24 CAATs is anything but equal. International college students tend to gravitate to major cities with multicultural populations and abundant job opportunities. For example, international college students in Ontario numbered more than 75,000 in 2018–2019, but more than half of them attended the five large colleges in the Greater Toronto Area (GTA) (Ontario Government, 2019). And this trend is likely to continue; the GTA is the most populous area in Canada (Statistics Canada, 2016), it has a strong economy, and it is one of the most multicultural jurisdictions in the world (Duncan & Popp, 2017)—all strong pull factors for international students.

Trend Two: Partnerships with Private Colleges

The overwhelming majority of international students opt for colleges in large cities, thus providing a large percentage of their revenues. As a result, colleges outside urban areas tend to be financially disadvantaged. To address this problem, the Government of Ontario has expanded the partnership agreements between the province's public and private career colleges. Like public colleges, private career colleges in Ontario offer vocational programs to domestic and international students. But international graduates of private colleges originally did not qualify for a postgraduate work permit (PGWP) and usually had to leave Canada after their studies. The partnership agreements allow international students admitted to community colleges in remote areas to attend private colleges in the GTA and receive a public-college credential that allows them to qualify for a PGWP (Ministry of Colleges and Universities, 2019). By December 2019, six publicly assisted Ontario colleges had such agreements—a trend that is likely to continue.

Trend Three: Campuses Exclusively for International Students

Another aspect of this phenomenon is that colleges that are in major urban centers and have large numbers of international students are setting up campuses exclusively for them. Canada's two largest public colleges, Seneca and Humber, both in the GTA, recently announced campuses for international students only (Humber College, 2020; Seneca College, 2020). The manifest reason is to address the unique needs of international students more effectively. Still, a critical observer might conclude that such campuses are creatively capitalizing on the international student bonanza. This approach is also controversial because students on such campuses will not have the opportunity to socialize with Canadian students and will miss out on that vital aspect of acculturation.

Simon Fraser University (SFU) in British Columbia opted for a slightly different approach when it established Fraser International College (FIC), a standalone institution run by a private company. For premium tuition fees, FIC offers international students smaller classes and more attention in their first year to help them transition to full SFU life (Simon Fraser University, n.d.).

Trend Four: Changing Countries of Origin of International College Students

International students at Canada's community colleges have traditionally come from China, India, and South Korea (Popovic, 2013). Even though these countries remain the top providers, India recently overtook China by a large margin as the colleges' top supplier of international students. According to CBIE (2020), there were 144,900 international Indian college students in Canada in 2019, followed by China (16,670), South Korea (7,420), Brazil (7,403), and Vietnam (6,955). The configuration of foreign students at Canada's universities was quite different, as shown in Figure 4.1.

This trend is most likely due to Canada's two-step immigration strategy as it pertains to international college graduates. The first step for a potential immigrant is to gain at least 12 months of full-time, or an equal amount of part-time, skilled work experience in Canada as a temporary

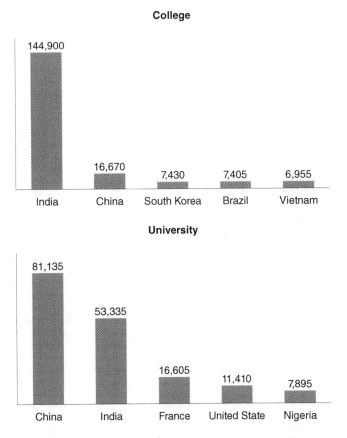

Figure 4.1 International Postsecondary Students in Canada

Source: CBIE (2020)

resident. After fulfilling this requirement, a temporary resident may apply for permanent residency under the Provincial Nominee Program (PNP) or the Canadian Experience Class (CEC) stream. International college graduates may obtain a PGWP allowing them to stay in Canada for up to three years (IRCC, 2020). Studies show that as many as 60 percent of international students in Canada plan to apply for permanent residency (PR) (CBIE, 2018). Not surprisingly, nearly 54,000 former students became permanent residents of Canada in 2018. Once international students qualify to apply for PR status, they are assigned points for their English and French language skills, education, work experience, and age, and are ranked against the other individuals in the pool under the Comprehensive Ranking System (CRS). The federal government periodically extends invitations to apply for permanent

Canadian Community Colleges 63

residency to those candidates in the Express Entry pool with the highest number of points.

Arguably, under such a system, international students from India and other countries where English is widely spoken enjoy two advantages over students from elsewhere. First, they tend to get higher points for their English-language skills. Second, because they are under no pressure to move to Canada at an earlier age to learn English, they often obtain their first educational credential and work experience in their home countries, which gives them additional points toward immigration. In essence, students from India are crowding out those from China.

The demographics of international college students in the predominantly French-speaking province of Quebec are strikingly different from those of the other Canadian provinces. Bégin-Caouette (2018) observed that although the overall diversity of international students in the province has increased since 2005, the number of students from France has increased more rapidly than the number from African countries. According to Bégin-Caouette, this outcome is due to the termination of agreements between Quebec and Reunion Island, Cameroon, and New Caledonia, whereby students from those countries paid no tuition fees.

Trend Five: Colleges' Reliance on Recruitment Agents

Canadian colleges use various means to recruit international students, the most important being recruitment agents. An agent is a third-party individual or company that provides advisory services to students who want to study abroad, in exchange for a fee paid by the students and their families and a commission paid by the institution that the agent represents (Coffey & Perry, 2014; Redden, 2013). According to International Consultants for Education and Fairs (ICEF) Monitor, there were more than 23,000 education agencies worldwide in 2019 (CICan, 2019).

Canadian colleges rely much more on agents to recruit international students than do universities. Unlike colleges, universities have a long history, differ little in their missions, and are better known around the world. In contrast, "community college" is an umbrella term that encompasses institutions that differ significantly from one jurisdiction to another. One of the agent's core functions is therefore to sell colleges in markets where people have a limited understanding of them. Moreover, the colleges' reliance on recruitment agents seems to increase as their populations of international students rise.

Legusov (2017, p. 10) analyzed how international students were recruited by agents from 1995 to 2014 for a large Ontario college. His findings show that "the percentage of students who solicited the help

64 Oleg Legusov and Hayfa F. Jafar

of an agent remained steady at about 30% from 1995 until 2007, after which it began to increase sharply and reached almost 60% in 2014." A more recent study revealed that 78.2 percent of 55 international graduates of GTA colleges used the services of a recruitment agent (Jafar & Legusov, 2020). This finding is in line with a study by Coffey and Perry (2014), who found that 78 percent of the educational institutions they surveyed used agents.

An exception was Quebec, where many institutions rely on ties with francophone nations, and the use of recruitment agents is minimal (Coffey & Perry, 2014). International student fees are still regulated to some extent in Quebec. In 2018, the provincial government moved to deregulate the university tuition fees paid by foreign students (CICan, 2019). Even so, the fees charged by Quebec's *collèges d'enseignement général et professionnel* (CEGEPs, or general and vocational colleges) and other colleges are still set by the province, so they charge foreign students lower tuition fees. But the government retains the bulk of the fees, so CEGEPs and other colleges have relatively little incentive to engage with agents or to invest otherwise in international market development. Partly because of Quebec's tuition-fee policy, its French-language institutions and schools have limited experience in international recruitment and in providing programs and services for international students. Those that are more involved in recruitment tend to be in places where domestic demographic declines are stronger, namely outside major urban centers. International recruitment is therefore a way to maintain program and service levels (CICan, 2019).

Trend Six: Shift to Online Education

Even though the trend to distance education began several years ago, it has accelerated rapidly during the COVID-19 pandemic. It is not clear whether many international students would prefer online courses, although they may take up to 50 percent of their programs online (Government of Canada, n.d.). A Hanover Research survey (2020) on COVID-19's impact on international students' program-delivery preferences showed that 66 percent favored online classes. Students who preferred the in-class format cited greater exposure to the new culture and language as their main reasons.

The time that international students spend studying online in their home countries is not normally counted in their PGWP application. IRCC has lifted this restriction until December 31, 2020, however (Government of Canada, n.d.). Thus thousands of international students, many for the first time, have found themselves studying online in Canada or from home. Even though such measures are temporary, one may assume that many more courses and programs will be offered through distance education than before the pandemic. Such a development will affect international students significantly. Some of them may be from cultures where distance education is not as prevalent as in Canada. They may also see their educational experience in Canada as an opportunity to learn about the country by interacting with other students on campus. Colleges will have to find ways to provide such opportunities virtually. Moreover, distance education will necessitate changes to immigration regulations governing international students.

Discussion and Conclusion

This study adds to the literature by exploring historical and emerging trends involving international students at Canadian community colleges and by highlighting possible developments. A number of studies have already examined the factors that influence international college students' choice of educational destination. They have looked at the matter primarily from the student's perspective, however. Our study contributes to the discussion by highlighting how provincial policies are affecting the number of international students on college campuses. It also identifies and explains the reasons for the major change in the configuration of the colleges' international student body from mostly Chinese to predominantly Indian.

The literature tells us that community colleges with large international populations rely heavily on recruitment agents (Jafar & Legusov, 2020). The French-speaking province of Quebec is an exception; its colleges rely mostly on their ties with francophone nations to attract international students.

The study also identifies new approaches used to increase the market share of international students, such as campuses exclusively for international students and partnerships with private career colleges. It gives a brief analysis of the latest development, namely the shift to online instruction in response to the COVID-19 pandemic, which at the time of writing had not been covered in the literature.

International students have become an integral part of community colleges in many developed countries. But geopolitical and socioeconomic changes are having a profound impact on the way the colleges function, accelerating established trends and setting in motion major new trends. Canada, with its wide variety of educational systems and long tradition of welcoming international college students, provides an ideal ground to explore such trends. The findings of this study can be generalized to other colleges and technical and vocational intuitions, such as junior colleges in the United States, further-education colleges in the United Kingdom, and technical and further-education (TAFE) institutes in Australia.

66 Oleg Legusov and Hayfa F. Jafar

This study identified and described several evolving trends in the internationalization of community college education. But, given the speed and scope of the changes affecting educational systems around the world, more trends are certain to emerge and will need to be studied if colleges and other educational institutions are to address such challenges effectively.

References

Altbach, P. G. (1998). *Comparative higher education: Knowledge, the university, and development*. Greenwood Publishing Group.

Bégin-Caouette, O. (2018). Le processus d'internationalisation des cégeps: Une analyse historique et géopolitique. *Canadian Journal of Higher Education/ Revue canadienne d'enseignement supérieur*, 48(1), 99–117.

Bohman, E. J. (2010). Headed for the heartland: Decision making process of community college bound international students. *Community College Journal of Research and Practice*, 34(1), 64–77. https://doi.org/10.1080/10668920903385848

CBIE. (2018). *The student's voice: National results of the 2018 CBIE international student survey*. https://cbie.ca/wp-content/uploads/2018/08/Student_Voice_Report-ENG.pdf

CBIE. (2020). *International students in Canada*. https://cbie.ca/infographic/

Chakma, A., Bisson, A., Côté, J., Dodds, C., Smith, L., & Wright, D. (2012). *International education: A key driver of Canada's future prosperity*. Government of Canada.

Chen, L. H. (2008). Internationalization or international marketing? Two frameworks for understanding international students' choice of Canadian universities. *Journal of Marketing for Higher Education*, *18*, 1–33. https://doi.org/10.1080/08841240802100113

CICan. (2019). *Emerging markets for international student recruitment to Canadian colleges and institutes*. https://www.collegesinstitutes.ca/wp-content/uploads/2019/06/CICan_Intl_Student_EmergingMarkets_Eng.pdf

Coffey, R., & Perry, L. M. (2014). *The role of education agents in Canada's deucation systems*. Council of Ministers of Education, Canada. https://www.cmec.ca/Publications/Lists/Publications/Attachments/326/The-Role-of-Education-Agents-EN.pdf

Duncan, H., & Popp, I. (2017). *World migration report 2018*. https://www.iom.int/sites/default/files/country/docs/china/r5_world_migration_report_2018_en.pdf

Dennison, J. D., & Gallagher, P. (1986). *Canada's community colleges: A critical analysis*. University of British Columbia Press.

Drea, C. (2004). Student attrition and retention in Ontario's Colleges. *College Quarterly*, 7(2), n2.

Fisher, R., & Saunders, M. (2017). International students and further education colleges in England: The context, policy tensions, and some aspects of practice. In L. Tran & K. Dempsey (Eds.), *Internationalization in vocational education and training (Technical and vocational education and training: Issues, concerns and prospects)* (Vol. 25). Springer. https://doi.org/10.1007/978-3-319-47859-3_6

Gallagher, P., & Dennison, J. D. (1995). Canada's community college systems: A study of diversity. *Community College Journal of Research and Practice, 19*(5), 381–393.

Galway, A. D. (2000). *Going global: Ontario colleges of applied arts and technology, international student recruitment and the export of education* [Doctoral dissertation]. http://www.nlcbnc.ca/obj/s4/f2/dsk1/tape3/PQDD_0023/NQ50012.pdf

Garcia, H., & De Lourdes Villarreal, M. (2014). The "redirecting" of international students: American higher education policy hindrances and implications. *Journal of International Students, 4*(2), 126–136.

Government of Canada. (n.d.). *Post-graduation work permit (PGWP) validity and application*. https://www.canada.ca/en/immigration-refugees-citizenship/corporate/publications-manuals/operational-bulletins-manuals/temporary-residents/study-permits/post-graduation-work-permit-program/permit.html

Government of Manitoba. (n.d.). *Manitoba provincial nominee program*. http://www.immigratemanitoba.com/immigrate-to-manitoba/

Government of New Brunswick. (2020, July 16). *New Brunswick provincial nominee program* (NBPNP). https://www.welcomenb.ca/content/wel-bien/en/immigrating/content/HowToImmigrate/NBProvincialNomineeProgram.html

Government of Saskatchewan. (n.d.a). *Saskatchewan immigrant nominee program (SINP)*. https://www.saskatchewan.ca/residents/moving-to-saskatchewan/immigrating-to-saskatchewan/saskatchewan-immigrant-nominee-program

Government of Saskatchewan. (n.d.b). *Graduate retention program*. https://www.saskatchewan.ca/residents/education-and-learning/graduate-retention-program

Hanover Research. (2020, August 05). *COVID-19's impact on international students' academic plans: Hanover*. https://www.hanoverresearch.com/reports-and-briefs/covid-19s-impact-on-international-students-academic-plans/

Hagedorn, L. S., & Lee, M. C. (2005). *International community college students: The neglected minority?* Retrieved from http://eric.ed.gov/?id=ED490516

Humber College. (2020). *International Graduate School*. https://international.humber.ca/study-at-humber/international-graduate-school.html

Hurabielle, J. (1998). *Canada's public colleges and postsecondary technical institutions involvement in international education* (Doctoral dissertation). University of Alberta. Retrieved from https://era.library.ualberta.ca/items/52defb5d-20a2-4395-93ba-4f97d8a834c7/view/6dae930d-b0f6-47b6-827a-d23f9a50840f/NQ34781.pdf

IRCC. (2020, July 13). *Work in Canada after you graduate: Who can apply*. https://www.canada.ca/en/immigration-refugees-citizenship/services/study-canada/work/after-graduation/eligibility.html

Jafar, H., & Legusov, O. (2020). Understanding the decision-making process of College-bound International students: A case study of Greater Toronto Area colleges of applied arts and technology. *Community College Journal of Research and Practice, 44*, 1–16.

Knight, J. (2006). Internationalization: Concepts, complexities and challenges. In J. Forest & P. Altbach (Eds.), *International handbook of Higher education* (pp. 207–228). Springer Academic Publishers.

Legusov, O. (2017). The growing reliance of Ontario colleges of applied arts and technology on educational agents for the recruitment of international students. *College Quarterly, 20*(1). http://collegequarterly.ca/2017-vol20-num01-winter/index.html

Mamiseishvili, K. (2012). Academic and social integration and persistence of international students at US two-year institutions. *Community College Journal of Research and Practice, 36*(1), 15–27. https://doi.org/10.1080/10668926.2012.619093

Mazzarol, T. W., & Soutar, G. N. (2008). Australian educational institutions' international markets: A correspondence analysis. *International Journal of Educational Management, 22*(3), 229–238.

Ministry of Colleges and Universities. (2019). Ontario creating more opportunities for college students. https://news.ontario.ca/maesd/en/2019/12/ontario-creating-more-opportunities-for-college-students.html

O'Leary, Z. (2014). *The essential guide to doing your research project* (2nd ed.). Sage Publications.

Ontario Government. (2019, October 25). *College enrolment.* Ontario Data Catalogue. https://data.ontario.ca/dataset/college-enrolment

Ortiz, A., Chang, L., & Fang, Y. (2015). *International student mobility trends 2015: An economic perspective.* WES Research & Advisory. https://wenr.wes.org/2015/02/international-student-mobility-trends-2015-an-economic-perspective

Perez-Encinas, A., Rodriguez-Pomeda, J., & de Wit, H. (2020). Factors influencing student mobility: A comparative European study. *Studies in Higher Education,* 1–14. DOI: 10.1080/03075079.2020.1725873

Popovic, T. (2013). *International education in Ontario's colleges.* College Student Alliance.

Redden, E. (2013). Giving agents the OK. *Inside Higher Education.* https://www.insidehighered.com/news/2013/09/23/admissionsassociation-lifts-ban-commissioned-agentsinternational-recruiting

Robertson, S. (2011). Cash cows, backdoor migrants, or activist citizens? International students, citizenship, and rights in Australia. *Ethnic and Racial Studies, 34*(12), 2192–2211. https://doi.org/10.1080/01419870.2011.558590

Ross, J. (2020, June 24). *Pandemic to redistribute international student flows: Report.* The Times Higher Education. https://www.timeshighereducation.com/news/pandemic-redistribute-international-student-flows-report

Scott, C., Safdar, S., Desai Trilokekar, R., & El Masri, A. (2015). International students as "ideal immigrants" in Canada: A disconnect between policy makers' assumptions and the lived experiences of international students. *Comparative and International Education/Éducation Comparée et Internationale, 43*(3), 5.

Seneca College. (2020). *Seneca International Academy.* https://www.senecacollege.ca/international/seneca-international-academy.html

Sheffield, E. F. (1962). *Education in Canada.* Statistics Canada.

Canadian Community Colleges 69

Simon Fraser University. (n.d.). *Fraser International College*. https://www.fraseric.ca/

Statistics Canada. (2016). *Census profile, 2016 census*. https://www12.statcan. gc.ca/census-recensement/2016/dp-pd/prof/details/page.cfm?Lang=E& Geo1=PR&Code1=01&Geo2=PR&Code2=01&Data=Count&SearchText =Canada&SearchType=Begins&SearchPR=01&B1=Ethnic%20 origin&TABID=1

Statistics Canada. (2018). *Table 17-10-0057-01 Projected population, by projection scenario, age and sex*. https://doi.org/10.25318/1710005701-eng

Statistics Canada. (2020). *Table 37-10-0086-01 Postsecondary enrolments, by status of student in Canada, country of citizenship and gender*. https://doi. org/10.25318/3710008601-eng

Usher, A. (2018). *The state of post-secondary education in Canada, 2018*. Toronto: Higher Education Strategy Associates.

Usher, A. (2019). *The state of post-secondary education in Canada, 2018*. Toronto: Higher Education Strategy Associates.

Wilkins, S., & Huisman, J. (2011). International student destination choice: The influence of home campus experience on the decision to consider branch campuses. *Journal of Marketing for Higher Education, 21*(1), 61–83. https://doi. org/10.1080/08841241.2011.573592

UNESCO. (2019). *Outbound internationally mobile students by host region*. http://data.uis.unesco.org/Index.aspx?queryid=172

Zhang, Y. (2016). An overlooked population in community college: International students' (in)validation experiences with academic advising. *Community College Review, 44*(2), 153–170. https://doi.org/10.1177/0091552116633293

Author Bios

Oleg Legusov is an international student advisor at Seneca College of Applied Arts and Technology. He previously worked as an agency coordinator, guiding the activities of student recruitment agents in multiple regions of the world. He is also a PhD candidate in Leadership, Adult and Higher Education at the Ontario Institute of Studies in Education. His research interests include the experience of international community college graduates in host-country labor markets and equity, diversity, and inclusion in multicultural societies. He has a BA (econ.) from McGill University and an MEd from Nipissing University (research on at-risk students) and studied Chinese culture and language at Beijing Language and Culture University.

Hayfa Jafar has worked at Centennial College of Applied Arts and Technology as an institutional research analyst since 2011. Her duties involve developing and improving student-retention data tools and taking part in projects related to international student retention and satisfaction. She was previously a quality assurance coordinator and a senior math and statistics instructor at a community college in the United Arab Emirates. She is pursuing a

PhD in Leadership, Adult and Higher Education at the Ontario Institute of Studies in Education. Her major area of research is the internationalization of higher education. She has master's degrees in applied statistics from Al Mustansrya University, Baghdad, Iraq, and in quality management from the University of Wollongong, Dubai, United Arab Emirates.

5 Community College Finances and International Student Enrollment

Ji Yeon Bae and Manuel S. González Canché

Introduction

Community colleges are public institutions that have contributed to the expansion and democratization of higher education in the United States. Established in the early 20th century as junior colleges that provided additional education beyond high school, community colleges have evolved to serve a wide range of functions such as workforce training, awarding of credentials and associate's degrees, and facilitating transfer to bachelor's degree programs (Baime & Baum, 2016; Meier, 2018). As reflected in their name, community colleges have historically served their local geographic communities by providing affordable education opportunities for local students.

These local institutions are also responding to an increasingly global world. Although foreign students have enrolled in community colleges in small numbers as early as the 1960s (Bevis & Lucas, 2007), community colleges have started to intentionally recruit international students in more recent years, recognizing the educational and financial benefits involved (Viggiano et al., 2018). According to the Institute of International Education [IIE] (2019b), the number of foreign students in community colleges increased from 70,616 in 2000 to 86,351 in 2019. Currently, foreign students studying at associate's colleges make up approximately 15 percent of total undergraduates studying in the United States (author's calculation using IIE, 2019a). Despite this increasing prevalence, the rhetoric and research around internationalization in the United States have revolved around 4-year institutions. Furthermore, existing research on international students in the 2-year sector have captured reasons behind the growth of international students (Anayah & Kuk, 2015) and some aspects of student experiences and outcomes (Mamiseishvili, 2012; Zhang, 2016), but the broader institutional implications of foreign student enrollment have yet to be examined in-depth.

We address this gap using a financial lens. Drawing from resource dependence and academic capitalism theories, we seek to understand foreign student enrollment in light of community colleges' fiscal and policy contexts. In addition to navigating volatility in public sources of funding, many community colleges have faced substantial declines in state funding in the past few decades, resulting in increased financial reliance on student tuition (Mullin et al., 2015; Palmer, 2013). In this context, we tested whether declines in public funding are associated with increases in international student enrollment, and whether international student enrollment is positively associated with tuition revenue. To test these hypotheses, we utilized data from publicly available sources on US higher education institutions and panel regression techniques. In light of the current unprecedented uncertainty in international student mobility and constrained public resources, understanding the financial implications of the ebb and flow of international student enrollment over time could help community college practitioners, policymakers, and researchers prepare for the future.

Literature Review

With increases in global mobility and connectivity across all sectors of society, the internationalization of higher education has been a much-discussed topic. Broadly defined as "the process of integrating an international, intercultural, or global dimension into the purpose, functions or delivery of postsecondary education," internationalization manifests in various ways at the national, sector, and institutional levels (Knight, 2015, p. 2). Among many dimensions of internationalization, the movement of students across borders has been of special interest to higher education researchers and practitioners. In 2013, 4.1 million students were globally mobile at the postsecondary level (United Nations Educational, Scientific and Cultural Organization, 2015). The United States has been a prominent destination, hosting 872,214 international students in 2018–2019 (IIE, 2019a).

Research in the United States has examined international student experiences (e.g. Lee & Rice, 2007) and institutional implications of international student enrollment (e.g. Cantwell, 2015; Shih, 2017); but has tended to focus on 4-year institutions. A small but important line of research has looked at factors motivating international student enrollment in the 2-year sector, finding that students are drawn to cheap tuition, lower barriers to entry, and transfer opportunities (Anayah & Kuk, 2015; Hagedorn, 2020; Zhang & Hagedorn, 2018) and institutional leaders are attracted to the revenue-generating potential of international students (Viggiano et al., 2018). However, further research that situates and examines international student enrollment in the broader institutional context of community colleges could provide insights into how these historically local institutions navigate a global world.

Community colleges are nested in policy contexts that govern the fiscal resources available for these institutions. While the federal government contributes via student financial aid (e.g. Pell grants), states play a more prominent role in the governance and funding of community colleges via appropriations. Furthermore, unlike other public 4-year institutions, many community colleges receive local appropriations (Dowd & Shieh, 2013). In aggregate, state and local appropriations constitute a bulk of public funding for community colleges. Across public 2-year institutions in 2016, state appropriations comprised about 25 percent of total revenues, followed by local appropriations (~20 percent), and tuition and fees (~16 percent) (Ginder et al., 2017). Nonetheless, the specific funding arrangement of community colleges vary widely across—and even within—states. Some states (e.g. California) are strongly state-supported; some (e.g. Vermont) are dependent on tuition revenue; some (e.g. Illinois) follow an equal share model that splits funding across the different sources (Mullin et al., 2015).

Despite these variations, a shift towards an increased reliance on tuition has been a trend in all US public higher education institutions. Appropriations for higher education are described as a balance wheel in state budgets, where appropriations are cut more severely than other spending categories during recessions because institutions have an alternative source of revenue via student tuition (Delaney & Doyle, 2011). Indeed, when state budgets fall short, institutions often respond by increasing tuition. The share of net tuition in the total education revenue of public institutions has increased from 28.8 percent in 1992 to 46.4 percent in 2017 (State Higher Education Executive Office, 2017). Community colleges have not been immune to this broader volatility and shifting balance of revenue. From 2004–2005 to 2014–2015, the average tuition revenue per student in community colleges has increased by 26 percent, while revenue from state and local sources has decreased (Baum et al., 2018). States vary in philosophies and policies around the setting of tuition in public institutions; however, institutions of higher education governing boards typically have more discretion in setting nonresident tuition, and a formalized policy around nonresident tuition—if it exists—often requires nonresident tuition to be higher than resident tuition (Carlson, 2013).

We utilized resource dependence and academic capitalism theories to situate international student enrollment in these contexts. Resource dependence theory sees the ecologies of organizations as crucial to understanding their behaviors: when their external environments shift, organizations adapt their behavior to secure necessary resources (Pfeffer & Salancik, 1978). Academic capitalism theory provides one lens into the changing ecology of public higher education. Slaughter and Rhoades (2004) have argued that the boundaries separating colleges, the state, and the market are blurred in the knowledge-based economy; colleges actively

74 *Ji Yeon Bae and Manuel S. González Canché*

engage in market-like behaviors, especially when public support is dwindling. The internationalization of higher education also represents a change in institutions' ecologies, as greater student mobility across borders gives access to foreign student markets. These changing environments could shape institutions' recruitment and enrollment management behaviors. For example, research on 4-year institutions has found that declines in state funding are associated with increases in higher-tuition-paying out-state (Jaquette & Curs, 2015) and foreign students (Bound et al., 2016). However, whether institutions can, indeed, leverage additional tuition revenue from foreign students could depend on their ability to attract sufficient numbers of such students (Cantwell, 2015). Drawing from these theoretical frameworks and prior research, we examine the relationships between institutional finances and foreign student enrollment for community colleges.

Research Method

Sample and Variables

Our main data source was the Integrated Postsecondary Education Data System (IPEDS, 2002–2014a; 2002–2014b), a system of annual surveys administered by the National Center for Education Statistics. IPEDS includes data on various institutional characteristics and outcomes for all US institutions receiving federal aid. For some enrollment and fiscal variables, we utilized the Delta Cost Project (DCP, 2002–2015), which standardizes fiscal variables from IPEDS across the years to enable easier longitudinal analyses. We also pulled county-level data that might influence community college finance and enrollment from the US Bureau of Labor Statistics (BLS, 2002–2015) and the National Bureau of Economic Research (NBER, 2002–2015)'s public-use data archive of US Census data.

The number of first-time international students in each community college for each year was a key variable. Consistent with prior research on international student enrollment (Bound et al., 2016; Cantwell, 2015), we operationalized this measure as the number of degree/certificate-seeking nonresident alien undergraduates in the IPEDS fall enrollment survey. The nonresident alien category captures non-US citizen students who are on a visa but could also include some undocumented students who have obtained lawful stay through Deferred Action for Childhood Arrivals (IPEDS, 2016). Despite the limitation, this measure represents the most extensive publicly available data on international students for all community colleges across multiple years.

Our main financial variables of interests—revenues from state and local appropriations and tuition—were obtained from DCP. Revenue from state and local appropriation combines revenues from the state through acts of a state legislative body or from governmental entities below the state level. We used two measures of tuition revenue: gross tuition revenue and net tuition revenue. The former is the total amount received from student tuition and fees, and the latter is the total amount net of institutional grant or aid applied to tuition. Both measures of tuition revenue include tuition and fees paid from federal, state, or local aid (DCP, n.d.).

We also included institutional-level controls from DCP that might influence the relationship between foreign student enrollment and institutional finances, drawing from relevant literature and our theoretical framework. First, we included in-district, in-state, and out-state tuition and fees. Domestic students could pay any of the tuition levels, while international students typically pay out-of-state tuition and fees. Second, we controlled for the number of domestic students by including the number of students paying in-district and in-state tuition as reported in the IPEDS Student Financial Aid survey. We did not include students who pay out-state tuition, because this could include international students. Third, in order to account for other revenue sources that may influence community colleges' enrollment management behavior, we included revenue from federal appropriations, and federal (excluding Pell), state, and local grants and contracts. Finally, we included total student aid, which combines student aid from federal (including Pell), state, local, and institutional sources. While widely used in higher education research, one limitation of DCP is that multi-campus institutions could be collapsed into one institution in the database, creating potentially misaligned or mismatched institutions between IPEDS and DCP (Jaquette & Parra, 2016). However, this limitation affected a small portion of institutions in our dataset: 13 percent of institutions represented a "grouped" institution and those grouped institutions were typically collapsed with only one or two other campuses. Furthermore, community colleges that were grouped with 4-year institutions in the DCP database (e.g. City College of New York) were excluded from the analysis.

Our models had two county-level controls. Prior research on 4-year institutions have used state-level economic indicators or population estimates (González Canché, 2014, 2017, 2018; Jaquette & Curs, 2015), but state-level aggregates may mask important variations within states since community colleges tend to serve their local communities. Therefore, we used county-level data to provide a more granular measure of local economic and demographic conditions than state aggregates. Specifically, we used unemployment rates from BLS and total population between the ages of 15 and 34 from NBER's compilation of Census data, both of which are typically predictive of community college enrollment (Long, 2015). The total population between the ages of 15 and 34 also serves as a proxy for the potential pool of local students

76 Ji Yeon Bae and Manuel S. González Canché

enrolling in community colleges, because the average age of community college students is 28 (American Association of Community Colleges, 2020).

Our analysis encompassed the academic years from 2002–2003 to 2014–2015, a period during which variables were most extensively available from our data sources. Defining community colleges as public 2-year institutions in IPEDS, we only kept institutions that reported data for all 13 panel years ($N = 931$). After merging relevant institutional and county-level data from DCP, BLS, and NBER, we removed 188 institutions that were missing observations on our key variables—international student freshmen enrollment, state and local appropriations, or tuition revenue—during any of the panel years. When institutions were missing control variables, we applied a linear interpolation using the imputeTS package in R, which fills-in missing years of data by fitting a straight line through the years in which observations exist (Moritz & Bartz-Beielstein, 2017). We applied the interpolation when there were less than three consecutive years of missing data and removed 24 institutions that still had missingness after this process. Our final analytic sample had 9,347 observations (719 institutions across 13 years).

Analytic Strategy

Utilizing panel data provides an opportunity to address bias from individual heterogeneity that might be present in cross-sectional data (Zhang, 2010). Our basic model specification was as follows:

$$log(Y_{it}) = \beta X_{i,t-j} + W_{i,t-j}\gamma + V_{i,t-j}\theta + \delta_i + \alpha_t + \varepsilon_{it} \qquad (1)$$

where, Y_{it} represented the number of international freshmen or tuition revenue at community college i at year t, depending on the model. X_{it-j} represented the main independent variables. In the model predicting international freshmen, $X_{i,t-j}$ represented state and local appropriations for community college i lagged by a year ($j = 1$). Appropriations were lagged because we hypothesized that the prior year's appropriations would inform institutions' enrollment management and recruitment efforts in the current year. In the model predicting tuition revenue, $X_{i,t-j}$ represented the number of international students in college i at the same year in which tuition revenue was measured ($j = 0$). In both models, β was our parameter of interest, capturing the relationship between the independent and the dependent variables. $W_{i,t-j}$ is a matrix of time-varying, institutional-level covariates (tuition and fees, in-district and in-state students, other revenue sources) and $V_{i,t-j}$ is a matrix of time-varying, county-level covariates (unemployment rates, population age 15–34). Similar to the rationale for lagging state and local appropriations, institutional and county-level covariates hypothesized

Community College Finances 77

to influence the institution's enrollment management behaviors were lagged 1 year. Finally, δ_i and α_t captured year-invariant institution-specific effects and institution-invariant year-specific effects, respectively, to control for unobserved individual- and year-specific factors.

All count and fiscal variables were log-transformed, so coefficients were interpreted as elasticities. Dollar variables were adjusted to 2015 dollars using the Consumer Price Index (DCP, n.d.). Heteroskedasticity-robust standard errors were clustered at the institutional level. Finally, we performed Hausman tests comparing random effects versus fixed effects model specifications: all tests yielded results favoring the latter, so all models were estimated with α_t and δ_i as fixed effects.

Results

Table 5.1 shows descriptive statistics for all variables at the beginning and end of the panel period. While the average number of first-time international students increased during this time, international students still represented a small proportion of the first-time student body at community colleges compared to in-district or in-state students. On average, county populations increased during the panel period, but

Table 5.1 Descriptive Statistics

	2002–2003 (N = 719)		2014–2015 (N = 719)	
	Mean	*St. Dev.*	*Mean*	*St. Dev.*
Foreign Enrollment (count)[a]	15	51	23	83
In-District/In-State Enrollment (count)[b]	592	641	748	791
County Pop. Age 15–34 (count)	177,150	450,939	189,173	462,677
County Unemployment (prop.)	0.06	0.02	0.06	0.02
In-District Tuition & Fees ($1)	2,169	1,090	3,229	1,237
In-State Tuition & Fees ($1)	2,729	1,711	3,814	1,804
Out-State Tuition & Fees ($1)	6,278	3,207	7,437	2,679
State & Local App. ($1K)	$27,734	$36,947	$31,329	$42,690
Gov't Grants & Contracts, Fed App. ($1K)	$7,382	$10,803	$8,254	$13,923
Gross Tuition Revenue ($1K)	$11,121	$12,320	$19,105	$21,947
Net Tuition Revenue ($1K)	$10,418	$11,487	$17,597	$19,932
Total Student Aid ($1K)	$7,817	$9,628	$15,222	$19,869

Source: IPEDS, DCP, BLS, Census (NBER)

Note: Rounded to the nearest whole number, except for county unemployment rates.

[a] Number of first-time, full-time and part-time, degree/certificate seeking undergraduates who are categorized as nonresident aliens (fall cohort).

[b] Number of first-time, full-time, local and in-state degree/certificate seeking undergraduates (fall cohort).

78 *Ji Yeon Bae and Manuel S. González Canché*

county unemployment rates stayed largely unchanged. Out-state tuition and fees were almost two times higher than in-district or in-state tuition, and all three tuition levels increased over time. While revenues increased across all sources and categories, the increases in tuition revenue were far more dramatic than increases in revenues from governmental sources. Furthermore, total student aid nearly doubled during the panel years.

Table 5.2 reports findings from our regression models. First, in modelling the relationship between the previous year's state and local appropriations and international student enrollment, we found no strong evidence of an association. The negative coefficient estimate indicates that a 1 percent decline in state and local appropriations is associated with a 0.05 percent increase in the number of foreign freshmen, while controlling for other variables in the model; however, the estimate is not statistically significant. Similarly, in modeling the relationship between foreign student enrollment and two measures of tuition revenue, we found no evidence of a statistically significant association. However, for the latter two models, the number of in-district or in-state students and total student aid were positively and significantly associated with tuition revenue.

Discussion and Conclusions

We found weak associations between international student enrollment and community college finances. While declines in state appropriations have been associated with increases in international or out-state students in the 4-year sector (Bound et al., 2016; Jaquette & Curs, 2015), this relationship was not statistically significant for community colleges. Furthermore, we found no significant association between international student enrollment and tuition revenue, consistent with Cantwell (2015)'s finding that the positive association between tuition revenue and foreign student enrollment depends on institutional type and prestige.

One interpretation of our findings is that international student enrollment is pursued by a few—but not all—community colleges (especially those located in California, see González Canché, 2018). Figure 5.1 shows the trends in international student enrollment by quantiles for each year. Any changes in foreign student enrollment are driven by institutions in the upper 95th percentile, but a majority of community colleges have near-zero numbers of foreign students throughout the years. The overall low numbers may reflect challenges in the recruitment process, such as a lack of awareness about community colleges in foreign countries (Loo, 2016). Nonetheless, that there are some institutions and states

Table 5.2 Regression Results

	Dependent Variable		
	International Enrollment	*Gross Tuition Revenue*	*Net Tuition Revenue*
	(1)	(2)	(3)
Log State & Local Appropriations (lag)	−0.048	0.021	0.021
	(0.090)	(0.017)	(0.019)
Log International Enrollment	–	0.002	0.002
		(0.001)	(0.002)
Log Gov't Grants & Contracts, Fed App. (lag)	0.011	0.015*	0.016*
	(0.074)	(0.008)	(0.009)
Log In-District/In-State Enrollment[a]	0.022	0.005**	0.006**
	(0.022)	(0.002)	(0.003)
Log County Pop. Age 15–34 (lag)	0.578	0.087	0.091
	(1.038)	(0.109)	(0.128)
County Unemployment (lag)	5.331	1.033**	1.032*
	(3.396)	(0.422)	(0.540)
Log Out-State Tuition & Fees	0.140	0.001	−0.019
	(0.101)	(0.030)	(0.025)
Log In-State Tuition & Fees	–	0.054*	0.071*
		(0.028)	(0.036)
Log In-District Tuition & Fees	–	0.123*	0.124**
		(0.069)	(0.049)
Log Total Student Aid	–	0.292***	0.206***
		(0.040)	(0.037)
Institution fixed effects	Yes	Yes	Yes
Year fixed effects	Yes	Yes	Yes
Observations	9,347	9,347	9,321[b]
R^2	0.688	0.974	0.957

Note: All enrollment and fiscal variables are logged. In the presence of 0s in the variable, we added a small constant for the log transformation (+0.01 for count variables, +1 for financial variables). Heteroskedasticity-robust standard errors, clustered at the institutional level, are shown in parentheses. Numbers are rounded to the nearest thousandths.

[a] In-District/In-State Enrollment is lagged for model (1) and contemporaneous for models (2) & (3).

[b] The number of observations in model (3) is smaller than (1) and (2), because a few cases of negative net tuition revenue were excluded.

*p<0.1, **p<0.05, ***p<0.01.

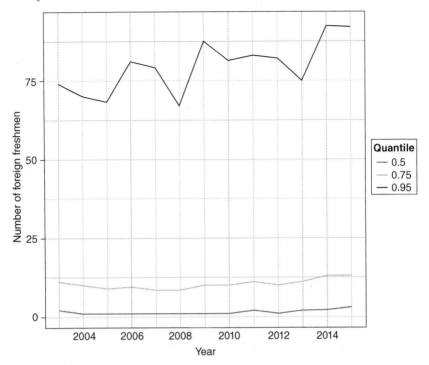

Figure 5.1 Line Trend Plot of Foreign Student Enrollment. (Source: IPEDS)

Note: Graph shows quantile trend for the 50%, 75%, and 95% percentile for each year

that still attract a sizable foreign student population warrants further exploration into institutional and state heterogeneity within the sector.

Our findings also suggest that the resource environments for community colleges are still strongly determined by local student demand and public sources of funding. Our models found in-district/in-state enrollment and total student aid to be positive and significant predictors of gross and net tuition revenue. In particular, as seen in Figure 5.2, the total amount of student aid has increased dramatically during the panel years. This increase was largely driven by increases in Pell grants, which are federal aid offered to low-income students in the United States. The total amount of Pell aid to community colleges grew from approximately $7 million in 2003 to over $17 million in 2011 (author's calculation using DCP, 2002–2015). In light of these considerations, resident students who represent a larger portion of the student body, and low-income students who are eligible for federal Pell aid, might play a more

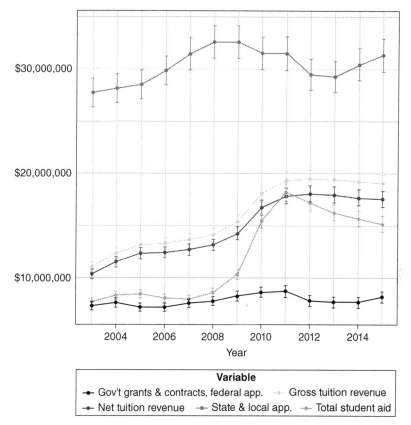

Figure 5.2 Trends in Fiscal Variables. (Source: DCP)

Note: Graph plots means with the errors for each fiscal variable by year

significant role in shaping the institution's enrollment management behavior than foreign students.

Implications

Our findings help to address a gap in research on US higher education institutions that have tended to overlook the public 2-year sector in its international dimension. We found that institutional finances and foreign student enrollment in community colleges do not mirror what is known from the 4-year sector. Furthermore, our research suggests that there is also heterogeneity within the community college sector. We found that foreign students were enrolled—often in large numbers—in a subset of institutions in some states, suggesting that there might be institutional- and state-level policies that create a particularly welcoming environment for foreign students. Previous work has found that states like California play a significant role in attracting international students to the 2-year sector (González Canché, 2018, p. 208) and that certain institutional practices successfully recruit and support international students (Hagedorn, 2020). Future research that continues to recognize, capture, and enhance our understanding of sector, state, and institutional heterogeneity could help paint a more accurate picture of how internationalization manifests across various levels and contexts.

For practitioners, it is important to remember that our findings paint a broad picture of institutional finances and require additional considerations when interpreting results in the context of specific institutions. One general implication from our research is that international student enrollment has not been a silver bullet for increased revenue. As such, rather than turn to international student recruitment for the sole purpose of revenue generation, institutions would benefit from considering and pursuing internationalization with a clear strategy and vision that accounts for the specific contexts of their institution. For policymakers at the federal, state, and local level, that the local and public nature of community colleges have largely been preserved over the years may come as good news. Policymakers could further benefit from paying more careful attention to how specific financial levers (e.g. appropriations, student aid) influence community college enrollment and use those levers in a way that is aligned with their expectations for these local institutions.

Finally, interpreting our findings in light of the unprecedented uncertainty in international student mobility and drains in public resources due to COVID-19 yields interesting insights. From one perspective, our findings suggest that community colleges' tuition revenues are generally cushioned from projected declines in international students, which is a concern for some 4-year institutions that are strongly dependent on foreign enrollment. However, public sources of revenue and resources are also facing huge drains as the United States grapples with the public health crisis. How these different moving pieces will affect institutions' enrollment management behavior and fiscal conditions remain to be observed and examined.

Acknowledgment

We thank our colleagues, Alan Ruby and Jeremy Wright-Kim, for the helpful discussions and feedback.

References

American Association of Community Colleges. (2020). *Fast facts from our fact sheet.* https://www.aacc.nche.edu/research-trends/fast-facts/

Anayah, B., & Kuk, L. (2015). The growth of international student enrollment at community colleges and implications. *Community College Journal of Research and Practice*, *39*(12), 1099–1110. https://doi.org/10.1080/10668926.2014.934409

Baime, D., & Baum, S. (2016). *Community colleges: Multiple missions, diverse student bodies, and a range of policy solutions*. Urban Institute. https://www.urban.org/research/publication/community-colleges-multiple-missions-diverse-student-bodies-and-range-policy-solutions

Baum, S., Mcpherson, M. S., Braga, B., & Minton, S. (2018). *Tuition and state appropriations using evidence and logic to gain perspective*. Urban Institute. https://www.urban.org/sites/default/files/publication/96791/tuition_and_state_appropriations_1.pdf

Bevis, T. B., & Lucas, C. J. (2007). *International students in American colleges and universities: A history*. Palgrave Macmillan. https://doi.org/10.1057/9780230609754

Bound, J., Braga, B., Khanna, G., & Turner, S. (2016). *A passage to America: University funding and international students* (Working Paper Series No. 22981). National Bureau of Economic Research. https://doi.org/10.3386/w22981

Cantwell, B. (2015). Are international students cash cows? Examining the relationship between new international undergraduate enrollments and institutional revenue at public colleges and universities in the US. *Journal of International Students*, *5*(4), 512–525.

Carlson, A. (2013). *State tuition, fee, and financial assistance policies for public colleges and universities*. State Higher Education Executive Officers. https://sheeo.org/wp-content/uploads/2019/04/Tuition-and-Fees-Policy-Report-2013.pdf

Delaney, J. A., & Doyle, W. R. (2011). State spending on higher education: Testing the balance wheel over time. *Journal of Education Finance*, *36*(4), 343–368. https://www.muse.jhu.edu/article/431700

Delta Cost Project (DCP). (n.d.). Data dictionary. *Delta Cost Project*. https://deltacostproject.org/delta-cost-project-database

Delta Cost Project (DCP). (2002–2015). Delta Cost Project database 1987–2015 (STATA) [Data Set]. American Institute for Research. https://deltacostproject.org/delta-cost-project-database

Dowd, A. C., & Shieh, L. T. (2013). Community college financing: Equity, efficiency and accountability. *NEA 2013 Almanac of Higher Education* 37–65. National Education Association.

Ginder, S., Kelly-Reid, J., & Mann, F. (2017). *Enrollment and employees in postsecondary institutions, fall 2016; and financial statistics and academic libraries, fiscal year 2016: First look (provisional data) (NCES 2018–002)*. U.S. Department of Education. National Center for Education Statistics. https://nces.ed.gov/pubsearch/

González Canché, M. S. (2014). Localized competition in the non-resident student market. *Economics of Education Review*, *43*, 21–35.

González Canché, M. S. (2017). The heterogeneous non-resident student body: Measuring the effect of out-of-state students' home-state wealth on tuition and fee price variations. *Research in Higher Education*, *58*(2), 141–183.

González Canché, M. S. (2018). Geographical network analysis and spatial econometrics as tools to enhance our understanding of student migration patterns and benefits in the US higher education network. *The Review of Higher Education*, 41(2), 169–216.

Hagedorn, L. S. (2020). *International students in community colleges: An unplanned diversity*. American Council on Education. https://www.acenet.edu/Documents/International-Students-in-Community-Colleges.pdf

Institute of International Education. (2019a). *International students by academic level, 2016/17–2018/19*, Open Doors report on international education exchange. https://opendoorsdata.org/data/international-students/academic-level/

Institute of International Education. (2019b). *International students community colleges, total students, 1999/00–2018/19*. Open Doors report on international education exchange.

Jaquette, O., & Curs, B. R. (2015). Creating the out-of-state university: Do public universities increase nonresident freshman enrollment in response to declining state appropriations? *Research in Higher Education*, 56, 535–565. https://doi.org/10.1007/s11162-015-9362-2

Jaquette, O., & Parra, E. (2016). The problem with the Delta cost project database. *Research in Higher Education*, 57(5), 630–651. https://doi.org/10.1007/s11162-015-9399-2

Knight, J. (2015). Updated definition of internationalization. *International Higher Education*, 33, 2–3. https://doi.org/10.6017/ihe.2003.33.7391

Lee, J. J., & Rice, C. (2007). Welcome to America? International student perceptions of discrimination. *Higher Education*, 53, 381–409. https://doi.org/10.1007/s10734-005-4508-3

Long, B. T. (2015). The financial crisis and college enrollment: How have students and their families responded? In J. R. Brown & C. M. Hoxby (Eds.), *How the financial crisis and Great Recession affected higher education* (pp. 209–233). University of Chicago Press. https://doi.org/10.7208/chicago/9780226201979.001.0001

Loo, B. K. (2016). Community colleges: An unexpected on-ramp for international students. *World Education News & Reviews*. https://wenr.wes.org/2016/11/international-students-u-s-community-colleges

Mamiseishvili, K. (2012). Academic and social integration and persistence of international students at U.S. two-year institutions. *Community College Journal of Research and Practice*, 36(1), 15–27. https://doi.org/10.1080/10668926.2012.619093

Meier, K. (2018). The historical origins of the comprehensive community college mission, 1901–1965. In J. S. Levine & S. T. Kater (Eds.), *Understanding Community colleges* (2nd ed., pp. 1–19). Routledge. https://doi.org/10.4324/9781315268071

Moritz, S., & Bartz-Beielstein, T. (2017). imputeTS: Time series missing value imputation in R. *R Journal*, 9(1), 207–218. https://doi.org/10.32614/rj-2017-009

Mullin, C., Baime, D. S., & Honeyman, D. (2015). *Community college finance: A guide for institutional leaders*. Jossey-Bass.

National Bureau of Economic Research (NBER). (2002–2015). *Census U.S. intercensal county population data by age, sex, race, and Hispanic origin [Data*

Set]. https://data.nber.org/data/census-intercensal-county-population-age-sex-race-hispanic.html

Palmer, J. (2013). State fiscal support for community colleges. In J. S. Levine & S. T. Kater (Eds.), *Understanding community colleges* (1st ed., pp. 171–183). Routledge.

Pfeffer, J., & Salancik, G. R. (1978). *The external control of organizations: A resource dependence perspective.* Harper & Row.

Shih, K. (2017). Do international students crowd-out or cross-subsidize Americans in higher education? *Journal of Public Economics, 156*(October), 170–184. https://doi.org/10.1016/j.jpubeco.2017.10.003

Slaughter, S., & Rhoades, G. (2004). *Academic capitalism and the new economy: Markets, state, and higher education.* Johns Hopkins University Press.

State Higher Education Executive Office. (2017) *State higher education finance: FY 2017.* Boulder, CO. https://shefstage.sheeo.org/wp-content/uploads/2020/04/SHEEO_SHEF_FY17_Report.pdf

United Nations Educational, Scientific and Cultural Organization. (2015). *UNESCO science report: Towards 2030.* https://en.unesco.org/node/252278

U.S. Bureau of Labor Statistics (BLS). (2002–2015). Local area unemployment statistics: County data [Data Set]. https://www.bls.gov/lau/#tables

U.S. Department of Education, National Center for Education Statistics, Integrated Postsecondary Education Data System (IPEDS). (2002–2014a). Fall Enrollment: Race/ethnicity, gender, attendance status, and level of student [Data set].https://nces.ed.gov/ipeds/datacenter/

U.S. Department of Education, National Center for Education Statistics, Integrated Postsecondary Education Data System (IPEDS). (2002–2014b). Institutional Characteristic: Directory information [Data set]. https://nces.ed.gov/ipeds/datacenter/

U.S. Department of Education, National Center for Education Statistics, Integrated Postsecondary Education Data System (IPEDS). (2016). *2015–16 survey materials FAQ: Fall enrollment.* https://nces.ed.gov/ipeds/UseTheData/ArchivedSurveyMaterialPdf?year=2015&fileName=package_6_77.pdf

Viggiano, T., López Damián, A. I., Morales Vázquez, E., & Levin, J. S. (2018). The others: Equitable access, international students, and the community college. *Journal of Studies in International Education, 22*(1), 71–85. https://doi.org/10.1177/1028315317725883

Zhang, L. (2010). The use of panel data models in higher education policy studies. In M. B. Paulsen (Ed.), *Higher education: Handbook of theory and research* (Vol. 25, pp. 307–349). Springer. https://doi.org/10.1080/01425690701737481

Zhang, Y. (2016). An overlooked population in community college: International students' (in)validation experiences with academic advising. *Community College Review, 44*(2), 153–170. https://doi.org/10.1177/0091552116633293

Zhang, Y., & Hagedorn, L. S. (2018). International student enrollment in U.S. community colleges. In J. S. Levine & S. T. Kater (Eds.), *Understanding community colleges* (2nd ed., pp. 89–108). Routledge. https://doi.org/10.4324/9781315268071

Author Bios

Ji Yeon Bae is a PhD student in Higher Education at the University of Pennsylvania. Her major interests are community colleges, internationalization, and the use of big data in higher education.

Manuel S. González Canché, PhD, is an Associate Professor in Higher Education at the University of Pennsylvania. He relies on network, spatial, and quasi-experimental methods to identify factors associated with improving the chances of success of low income and minoritized students.

Part II

Understanding Support System and Challenges of International Students at Community Colleges

6 International Students' Career Development Preparation at the American Community College

Hannah Rapp, Yi-jung Wu,
Ran Liu, and Xiaoli Jing

Introduction

With the accelerating trends of globalization and the neoliberalism development of modern education systems, an increasing number of students now choose to study abroad to develop intercultural understanding and to enhance global competence. For the past several decades, the United States has been the most popular study destination for international students around the world (United Nations Educational, Scientific, and Cultural Organization Institute for Statistics, 2020). According to the Open Doors report by the Institute of International Education (IIE) (2020), over 1 million international students studied in the United States during the 2019/2020 academic year, among whom 7.4 percent attended community colleges. However, while much research has been dedicated to the study of international students at universities, there is a dearth of knowledge regarding international students at community colleges. Similar to their peers at 4-year institutions, many international students in US community colleges have expressed a desire to stay and work in the United States after graduation (Crockett & Hays, 2011). Alternatively, other students plan to leverage their US degrees in their home countries or third countries for better career outcomes (Adams, 2016). Regardless of whether these students pursue a career in the United States or not, it is crucial for researchers and college leaders to understand international students' unique career development paths in order to develop effective college practices and policies.

The present chapter seeks to: (1) review the career expectations and aspirations of international students attending community colleges; (2) review the common challenges of career development that international students attending community colleges face; and (3) provide an overview of career services provided by community colleges to international students. We conclude by discussing the limitations in current research and future research directions, and by providing implications for improving community college policies and practices to better address the specific career development needs of international students.

Career Expectations and Aspirations of International Students in Community Colleges

As reflected in the existing literature, international students studying in US community colleges have three major expectations and aspirations when it comes to career development. Firstly, one reason for international students to choose the United States as their study destination is that they value American higher education credentials and believe that they can receive better career training in the United States than in their home countries (Anayah & Kuk, 2015; Bohman, 2009; Zeszotarski, 2004). For example, James, an international student with entrepreneurial ambitions attending community college in Iowa, shared that he came to the United States to study business because the education is better than what is offered in Central America (Adams, 2016). In addition, several international students in a California community college indicated that a US degree would make them more competitive in the job market in their home country and lead to better job opportunities (Zeszotarski, 2004). Furthermore, US colleges may offer degrees or courses that are not common or even available in other countries. Adams (2016) cites that programs in more technical areas such as fire science or nursing assisting may be less available in international students' home countries. For example, an international student from Japan shared that he was interested in a career in the film industry, but he could not find courses meeting his career goals at Japanese universities (Zeszotarski, 2004).

Secondly, international students attending US community colleges may hope to demonstrate cultural advantages that are indirectly related to their future careers. International students in the United States expect to enhance particular capacities such as foreign language fluency, global social networks, knowledge of other cultures, open-mindedness, independence, and the ability to work in an international setting and quickly adapt to new situations (Zeszotarski, 2004). Adams (2016) found that half of the six participants she interviewed indicated that studying the English language was a factor in their decision to attend US community college. According to the IIE (2019a), the plurality of international students who attend US community colleges are from China (18.6 percent), Vietnam (11 percent), Japan (5.8 percent), and South Korea (5.6 percent). According to the US Census Bureau (2020), these four nations are also among the top ten nations that do business with the United States. Studying overseas may put an international student in an advantageous position for working with a multinational or US company. Thus, non-academic skills that students expect to acquire while studying in the United States should not be overlooked.

International students may enroll in community colleges as a starting point with the expectation that it will facilitate their access to more prestigious 4-year institutions (Adams, 2016; Zeszotarski, 2004). The *US News* reported that Santa Monica College, the leading transfer institution to the University of California for 29 consecutive years, transferred 467 international students into the California State University and University of California systems at the end of the 2019 school year (Durrani, 2020). Other peer-reviewed studies support the observation that international students attend community colleges in order to transfer to 4-year institutions. Ghazzawi et al. (2020) examined longitudinal data at a large community college district in Texas and reported that 32.6 percent of the 543 international students transferred from a community college to a 4-year institution. Similarly, Hagedorn and Mi-Chung (2005) surveyed international students in the Los Angeles Community College District and found that 79 percent of the 466 students intended to transfer to a 4-year institution.

On the other hand, students also recognize some advantages of community colleges in terms of career development. Findings in Ghazzawi et al. (2020) indicate that 19 percent of community college international students opt for a nontransfer degree, or a degree that cannot transfer credits to a 4-year institution. Similarly, Hagedorn and Mi-Chung (2005) show that 55.4 percent of international students in community college indicated the goal of attaining an associate degree. One of the most common reasons that international students choose community colleges over 4-year colleges is the relatively affordable tuition and fees (Bohman, 2009). Therefore, community colleges provide an opportunity for students with relatively lower family socioeconomic status (SES) to gain overseas experiences. Also, different from most 4-year institutions, community colleges typically do not require SAT scores and tend to have lower levels of selectiveness and competitiveness (Anayah & Kuk, 2015). Some students also believe that the relatively smaller class sizes at community colleges offer better support for their limited English proficiency (Adams, 2016; Bohman, 2009). Students may also expect higher levels of flexibility, better course placement, and more interactions with native students at small-scale community colleges (Zeszotarski, 2004). These characteristics thus make community colleges an attractive alternative for international students with less competitive academic backgrounds but clear career goals.

Challenges Faced by International Students during Career Preparations

International students who transition from school to work in the United States face many obstacles such as language and cultural barriers, lack of social capital, unfavorable immigration policies, and perceived employer biases. Although research on the career development of international

92 *Hannah Rapp et al.*

students in the US community colleges is very limited, we can still learn from broader studies on international students in other US educational institutions about the common obstacles they face during career preparation.

Language and Culture Barriers

Language and cultural barriers are prevalent challenges faced by international students in seeking jobs (Yeh & Inose, 2003; Zhang, 2016). Language barriers influence how international students receive and understand information (Yeh & Inose, 2003), their ability to acculturate and adjust to a new culture (Poyrazli et al., 2001), and their mental health (Mori, 2000). In terms of career transitions to US workplaces, international students hold unique strengths in cultural diversity and multilingual ability. However, since English is usually their second language, they face additional challenges in speaking in a culturally "appropriate" manner to potential American employers (Sangganjanavanich et al., 2011). In addition to this, the career development outcomes of international college students can be significantly impacted by their levels of cross-cultural adjustment. Based on surveys with 261 African, Asian, and Latin-American international college students in the United States, Reynolds and Constantine (2007) revealed that higher levels of acculturative stress and greater intercultural competence concerns are associated with lower levels of career outcome expectations among international students. Research also shows that highly acculturated international students face fewer difficulties in finding jobs in the United States because they are more willing to interact with people and understand how things are done in the host culture (Crockett & Hays, 2011).

Lack of Social Capital

Previous studies demonstrate that social capital plays an integral role in the career development of international students (Popadiuk & Arthur, 2014; Reynolds & Constantine, 2007). Social capital here refers to the network of relationships between an international student and other individuals in their host country and back home. For example, Reynolds and Constantine (2007) found that distancing international students from their primary social support systems, such as family and friends, makes it difficult for these students to focus on career preparation and other future-oriented planning. By contrast, friends and acquaintances can provide information and support for international students when they search for jobs in the host country. After interviewing international students in their last year of transition from university to work in the country they were studying in, Popadiuk and Arthur (2014) found that

International Student's Career Development   93

building strong friendships support their decision to stay in the host country, and that relational networks help them make career decisions (e.g. host country friends may offer realistic analysis of job prospects) and gain their first job. In addition, half of the interviewees expressed a desire for mentoring from international alumni who work in their field. Among international graduate students, faculty-led mentorship groups were shown to benefit students by allowing them to relax and form meaningful relationships as well as discuss career-related knowledge (Ku et al., 2008).

Unfavorable Immigration Policies

Unlike native students, international students must obey immigration policies to enter, remain, and work in the host country. An F-1 student visa allows international students entrance into the United States as full-time students. While holding an F-1 visa, students can take part in two types of practical training, Curricular Practical Training (CPT) and Optional Practical Training (OPT). International students may use their CPT or pre-OPT after the first year of full-time study to hold an academic appointment, internship, or off-campus employment limited to up to 20 hours a week (US Immigration and Customs Enforcement, 2020). Although CPT is usually a favorable immigration policy, it has some limitations. For example, students must do CPT in their current areas of study to receive CPT authorization from their institution (US Immigration and Customs Enforcement, 2020), which limits their exploration of other fields. Another limitation of CPT is that the federal regulations are quite vague, so it is up to each institution to create procedures for CPT approval (Durrani, 2019). For example, some institution's established curriculums may not require internship opportunities for their students and may not allow international students to work for off-campus jobs or internships related to their majors. In this case, students may miss out on experiential learning that can help them prepare for a future career.

After completing their degree studies, OPT is the primary way in which international students get work experience after graduation in their host country. OPT also requires that the student's work experience be directly related to their major area of study (US Immigration and Customs Enforcement, 2019), which means that the jobs an international student applies for after graduation must relate to their degree. In addition to this, the OPT authorization process takes at least three months and costs $410 (The University of Chicago, 2020). International students can apply for an Employment Authorization Document (EAD) to legally work in the United States for 12 months, but that requires them to find a job within ninety days of graduation (Department of Homeland Security, 2020; US Immigration and Customs Enforcement,

94 *Hannah Rapp et al.*

2020). Otherwise, they must leave the United States according to immigration policies (US Citizenship and Immigration Services, 2020). These immigration regulations put serious constraints on international students' career opportunities.

Employer Biases

Another challenge for international students' school-to-career transition is the perceived or actual employer biases. According to a National Association of Colleges and Employers survey, among the 201 US employer respondents, only 23.4 percent hired international students in 2018 (National Association of Colleges and Employers, 2018). Studies have shown that when other conditions are all the same, having an accent can negatively affect employability (Cargile, 2000; Carlson & McHenry, 2006; Deprez-Sims & Morris, 2010). Additionally, in a study documenting the career exploration of international students in the United States, all eight participants believed that immigration policy issues contributed to employers' hiring decisions in a way that makes them prefer hiring domestic over international applicants (Sangganjanavanich et al., 2011). As a result, these international students perceive themselves as less competitive and more disadvantaged compared with domestic applicants.

Challenges of On-campus Career Services

An important consideration in international students' career preparations is the educational institution's career counseling or career development services. Research shows that career preparation (Lin & Flores, 2013) and counseling (Shen & Herr, 2004) services are effective methods that can help international students at community colleges deal with the challenges in the host country's labor market. International students also express a need for timely information about services at community colleges that could help them with career planning (Jachowicz, 2007). Career counselors may help international students to integrate their academic learning, networking skills, and career aspirations into a feasible plan (Nadermann & Eissenstat, 2018; Shen & Herr, 2004). They can also evaluate international students' acculturation levels and guide them in a way that they are comfortable networking (Nadermann & Eissenstat, 2018).

However, international students face many challenges in using career counseling services. First of all, they may simply not know of the existence or make use of the service. A study that analyzes data from 6,043 international students in the Community College Survey of Student Engagement reveals that the least used on-campus services were job placement (38.7 percent) and career counseling (37.5 percent) (Lau et al., 2019). Follow-up interviews are necessary to ascertain whether this is due to students not knowing about the existence of these services, or whether many students are not expecting to look for employment in the United States after graduation. Secondly, international students may face more barriers in seeking career counseling services than their US counterparts. Crockett and Hays (2011) identify a series of barriers preventing international college students from accessing on-campus counseling services, which include language barriers, differences in cultural norms and values, and little to no previous counseling experience. Thirdly, the career counselors themselves may not be adequately prepared to cater to the heterogeneous needs of international students. A study within the community college setting revealed that the utilization of career counseling among international students was limited and produced varying levels of satisfaction (Jachowicz, 2007). In this study, participants expressed that academic and career counselors should be more knowledgeable about cultural differences, especially with regard to potential family influence on student career choices in some cultures. In addition, international students who have been in the United States for a long time may have different career needs than those who are newer to the United States or who are less comfortable fully engaging in the US culture (Reynolds & Constantine, 2007). Therefore, career counselors need to develop specific types of counseling strategies that can tailor to the differential needs of international students who may be at different stages of the acculturative process.

Discussion

Community colleges in the United States are attracting an increasing number of international students, and there is a pressing need for researchers, college leaders, and state and federal policymakers to better understand their career development paths. Although a few studies provide valuable findings through large-sample surveys and small-sample qualitative interviews, we have yet to develop a comprehensive understanding of the career paths of international students in community colleges due to the lack of representative and systematic data. Moreover, there can be important regional variations in the career development experiences of international students studying in community colleges. In the academic year 2018–2019, one out of three international students studied in New York, California, or Texas (Institute of International Education, 2019b). However, international students attending community colleges in regions with a smaller immigrant population, a lower level of ethnic diversity, and fewer job opportunities may face additional challenges in career preparation and development. Further, career development is a long-term process, yet current research mostly collects data at one time point, usually before students graduate. Consequently, we are unable to track how students' career decisions may change during

96 *Hannah Rapp et al.*

their college years or to evaluate and compare the actual outcomes of school career services and students' career outcomes. Considering these limitations, we suggest future studies to consider utilizing large-scale, cross-institutional, and longitudinal survey designs to lay the foundation of a systematic examination of international students' career development in US community colleges. This can be a joint effort across multiple regions and institutions.

It is also worth noting that due to the small sample and limited scope of current studies, international students are often regarded as highly homogenous or simply clustered by nationality when it comes to their experiences in community colleges. This overgeneralization has led to the under-examination of the heterogeneity in international students' experiences based on personal, familial, institutional, and regional factors (Heng, 2019). A few studies in 4-year higher education institutions have pointed out the diverse experience and potential inequality among international students. For example, international students with less financial resources are more likely to experience negative encounters with professors (Glass et al., 2015), quite possibly due to the relationship between financial stress, and reduced coursework or poor academic performance (Northern et al., 2010). It has also been found that female international students experience more stress than their male counterparts (Bang et al., 2008). Despite existing empirical evidence from 4-year institutions, no research has ever examined the diversity of student backgrounds and career development experiences in US community colleges. Considering the unique academic and financial challenges faced by community college students (Jachowicz, 2007), future studies should pay more attention to the potentially unequal experiences among this group by recruiting research respondents with a more diverse background and linking the analyses with theoretical and empirical findings from the inequality and intersectionality literature.

Another important limitation of current research is the lack of connections between theories and empirical findings. It is also worth noticing that classic theories of career development may not fully capture the complexities of career development of international students in US community colleges. The early vocational interest theory derived by Holland (1959) denotes that career choices are an expression of the student's vocational interests. Holland's theory can be used at the individual level to explain, for example, why a Chinese international student chooses a US school—they may regard US colleges as better aligning with their specific vocational interests. However, Holland's theory is not suitable to discuss the unique challenges faced by international students, such as immigration policies and societal discriminations. Donald Super's stage theory (1953), on the other hand, defines different life roles and career developmental stages to explain life transitions.

Moreover, it acknowledges that determinants such as immigration policies, historical prejudice, family SES, and individual psychological and biological well-being all play a role in a student's exploration of courses, internships, hobbies, and future careers. However, it does not examine the potential impact of any given determinant or its connection to other factors in detail. Thus, it is not adequate to explain the interaction of factors such as race, immigration status, language ability, geographical locations, and so on. Another important career development theory is the Social Cognitive Career Trajectory Theory (SCCT), which focuses on the relationship between cultural and environmental factors and individual career outcomes (Flores & O'Brien, 2002). SCCT lends itself to more diverse groups as it recognizes that race, gender, SES, and other contextual factors affect cognitive factors related to career development (Lent et al., 1994). For example, Kantamneni et al., (2018) used the SCCT model to demonstrate how higher levels of internalized stereotype and ethnic values affects Asian American's self-efficacy in different occupations, which in turn lead to stereotypical career paths. SCCT thus encourages examining the unique experiences of subgroups. To thoroughly account for the career development experiences of international students at community colleges, we suggest combining these existing theories to complement each other and further developing a theoretical framework that incorporates career development theories with immigration theories and macro-level development theories such as the world cultural theory. It is also crucial for this framework to emphasize the intersectionality in challenges faced by each particular subgroup within the international student community.

It is also worth pointing out that there is an urgent need to study the short-term and long-term impact of the COVID-19 pandemic and recent immigration policy changes on international students' career development. A new survey on international students in Australian universities has shown a dramatic decrease in job opportunities and an increase in financial and housing stress among international students; these challenges have inevitably impacted their academic performance and psychological health (Morris et al., 2020). A similar study in the United States is necessary for schools and policymakers to address the concerns of international students during and after the pandemic. Furthermore, the initial guidance from the US Immigration and Customs Enforcement banning international students from legally entering and staying in the United States for a fully online fall 2020 semester led to immediate confusion and panic among international students (Jordan et al., 2020). Although the guidance has been rescinded following a legal challenge initiated by multiple higher education institutions, international students may still feel their legal status is under constant threat amidst this era of uncertainty. The temporary

98 *Hannah Rapp et al.*

suspension of entry of aliens with nonimmigrant visa (H-1B, H-2B, J, and L) in the name of protecting the US labor market following the coronavirus outbreak (Trump, 2020) has also invoked rage and fear among immigrant workers (Brandom, 2020), which can further disrupt international students' career plans after graduation and pose psychological and financial challenges to those currently enrolled. It is thus important to study how the pandemic and new immigration policies affect the career decisions of international students and how community colleges can better support and advise students in light of these changes.

Policy Implications

The current research findings point to several important directions of practices for community colleges to improve career development experiences for international students. First, since studies have shown challenges for international students to actively utilize existing on-campus career counselling services (Crockett & Hays, 2011; Lau et al., 2019; Reynolds & Constantine, 2007), it is thus crucial for community colleges to develop effective outreach programs to address international students' career needs and concerns rather than waiting for them to present these at the counseling center. In particular, as Crockett and Hays (2011) have suggested, career counselors should form liaison relationships with the International Students' Office and existing campus international student groups to increase students' familiarity with available career development services, as well as to increase career counselors' awareness of special needs and concerns from international students. Active organization of peer counseling sessions, support groups, and culturally relevant activities can also work as good ways to reach international students. Students may also find support groups with others who share similar cultural backgrounds less intimidating than one-on-one counseling sessions since some students may identify with a more collectivist worldview (Flores & Heppners, 2002). By providing career services in settings and contexts that are familiar and comfortable to international students (e.g. international student lounges, cultural fairs, or similar facilities and events on campus), community colleges may observe an increase in the use of career counseling services of international students.

Second, academic and career counselors should increase their awareness and knowledge of the diverse and specific challenges and obstacles that international students face during career development. Further, institutions should provide training programs for career development professionals to develop and employ culturally appropriate career counseling practices. Early studies have argued for an

International Student's Career Development 99

integrative training approach that incorporates multicultural counseling theory for college career counselors to adequately serve culturally diverse student groups (Flores & Heppner, 2002). In particular, they should be aware of the discrimination and oppression that students may encounter, understand students in their own historical and cultural contexts and how these contexts may be associated to different worldviews, learn about racial/cultural identity development theories and non-Western practices, and critique traditional intervention strategies for cultural applicability. It is also important for career counselors to develop a broad understanding of a global economy and its impacts on the career choices of international students to provide enough resources and support.

Last but not least, community colleges should be aware of the tremendous impact of immigration regulations on international students' learning and career preparation experiences and respond quickly to policy changes. Institutions should continuously strive for friendly and fair immigration policies and actively speak out when their students are unfairly treated.

Conclusion

This chapter provided an overview of issues in the career development of international students in US community colleges. In order to understand these students' unique career development path, our chapter reviews the career expectations and aspirations of international students attending US community colleges, the common challenges during their career preparations, and provides an overview of on-campus career services provided by community colleges. We found that international students value American higher education because it provides high-level career training, more specialized degree options, and can lead to a degree that will make the student more competitive in the international job market. We noted several challenges faced by international students during their career preparations, including language and cultural barriers, lack of social capital, unfavorable immigration policies, and perceived employer biases. We also found that community college career services may be more helpful to international students if counselors familiarize themselves with an international student's differential cultural norms and language ability, and are prepared to address common topics such as Immigration policies that affect an international student's legal status and future employment in the United States. The current research findings suggest that preparations can be made by campus career counselors, mental health professionals, academic advisors, and institutional leadership to improve career development experiences for international students.

References

Adams, S. E. (2016). *International students' decision to attend a small, rural community college in Iowa* [Unpublished doctoral dissertation]. Iowa State University.

Anayah, B., & Kuk, L. (2015). The growth of international student enrollment at community colleges and implications. *Community College Journal of Research and Practice, 39*(12), 1099–1110.

Bang, E. J., Muriuki, A., & Hodges, J. Q. (2008). International students at a Midwestern University: Gender, stress, and perceived social support. *International Journal of Diversity in Organisations, Communities & Nations, 8*(4), 109–116.

Bohman, E. (2009). Headed for the heartland: Decision making process of community college bound international students. *Community College Journal of Research and Practice, 34*(1–2), 64–77.

Brandom, R. (2020, June 29). The human cost of Trump's guest worker ban. *The Verge.* https://www.theverge.com/21306188/guest-worker-ban-trump-h1b-visa-immigration-stamp-entry

Cargile, A. C. (2000). Evaluations of employment suitability: Does accent always matter? *Journal of Employment Counseling, 37*(3), 165–177.

Carlson, H. K., & McHenry, M. A. (2006). Effect of accent and dialect on employability. *Journal of Employment Counseling, 43*(2), 70–83.

Crockett, S. A., & Hays, D. G. (2011). Understanding and responding to the career counseling needs of international college students on U.S. campuses. *Journal of College Counseling, 14*(1), 65–79.

Department of Homeland Security. (2020). *Unemployment counter: Study in the states.* https://studyinthestates.dhs.gov/sevis-help-hub/student-records/fm-student-employment/unemployment-counter

Deprez-Sims, A. S., & Morris, S. B. (2010). Accents in the workplace: Their effects during a job interview. *International Journal of Psychology, 45*(6), 417–426.

Durrani, A. (2020, July 14). International students: Find community college fit. *US News & World Report.* https://www.usnews.com/education/community-colleges/articles/ways-international-students-can-find-the-right-community-college-fit

Durrani, A. (2019, May 21). What to know about curricular practical training. *US News & World Report.* https://www.usnews.com/education/best-colleges/articles/2019-05-21/curricular-practical-training-what-international-students-should-know

Flores, L. Y., & Heppner, M. J. (2002). Multicultural career counseling: Ten essentials for training. *Journal of Career Development, 28*(3), 181–202.

Flores, L. Y., & O'brien, K. M. (2002). The career development of Mexican American adolescent women: A test of social cognitive career theory. *Journal of Counseling Psychology, 49*(1), 14.

Ghazzawi, D., McKinney, L., Horn, C. L., Carales, V., & Burridge, A. (2020). The Road to the baccalaureate. *Journal of International Students, 10*(2), 420–442. https://doi.org/10.32674/jis.v10i2.339

Glass, C. R., Kociolek, E., Wongtrirat, R., Lynch, R. J., & Cong, S. (2015). Uneven experiences: The impact of student-faculty interactions on international students' sense of belonging. *Journal of International Students, 5*(4), 353–367.

Hagedorn, L. S., & Mi-Chung, L. (2005). International community college students: The neglected minority? *Online Submission*. https://files.eric.ed.gov/fulltext/ED490516.pdf

Heng, T. T. (2019). Understanding the heterogeneity of international students' experiences: A case study of Chinese international students in U.S. universities. *Journal of Studies in International Education, 23*(5), 607–623.

Holland, J. L. (1959). A theory of vocational choice. *Journal of counseling psychology, 6*(1), 35.

Institute of International Education. (2019a). *Open Doors: Community colleges leading places of origin.* https://opendoorsdata.org/data/international-students/community-colleges-leading-places-of-origin/

Institute of International Education. (2019b). *Open Doors: International students-leading institutions.* https://opendoorsdata.org/data/international-students/leading-institutions/

Institute of International Education. (2020). *Open Doors: Community college total students.* https://opendoorsdata.org/data/international-students/community-colleges-total-students/

Jachowicz, P. L. (2007). *Influences on career decisions of international students attending community colleges in the United States.* [Unpublished doctoral dissertation]. Northern Illinois University.

Jordan, M., Kanno-Youngs, Z., & Levin, D. (2020, July 7). Trump visa rules seen as way to pressure colleges on reopening. *The New York Times.* https://www.nytimes.com/2020/07/07/us/student-visas-coronavirus.html

Kantamneni, N., Dharmalingam, K., Orley, G., & Kanagasingam, S. K. (2018). Cultural factors, perceived barriers, and Asian American career development: An application of social cognitive career theory. *Journal of Career Assessment, 26*(4), 649–665. https://doi.org/10.1177/1069072717723097

Ku, H. Y., Lahman, M. K., Yeh, H. T., & Cheng, Y. C. (2008). Into the academy: Preparing and mentoring international doctoral students. *Educational Technology Research and Development, 56*(3), 365–377.

Lau, J., Garza, T., & Garcia, H. (2019). International students in community colleges: On-campus services used and its effect on sense of belonging. *Community College Journal of Research and Practice, 43*(2), 109–121.

Lent, R. W., Brown, S. D., & Hackett, G. (1994). Toward a unifying social cognitive theory of career and academic interest, choice, and performance. *Journal of Vocational Behavior, 45*(1), 79–122.

Lin, Y. J., & Flores, L. Y. (2013). Job search self-efficacy of East Asian international graduate students. *Journal of Career Development, 40*(3), 186–202.

Mori, S. (2000). Addressing the mental health concerns of international students. *Journal of Counseling and Development, 78*(2), 137–144.

Morris, A., Hastings, C., Mitchell, E., Ramia, G., Wilson, S., & Overgaard, C. (2020, July). The experience of international students before and during COVID-19: Housing, work, study and wellbeing. In *The experience of international students before and during COVID-19.* University of Technology Sydney.

National Association of Colleges and Employers. (2018, January 22). *Hiring of international students continues to decline.* https://www.naceweb.org/job-market/trends-and-predictions/hiring-of-international-students-continues-decline/

Nadermann, K., & Eissenstat, S. J. (2018). Career decision making for Korean international college students: Acculturation and networking. *The Career Development Quarterly*, 66(1), 49–63.

Northern, J. J., O'Brien, W. H., & Goetz, P. W. (2010). The development, evaluation, and validation of a financial stress scale for undergraduate students. *Journal of College Student Development*, 51(1), 79–92.

Popadiuk, N. E., & Arthur, N. M. (2014). Key relationships for international student university-to-work transitions. *Journal of Career Development*, 41(2), 122–140.

Poyrazli, S., Arbona, C., Bullington, R., & Pisecco, S. (2001). Adjustment issues of Turkish college students studying in the United States. *College Student Journal*, 35(1), 52–52.

Reynolds, A. L., & Constantine, M. G. (2007). Cultural adjustment difficulties and career development or international college students. *Journal of Career Assessment*, 15(3), 338–350.

Sangganjanavanich, V. F., Lenz, A. S., & Cavazos, J. (2011). International students' employment search in the United States: A phenomenological study. *Journal of Employment Counseling*, 48(1), 17–26.

Shen, Y. J., & Herr, E. L. (2004). Career placement concerns of international graduate students: A qualitative study. *Journal of Career Development*, 31(1), 15–29.

Super, D. E. (1953). A theory of vocational development. *American Psychologist*, 8(5), 185–190.

The University of Chicago. (2020). *OPT (Optional Practical Training)*. https://internationalaffairs.uchicago.edu/page/opt-optional-practical-training

Trump, D. J. (2020). *Proclamation suspending entry of aliens who present a risk to the U.S. labor market following the coronavirus outbreak*. Presidential proclamation. https://www.whitehouse.gov/presidential-actions/proclamation-suspending-entry-aliens-present-risk-u-s-labor-market-following-coronavirus-outbreak/

United Nations Educational, Scientific and Cultural Organization Institute for Statistics. (2020). *Education: Inbound internationally mobile students by continent of origin*. http://data.uis.unesco.org/Index.aspx?queryid=172

U.S. Census Bureau. (2020). *Foreign trade: Top trading partners*. https://www.census.gov/foreign-trade/statistics/highlights/toppartners.html

U.S. Citizenship and Immigration Services. (2020). *Students and employment*. https://www.uscis.gov/working-united-states/students-and-exchange-visitors/students-and-employment

U.S. Immigration and Customs Enforcement. (2019, September 27). *SEVP policy guidance: Practical training-determining a direct relationship between employment and a student's major area of study*. https://www.ice.gov/doclib/sevis/pdf/optDirectlyRelatedGuidance.pdf

U.S. Immigration and Customs Enforcement. (2020, June 15). *Practical training*. https://www.ice.gov/sevis/practical-training

Yeh, C. J., & Inose, M. (2003). International students' reported English fluency, social support satisfaction, and social connectedness as predictors of acculturative stress. *Counselling Psychology Quarterly*, 16(1), 15–28.

Zeszotarski, P. (2004). *Expectations and experiences of international students in an American community college in the context of globalization* [Unpublished doctoral dissertation]. University of California, Los Angeles.

Zhang, Y. (2016). An overlooked population in community college: International students' (in) validation experiences with academic advising. *Community College Review*, 44(2), 153–170.

Authors Bios

Hannah Rapp is a PhD student in the Department of Educational Psychology at the University of Wisconsin-Madison, United States. She is interested in a range of research topics: social-emotional learning in schools, career development of international students, and student understanding of inherent worth and interpersonal forgiveness. She was recently awarded a scholarship from the Future Institute Research Center to qualitatively explore the career development needs of international students.

Yi-jung Wu is a PhD student at the Department of Educational Leadership and Policy Analysis, University of Wisconsin-Madison, United States. Her research interests include international education, career development, STEM education, and K-12 school leadership. She has published papers in peer-review journals such as *Change: The Magazine of Higher Learning* and *Attention, Perception, & Psychophysics*.

Ran Liu is an assistant professor at the Department of Educational Policy Studies, School of Education, University of Wisconsin-Madison. Her research examines cross-national differences in gender inequality in STEM education, with a particular focus on East Asian societies. More broadly, she studies the intersection of race, gender, class, and immigration status in education and the labor market. She is also interested in survey and statistical methods and applying machine learning models to social science research. Her recent publications appear in *Social Forces, American Educational Research Journal, Comparative Education Review*, and *Comparative Education*.

Xiaoli Jing is a PhD candidate at the Department of Integrated Studies in Education, McGill University, Canada, funded by China Scholarship Council-McGill University Joint Scholarship. Her research interests include international education, transnational education, and international student mobility. She has published over ten papers in peer-review journals such as *Higher Education, Journal of Higher Education Policy and Management,* and *Comparative Education Review in China*.

7 Latinx ESL Students' Successful English Language Transition at Community Colleges

DuEwa M. Frazier

Introduction

According to the 2020 Census Facts report, Latinos comprise 18.3 percent of the total American population (US Census Bureau, 2020). Latinx community college enrollment was at 27 percent as of Fall 2018 (Zerquera et al., 2018). Since the COVID-19 pandemic, Latinx enrollment in community colleges has dropped by 5.9 percent (National Student Clearinghouse Research Center, 2020). Latinx English as a second language (ESL) learners need to complete college English courses for a multitude of reasons. According to Suh (2016), US community colleges offer language courses for ESL students to increase their competitiveness in a global job market. Ling et al. (2014) noted ESL students attend community colleges to improve their English language skills before transferring to a 4-year university. However, community college practitioners may generalize that all ESL students are alike in their limited English skills, which does not consider the range of backgrounds, experiences, and needs these learners have (Janis, 2013).

Latinx community college students are among the following broadly defined populations of students with diverse ethnic and cultural backgrounds who need ESL courses: (a) generation 1.5 students who completed secondary education in the United States, yet have not achieved English language proficiency for postsecondary studies; (b) young adult immigrants who have recently arrived in the United States; (c) international students who came to the United States on a student visa; and (d) adult immigrants who need English language skills to advance careers in the United States (Chang, 2016). Latinx college students with strong efficacy and coping skills can persist through challenges in pursuit of their academic studies (Watson & Watson, 2016). Indeed, Schunk and DiBenedetto (2016) reported college students who engage in goal-setting and collaborative peer support have greater academic success. Furthermore, a study by Tovar (2014) examined how regular communication with administration, faculty, and counseling staff contributes to Latinx student success through academic support services. While these supports can bolster Latinx student success, barriers still exist. For example, Murphy and Murphy (2018) found that the following barriers put Latinx students at risk for academic failure and withdrawal: working more than 30 hours per week, inadequate academic preparation, lack of cultural pedagogy to support academic persistence, and being the first in their family to attend college. Therefore, the purpose of this qualitative study with a phenomenological approach was to illuminate the factors in the successful language transition of Latinx ESL students to college English at community colleges.

Literature Review

Active Learning Pedagogy for English as a Second Language Students at Community Colleges

This literature review is focused on active learning methods found to be successful in actively engaging ESL students to prepare for college-level English. Active learning occurs when instructional methods are used that engage students in a meaningful process of learning and reflection (Prince, 2004). Various instructional strategies, such as blog writing and speed-reading, show examples of active learning methods which resulted in successful ESL student progress in English language acquisition. According to Chae (2014), writing pedagogy for ESL students in the community college has included the use of online discussion forums and blogs. Indeed, Gerich (2013) found online conversations and blogging provide second language learners an opportunity to reflect their learning through both traditional writing processes and online writing. Further, faculty at one community college use literacy narratives with a strategy called "translanguaging" which encourages ESL students to write in Spanish and then translate their essays into English while also teaching students technical aspects of academic writing (Parmegiani, 2014). On improving English reading skills, Haupt (2015) examined speed-reading programs for ESL students and discovered such programs improve English reading rates and increase reading comprehension scores above 70 percent. Additionally, Doman and Webb (2016) studied a flipped classroom model within an ESL class at a 2-year community college and highlighted the increased language and grammar support given to ESL students through this pedagogical approach.

Theoretical Framework

Dörnyei's (2009) L2 (meaning "second language") motivational self-system was applied to the study to explain how Latinx ESL students

106 *DuEwa M. Frazier*

incorporate the target language—English—into their self-motivation and academic goals to successfully transition to college English. Second language learners who desire to become proficient in the L2, are motivated to reduce the disparity between their ideal and actual selves (Dörnyei, 2009). According to Dörnyei, L2 motivational self-system is made up of three constituents: the Ideal L2 self; the Ought-to-L2 self; and the L2 Learning experience. The Ideal L2 self represents the self-image the learner envisions: being a fluent speaker who interacts with others (Dörnyei, 2009). The Ought-to L2 self is most concerned with the expectations of possessing attributes to "avoid possible negative outcomes" (Dörnyei, 2009, p. 29). This dimension is considered a key motivation for L2 learning for extrinsic rewards. In the last dimension, the L2 Learning experience is connected to the L2 learners' environment and who influences their learning and proficiency (Papi, 2010). The three dimensions combine to form the Latinx ESL learners' self-actualization to motivate them to successfully transition from ESL courses to college-level English.

Research Method

Qualitative research designs are used to collect narrative data and draw conclusions without statistical analysis (Ahlgrim-Delzell & Privitera, 2019). It was important to use the phenomenological approach to gain first-hand knowledge of participants' experiences and to understand the context or situation that influenced the phenomenon (Creswell, 2013). The phenomenological approach was also chosen to understand how Latinx ESL students succeed in second language (L2) study in order to persist in college English at three community colleges. This approach was chosen over the case study method due to the small sample size of students and the narrative nature of the data collected. This approach was chosen over ethnographic study because the study did not focus on observing the participants in their social or academic environment. Narrative data were collected via one-on-one interviews with five Latinx ESL students currently enrolled in three community colleges in the United States. The data from participant interviews informed on the lived academic experiences of Latinx ESL students studying English at three community colleges.

Research Question

The research question for this study was, "What are the lived academic experiences of Latinx ESL students who matriculate to college English at community colleges?"

Context of the Study

The recruitment sites included one community college in the Northeastern United States and two community colleges in the Mid-Atlantic region. I submitted application to and was approved by the Institutional Review Board (IRB) of each of the three institutions. Two of the community colleges are Hispanic Serving Institutions (HSIs) with at least 25 percent Latinx student enrollment. Two of the institutions were selected using purposive sampling due to my knowledge of their ESL programs from the literature. A third community college was obtained through snowball sampling from a faculty member at one of the previously identified recruitment sites. Each of the community colleges was selected for its available demographic of Latinx ESL students who had completed ESL courses and English Composition I (101) and/or English Composition II (102).

Participants

In this study, ten participants who self-identified as Latinx were interviewed. However, for the sake of highlighting students who completed both English Composition I and English Composition II at the community college by the time of our one-on-one interview, five Latinx ESL students' academic experiences will be discussed in this chapter. The inclusion criteria for the study was that participants must: be 18–25 years of age; self-identify as Latinx; be currently enrolled as a student at one of the selected community colleges; have completed an ESL class or program of classes and earned at least one credit; and have completed English Composition I and/or English Composition II college-level courses. I requested and received a list of names and email addresses of prospective Latinx ESL student participants at each of the three community colleges; these prospective participants were selected by ESL and English faculty at their respective institutions.

I initially reached out to prospective participants via email to introduce the study and share the recruitment flyer, informed consent, and link to the Qualtrics eligibility screener and demographics survey. In relation to their student status, all participants were currently enrolled at one of the three selected community college sites. Potential participants were sent an 11-question survey, which included questions related to age, community college enrollment, number of credits earned, GPA, gender, self-identification of ethnic identity, English Composition I and II completion, chosen pseudonym, and preferred method of contact, as well as one question confirming the participant's acceptance of informed consent. Interested students who completed the survey and met the eligibility criteria were asked to create pseudonyms to protect their identities to ensure confidentiality throughout their participation in the

108 DuEwa M. Frazier

Table 7.1 Participant Information

Pseudonym	Age	Gender	GPA	English Courses Completed
Eva	20	F	2.5	I, II
Robert	20	M	2.7	I, II
Rose	25	F	3.4	I, II
Charly	23	F	3.5	I, II
Laura	25	F	2.7	I, II

study. Participants created first-name pseudonyms of their own choosing without guidance from me. I emailed eligible students to inquire about their availability for a one-on-one interview.

The participants' majors of study included Accounting, Biology, and Criminal Justice. Participants currently live in the United States in the areas where they are enrolled at the community colleges, yet they referenced their native countries including the Dominican Republic, Venezuela, and Honduras. Participants were asked to create pseudonyms. Quotations from interviews are identified by participants' first name pseudonyms. Participant information is shown in Table 7.1.

Data Collection and Analysis

I conducted semi-structured interviews in-person or via Zoom web conferencing software. I conducted the interviews in English as all of the participants were proficient in English. The semi-structured approach allowed participants to offer in-depth responses and allowed me to clarify and ask probing questions when needed. Participants signed and returned the informed consent to me before their interview. The interviews were between 30 minutes to one hour in length depending on participant responses. Each recorded interview file was transcribed verbatim using a transcription service. I conducted member checks to validate participants' responses within two weeks of their completed interviews to ensure accuracy. Member checks were completed throughout the study. The study participants' did not request revisions to their initial interview responses. Rather, the students responded that they approved of their interview responses and did not have further additions.

Thematic analysis was used to allow research findings to emerge from frequent, dominant, or significant themes within the raw data (Thomas, 2006). Initial codes were taken from the narrative by looking for common themes in context. After reviewing participant transcripts through coding and themes, I organized the data into themes and subthemes. I re-reviewed each theme and code for accuracy and

ESL Students' English Language Transition   109

then developed meaning to highlight the participants' lived experiences persisting in college English.

After observing I had reached a point of saturation of participant responses, I was able to identify repeated patterns of words and phrases from the participants' quotes. I was able to extract words from these quotes to begin the process of coding. Comparing what the codes had in common, I then combined these initial codes to create themes. As I coded and analyzed participant narratives, themes emerged based on commonalities between participant experiences; the emergent themes provided a detailed description of the data (Creswell, 2013).

I discovered three themes within the data, which revealed the successful English language transitions of the Latinx ESL participants as they persisted in college English at community colleges. The themes answered the research question of the study. The three emergent themes were: (a) student engagement in active learning opportunities; (b) students' motivation to learn English; and (c) faculty communication that guides English language learning. I explore these themes in the results section using the participants' narratives to support the analysis.

Ethics

Trustworthiness in this study was achieved with the use of consent forms, member checking, and journal keeping. Participants received informed consent, and each returned the signed consent form to me before data collection began. I ensured confidentiality by using pseudonyms for the participants. Further, member checking was important in building trust and transparency with participants and to articulate my commitment to convey their experiences as they reported them to me. I performed frequent member checking via email to ensure I had validated participants' responses and they were represented in the way they wanted to appear in the study. Additionally, I kept a reflexive journal throughout my process of data collection to record my thoughts or any potential biases I may have felt during the interview process that would not show up in the audio-recorded interviews. During the data analysis process, I reviewed my journal notes to recall details that I believe have added greater depth to the analysis.

Results

Students' Motivation to Learn English

Latinx ESL students discussed the difficult language transition they experienced when they came to the United States and enrolled at the community college. I asked participants to share their motivations to learn English. Robert, a 20-year-old student, completed ESL courses,

110   DuEwa M. Frazier

and English Composition I and II by the time of our interview. Robert reported, "When I first came, it was hard for me because I was not used to speaking English well." Rose, a 25-year-old student, completed ESL courses, and English Composition I and II by the time of our interview. Similar to Robert, Rose stated,

> At first it was difficult because I didn't speak any English at all. I studied in a classroom where everybody was speaking English, and sometimes I didn't understand what they were saying ... now I think I speak like 80% better than when I came.

Charly, a 23-year-old student, who completed ESL courses, and English Composition I and II by the time of our interview, also shared her difficult language transition. She expressed,

> It was hard for me because I didn't learn anything about English in my country ... when you come here you have to learn another language ... it was hard for me trying to practice because I was kind of shy and afraid ... to pronounce the words.

Latinx ESL students discussed their difficult language transitions as second language learners who were motivated to learn English.

The motivation to learn English and pursue both academic and career goals was a common thread among participants. Rose connected her pursuit of academic goals with professional growth. She shared, "The motivation was to learn. To study an associate's for a career that can help me to grow as a professional person." Latinx ESL students also connected their motivation to learn English with career placement and greater earning potential. Charly stated, "I want to try my best to get my degree and get a good job ... get good payment ... do what I want, what I love to do." Robert expressed his motivation to learn English connected to his goal to earn a bachelor's degree and a master's degree. He expressed, "I would like to do a bachelor and go for a master." Robert further described his career aspirations: "I would like to ... open my own business ... taxes service in accounting ..." Latinx ESL students shared their motivation for learning English: improving English language skills was connected to the pursuit of degree completion and careers.

Student Engagement in Active Learning

Latinx ESL students revealed engagement in active learning helped them to develop English language skills. Eva, a 20-year old student, completed ESL courses, and English Composition I and II by the time of our interview. She reported,

ESL Students' English Language Transition   111

> It helped me a lot because my writing was the worst thing … When I took ESL … almost every day we had to do a different essay. I learned a lot. We had to read. We had to watch movies about everything that we read every day.

Eva further discussed, "I learned a lot by watching movies and writing essays about the movies … also making a comparison between history, a movie, and a book." Eva shared writing daily essays, reading books, and watching movies in ESL courses was the engagement in active learning that helped to improve her English language skills.

Laura, a 25-year-old student, who completed ESL courses, and English Composition I and II by the time of our interview, shared reading poetry in ESL courses helped her build reading comprehension skills. She noted, "We were doing a lot of reading poems. ESL helped me to understand those poems … the grammar helped me to match my ideas when I was reading." Additionally, like Eva, Laura engaged in active learning that connected book reading with watching a movie adaptation. She continued, "Watching movies in the classroom … reading and listening at the same time. Of course, doing exercises in the book." Latinx ESL students expressed their engagement in active learning methods that helped them to improve their English language skills. These methods included: essay writing, reading books, watching movies to compare with what they read, and reading poetry. Students engaged in active learning which helped them to successfully transition to college English.

Faculty Communication That Guides English Language Learning

Latinx ESL students valued faculty communication that was attentive and specific about steps for English language development. When asked to recall what faculty did that helped them to be successful in college English, students' responses revealed their value for faculty communication that guides their comprehension as English language learners. Laura recalled when she did well on an essay in class. She reflected on what the professor did that helped her. She stated,

> It was my essay, one that I did for a compare and contrast. I was comparing two novels and I got a good grade. The teacher told me that I was using my ideas in the way that I was supposed to do it. He showed us the first example about the project that we were supposed to do … he explained how he was connecting ideas.

Laura attributed her good grade to the model essay her professor shared. Robert discussed how his professor communicated steps for writing.

112 *DuEwa M. Frazier*

Robert shared, "The professor always says that once you type a paragraph, stop there, review that paragraph and then continue to do the other one." Similarly, Rose contributed, "For every essay that you write, the professor gives you feedback. If I wrote a sentence that was not in order ... he told me that I need to structure that sentence."

Charly discussed an experience with a professor who communicated a passion for English. She expressed, "The professor in 101 she was fantastic with a lot of knowledge ... with passions to teach. I mean you can really see that she enjoys teaching." Latinx ESL participants expressed how effective faculty communication helped them make connections between feedback, what they read, and how they wrote. Repeated responses about faculty communication revealed the attentiveness given for students to develop academic writing skills.

Discussion and Conclusions

Discussion

In response to the research question, "What are the lived academic experiences of Latinx ESL students who matriculate to college English at community colleges?" the present study found factors influencing the successful language transition of participants in college English were: student engagement in active learning; students' motivation to learn English; and faculty communication that guides English language learning. From the interview responses, I deduced Latinx ESL students are motivated to learn English to complete English coursework, accomplish degree attainment, and prepare for future careers. Students communicated the specific engagement in literacy activities that helped them develop English skills and the influencing style of faculty communication and guidance that helped them learn.

Latinx ESL students reported their motivation to learn English stemmed from having limited English language skills when they first came to the United States and enrolled at the community college. They desired to improve their English communication abilities. This finding is supported by Dörnyei's (2005) L2 Motivation Self System. The Ideal L2 Self contains the learners' image of a competent speaker of the target language. Motivation serves as the driving force for the L2 learner—in this case, Latinx ESL students—to sustain a tedious process in acquiring English language skills (Dörnyei, 2005). Robert shared, "... it was hard for me because I was not used to speaking English well." Charly expressed a similar sentiment, "... when you come here you have to learn another language ... it was hard for me trying to practice because I was kind of shy and afraid ... to pronounce the words." Rose contributed, "I studied in a classroom where everybody was speaking English, and sometimes I didn't understand what they were saying ..."

Latinx ESL students' motivation to learn English was also connected to their pursuit of degree attainment and careers. Rose revealed her motivation to learn English was to earn "an associate's for a career that can help me to grow as a professional person." Similarly, Charly offered, "I want to try my best to get my degree and get a good job ..." This finding links to the L2 learners' desire to incorporate the L2 into one's self-concept (Dörnyei, 2005). In this case, Latinx ESL learners incorporate their second language skills into their identity to complete English coursework, and eventually earn degrees that will lead to satisfying careers.

Engagement in active learning was an influencing factor in participants' English language development. Piaget's (1964, 2000) constructivist learning theory proposes students engage in active learning through connecting new ideas and experiences with existing experiences to build knowledge.

The premise of active learning is to apply the concepts that students have learned during in-class reading and writing activities to influence a greater depth of learning to occur (Alves, 2015).

Participants reported active learning through reading books, watching film adaptations of books to write essays, and studying poetry, helped them to develop the reading comprehension, verbal communication, and writing skills needed to successfully complete English Composition I and II. Eva reported writing daily essays and making comparisons between a movie and a book influenced her English language development. She stated, "I learned a lot by watching movies and writing essays ... also making a comparison between ... a movie, and a book." Movies shown in the ESL classroom enhances English pronunciation and provides variation in second language study for ESL students (Mei-Ling, 2012). Laura expressed the grammar in poetry helped her reading comprehension skills. She shared, "... the grammar helped me to match my ideas when I was reading." The use of poetry in the ESL classroom can broaden intellectual perspective, teach grammar and vocabulary, and develop an in-depth understanding of the second language (Antika, 2016).

Cole and Griffin (2013) found that Latinx students are more likely to persist when faculty show concern and attentiveness for their academic achievement. Latinx ESL students revealed the importance of faculty communication that helped them academically persist, which guided their English language development. Both the frequency and quality of interactions Latinx students have with faculty have a positive impact on their academic progress (Cole & Griffin, 2013). Faculty provided students with model writing to support their understanding of writing

114   *DuEwa M. Frazier*

essays. Laura expressed, "I was comparing two novels and I got a good grade ... The teacher told me that I was using my ideas in the way that I was supposed to do it. He showed us the first example ..." Dörnyei (2007) stated the motivating factors of learning contexts can be bolstered by the language teacher. Both Robert and Rose discussed how faculty helped to guide their writing process through thoughtful and intentional feedback. Additionally, participants highlighted the importance of faculty displaying a passion for teaching English. Charly reported, "The professor in 101 she was fantastic with a lot of knowledge ... with passions to teach." As reported by the students, faculty guidance was an influencing factor in their successful English language transition in college English.

Limitations

Findings from this study were based on the lived academic experiences of five Latinx ESL students and, therefore, do not reflect the entire Latinx ESL student population at their respective community colleges. Given the factors that influenced academic persistence shared by participants, future research should continue to examine the successful English language learning transition and motivations to learn for Latinx ESL students in other institutions including other community colleges on the West Coast, in southern and rural regions, 4-year colleges and universities, and HSIs.

Conclusion

The findings provide key insights about the academic goals Latinx ESL students set for themselves as well as their motivations to learn English. This study highlighted the influencing factors on the successful English language transitions of Latinx ESL learners who matriculate to college English at three community colleges. For example, students' motivations to learn English stem from their desire to verbally communicate in English and attain college degrees and future job placement. Students expressed how their successful English language transition in college English was influenced by active learning which allowed them to practice academic writing and reading comprehension skills. In addition, faculty who communicated with the intent to guide students' English language development through modeling and constructive feedback helped Latinx ESL students achieve their learning goals. Further studies are necessary to provide additional insight into the preferred instructional strategies and learning tools Latinx ESL students use to successfully complete college English courses and motivate themselves to achieve success in college and beyond.

Implications

The study has implications for teaching, curriculum, and student services to support Latinx ESL students enrolled at community colleges. This study contributes to the lived academic experiences of Latinx ESL students in their own words, revealing their successful transition from ESL courses to college English. Adding to the current literature on faculty interactions that support the academic success of ESL community college students, this study contributes that Latinx ESL students value active learning methods that incorporate a responsive, learner-centered curriculum. Examples of this include: the use of poetry which connects the oral nature of language with reading comprehension; book readings paired with film adaptations so that ESL students connect what the text states with what they see and hear; and faculty scaffolding, which provides step by step instructions for ESL students.

Latinx ESL student responses conveyed a value for consistent guidance, encouraging feedback, and faculty communication that helps them progress to English proficiency. Faculty working with Latinx ESL students at community colleges can incorporate into the curriculum the diverse learning styles and language differences students bring to the classroom to maintain an equitable learning environment (Maldonado-Torres, 2016). Latinx ESL participants expressed an appreciation for academic support both in and outside of the classroom. These students benefit from tutoring, study groups, advisement for transfer to 4-year institutions, counseling therapy, career services, and mentoring (Murphy & Murphy, 2018). Participation in mentoring programs influences positive academic outcomes for Latinx community college students (Tovar, 2014).

This study shows the educational goals of the Latinx ESL students in community colleges are based in skills development, degree attainment, academic transfer, and career. The students' goals suggest community college ESL programs should focus on curriculum objectives that prepare students to develop strong verbal and written English language skills needed for career placement in addition to developing communication skills to function in daily life. Additionally, a program that focuses on the development of English language proficiency for Latinx ESL students seeking academic transfer to 4-year institutions to pursue bachelors' and master's degrees should be included.

References

Ahlgrim-Delzell, L., & Privitera, G. J. (2019). *Research methods for education.* Sage.

Alves, M. J. (2015). Ways to apply active learning in the college ESL classroom: The old, the new, and experiments in teaching. *College ESL Quarterly,* 1–4. College ESL Quarterly (languageartspress.com)

116 DuEwa M. Frazier

Antika, R. (2016). Poetry in the EFL classroom. *Tell-Us Journal*, 2(2), 20–35. DOI: 10.22202/tus.2016.v2i2.1335

Chae, S. E. (2014). Blogging and conversing: Community college students' sharing their experiences in an ESL writing class. *English Teaching*, 69(2), 31–50. http://journal.kate.or.kr/?p=154

Chang, Y. (2016). Discourses, identities and investment in English as second language learning: Voices from two U.S. community college students. *International Journal of Education & Literacy Studies*, 4(4), 38–49. https://www.journals.aiac.org.au/index.php/IJELS/article/view/2877

Cole, D., & Griffin, K. A. (2013). Advancing the study of student-faculty interaction: A focus on diverse students and faculty. In M. B. Paulsen (Ed.), *Higher education: Handbook of theory and research* (pp. 561–611). Springer.

Creswell, J. W. (2013). *Qualitative inquiry and research design: Choosing among five approaches* (3rd ed.). SAGE Publications.

Doman, E., & Webb, M. (2016). Does the flipped classroom lead to increased gains on learning outcomes in ESL/EFL contexts? *CATESOL Journal*, 28(1), 39–67. https://eric.ed.gov/?id=EJ1111606

Dörnyei, Z. (2005). *The psychology of the language learner: Individual differences in second language acquisition*. Routledge.

Dörnyei, Z. (2007). Creating a motivating classroom environment. In J. Cummins & C. Davison (Eds.), *International handbook of English language teaching* (pp. 719–731). Springer.

Dörnyei, Z. (2009). The L2 motivational self-system. In Z. Dörnyei & E. Ushioda (Eds.), *Motivation, language identity and the L2 self* (pp. 9–42). Multilingual Matters.

Gerich, D. (2013). Beyond the class blog: Creative and practical uses of blogger for the ESL classroom. *TESOL Journal*, 4(1), 175–180. https://doi.org/10.1002/tesj.68

Haupt, J. (2015). The use of a computer-based reading rate development program on pre-university intermediate level ESL learners' reading speeds. *Reading Matrix: An International Online Journal*, 15(1), 1–14. https://eric.ed.gov/?id=EJ1066232

Janis, T. (2013). The community college: Bridge or roadblock to higher education for U.S. adult immigrant English-language learners? *Research in Comparative and International Education*, 8(2), 149–165. https://doi.org/10.2304/rcie.2013.8.2.149

Ling, G., Wolf, M. K., Cho, Y., & Wang, Y. (2014). English-as-a-second-language programs for matriculated students in the United States: An exploratory survey and some issues. *ETS Research Report Series*, 14(11), 1–21. https://doi.org/10.1002/ets2.12010

Maldonado-Torres, S. E. (2016). Understanding the relationship between Latino students' preferred learning styles and their language spoken at home. *Journal of Latinos & Education*, 15(3), 244–252. https://doi.org/10.1080/15348431.2015.1131694

Mei-Ling, C. (2012). Effects of the order of reading text or viewing a film and l1/l2 captions on reading comprehension. *Perceptual & Motor Skills*, 115(1), 18–26. https://doi.org/10.2466/23.PMS.115.4.18-26

Murphy, J. P., & Murphy, S. A. (2018). Get ready, get in, get through: Factors that influence Latino college student success. *Journal of Latinos & Education,* *17*(1), 3–17. https://doi.org/10.1080/15348431.2016.1268139

National Student Clearinghouse Research Center. (2020). *Fall 2020 enrollment.* https://nscresearchcenter.org/stay-informed/

Papi, M. (2010). The L2 motivational self system, L2 anxiety, and motivated behavior: A structural equation modeling approach. *System, 38*(3), 467–479. https://doi.org/10.1016/j.system.2010.06.011

Parmegiani, A. (2014). Bridging literacy practices through storytelling, translanguaging, and an ethnographic partnership: A case study of Dominican students at Bronx Community College. *Journal of Basic Writing, 33*(1), 23–51. https://www.jstor.org/stable/43858446?seq=1

Piaget, J. (1964). Cognitive development in children: Development and learning. *Journal of Research in Science Teaching, 2,* 176–186. http://dx.doi.org/10.1002/tea.3660020306

Piaget, J. (2000) *The psychology of the child.* Basic Books.

Prince, M. (2004). Does active learning work? A review of the research. *Journal of Engineering Education, 93*(3), 223–231. https://doi.org/10.1002/j.2168-9830.2004.tb00809.x

Schunk, D. H., & DiBenedetto, M. K. (2016). Self-efficacy theory in education. In K. R. Wentzel & D. B. Miele (Eds.), *Handbook of motivation at school* (pp. 34–54). Routledge Handbooks Online.

Suh, E. (2016). Language minority student transitions. *Journal of Developmental Education, 40*(1), 26–28.

Thomas, D. R. (2006). A general inductive approach for analyzing qualitative evaluation data. *American Journal of Evaluation, 27*(2), 237–246.

Tovar, E. (2014). The role of faculty, counselors, and support programs on Latina/o community college students' success and intent to persist. *Community College Review, 43*(1), 46–71. https://doi.org/10.1177/0091552114553788

U.S. Census Bureau. (2020). *Census facts.* Retrieved from the U.S. Census Bureau website: https://www.census.gov/quickfacts/fact/table/US/RHI725218

Watson, J. C., & Watson, A. A. (2016). Coping self-efficacy and academic stress among Latina/o first-year college students: The moderating role of emotional intelligence. *Journal of College Counseling, 19*(3), 218–230. DOI: 10.1002/jocc.12045

Zerquera, D. D., Acevedo-Gil, N., Flores, E., & Marantal, P. (2018). Repositioning trends of Latina/o/x student enrollments in community colleges. *Association of Mexican American Educators Journal, 12*(1), 86–106. https://doi.org/10.24974/amae.12.1.379

Author Bio

DuEwa M. Frazier, EdD, is an Instructor and Course Author in the College of Arts and Sciences, Maryville University, United States. Her research interests include Latinx ESL student persistence in college English, literacy studies, and culturally responsive pedagogy.

8 Assessing Acculturative Stress of International Students at a US Community College

Hardaye R. Hansen, Yuliya Shneyderman, Gloria S. McNamara, and Lisa Grace

Introduction

International students experiencing the US education system for the first time are vulnerable to acculturation stress. The acculturation process of adapting to the host nation exposes international students to acculturation stress. Factors such as country of origin, family support, immersion in the host culture, and host language are sources of acculturative stress. The purpose of the current study was to assess the degree of acculturation stress experienced by international undergraduates at a diverse, metropolitan community college. This will lend support to college administrators in addressing the academic success needs of international students.

The concept of acculturation was first introduced as an anthropological phenomenon "which results when a group of individuals having different cultures comes into continuous firsthand contact with subsequent changes in the original cultural patterns of either or both groups" (Redfield et al., 1936, p. 149). Two separate definitions emerged, led by Graves (1967), who defined acculturation in two distinctive levels: (a) The group level as a collective process in which there is a change in either the native culture or the host culture members or both; and (b) the individual level as the psychological change within the individual as a result of contact with the host society.

Subsequent researchers categorized psychological acculturation into two dimensions (Berry et al., 1987; Ward & Kennedy, 1994). The first is the psychological dimension that relates to values, ideologies, beliefs, and attitudes that define a culture. The second is related to the behavioral aspects which are about how the individual learns and adapts to external aspects of the dominant culture. Berry (2005) has identified the behaviors of integration, assimilation, separation, and marginalization as acculturation strategies. However, despite such extensive efforts to define acculturation, researchers have not yet reached a consensual definition (Mehta, 1998).

Acculturation and Stress

One important phenomenon that has been at the heart of acculturation research is related to the manifestation of acculturation, namely acculturative stress. According to Berry et al. (1987), acculturative stress is defined as impaired physical and psychosocial health in individuals who must adapt to a new culture, and operate in an environment lacking the strength of accustomed cultural attachment, status, and social support. Desa et al. (2012) describe acculturative stress as comprised of social, attitudinal, family, and environmental factors, often measured by a scale of the same name—the Social, Attitudinal, Familial, and Environmental (SAFE) Acculturation Stress Scale. Berry et al. (1987) argued that the relationship between acculturation and stress is sometimes inevitable, and depends on the group of individuals and their characteristics as they enter the acculturation process. The outcome of this process can be enhancement or deterioration of mental health. For example, Torres et al. (2012) found that acculturative stress mediated psychological distress among over 600 Latino adults.

Five factors that moderate the relationship between acculturation and stress are: (a) the multicultural ideology of the host society; (b) the nature of the acculturating group; (c) the mode of acculturation used by an individual as they adjust to the new environment, which include marginalization, separation, assimilation, or integration; (d) the demographic and social characteristics of the groups (age, gender, length of stay, socioeconomic status, prior intercultural experiences); and (e) the psychological characteristics of the individual (cognitive style). Empirical studies have validated the special association between acculturative stress and several predictive factors (e.g. Berry et al., 1987). However, the relationship between acculturative stressors and acculturative stress has not yet been clearly established.

Acculturative Stress and International College Students

Increasing numbers of foreign students, particularly from China, India, and South Korea, are accessing higher education in the United States. Moon and Larke (2020) found students from Asia studying in America had higher levels of acculturative stress than international students from Europe. Lian and Wallace (2020) found that, of a sample of 222 Chinese international students, 74 percent reported symptoms of anxiety and depression. Smiljanic (2017) found that lower TOEFL (Test of English as Foreign Language) scores for international students were related to higher levels of acculturative stress. Similarly, Zhang and Jung (2017) found a complementary scenario; as English competency increased, acculturative stress decreased. Feelings of isolation and alienation, particularly during the initial phase of the acculturation process, require social, cultural, and often academic adjustments that foster a successful integration into university life.

The variety of coping behaviors used to manage stress produced by the acculturation process has significant health and academic performance implications (Kuo, 2014). Ra and Trusty (2017) found among East Asian international students studying in the United States that social support and coping mediates the relationship between acculturation and acculturative stress. Furthermore, higher levels of attachment anxiety are related to higher levels of acculturative stress (Smiljanic, 2017). Also, Cho (2014) found among international teens studying in the United States that those using problem-focused or social support coping strategies had more positive school adjustment, while those relying on emotionally focused coping strategies had greater satisfaction of life scores. Kim and Cronley (2020) also found that the relationship between acculturative stress and binge drinking was mediated by resilience among international students.

Literature reviews pertaining to the salient variables of acculturation for international students, including acculturative stressors frequently encountered by international students, found language barriers, academic burden, lack of social support, and barriers to seeking professional help (Bai, 2016). However, Yakunina et al. (2013) reported that personal and multicultural strengths such as growth initiative, hardiness, and universal diverse orientation can reduce acculturative stress.

For those international students experiencing high levels of acculturative stress, seeking support for issues such as stress management and depression can be daunting. Compounding the challenge of seeking support for acculturative stress is the language challenge some international students face, having a more limited ability to articulate the systems they are experiencing. Maeshima and Parent (2020) found that perceived stigma has a negative relationship with students' professional mental help-seeking. Matic and Russell (2020) further found that social statuses that are treated differently in international students' home and host countries pose a unique challenge for counseling prior to re-entry. Lewthwaite (1996) noted that students use host families, academic supervisors, and mentors, as "counselors" during the acculturative process. By developing a more comprehensive understanding of how students self-identify their acculturative stress, universities and their constituents can develop a deeper understanding of the potential challenges and how to responsibly assist students during their stay in a new culture. As a result, international students will have the opportunity of experiencing positive academic and social outcomes.

Hypotheses

The following hypotheses were proposed:

H1: The self-reported levels of acculturation in the dominant and ethnic culture of international college students are related to their acculturative stress levels during their college experience.

H2: Demographic factors like age, country of origin, and native language, will be associated with levels of acculturative stress.

The goal of this investigation is to assess whether international students at a community college experience high levels of acculturative stress. The current research study will contribute to the understanding of acculturative stress faced by international community college students and, in turn, it will contribute to higher education administrators addressing acculturative stress in the international student's enrollment. This study is unique because it focuses on international students attending a community college (2-year degree programs) in a major urban city. Community colleges are less expensive than private universities and other colleges in the United States, which attracts an ethnically and economically diverse student body. Much of the other research done on international students was conducted with 4-year colleges or postgraduate university students.

Research Method

Participants

The setting for the current study is at Borough of Manhattan Community College (BMCC) which is in New York City, the institution has a population of over 23,000 plus students enrolled each semester. Additionally, international students attending this college come from 161 different countries. Each semester there are approximately 800 students who are registered at this college on a student visa and 20 plus students on a temporary visa (BMCC Factsheet, 2016). Participants were recruited through the Office of International Students enrolled at the college, which ranks fifth nationwide in the number of international students enrolled (Institute of International Education, 2013).

Eligible participants were invited via posted flyers, bulletin boards, and email notifications, as well as by invitation during the first-class meeting in various introductory courses among several majors throughout the college that semester. Participation was strictly voluntary and all participants were informed that they could withdraw from the study at any time. One week prior to the administration of the surveys, participants

122   Hardaye R. Hansen et al.

were given a consent form to sign. Institutional Review Board approval was obtained for the protocol described in this study in August 2015. Participants took a pen-and-paper questionnaire which consisted of demographic questions and two scales described below.

Measures

The measures in the study were carefully chosen to examine acculturation, acculturative stressors, the welfare of international students, and whether their general social status diminishes the relationship amongst acculturation, the welfare of international students, and acculturative stress. These measures are commonly accepted in the field of acculturation. The demographic questionnaire addressed students' ages, relationship status, purpose for migrating to the United States, country of origin, and other items.

The SAFE Acculturation Stress Scale was used to measure international students' acculturative stress. The SAFE is composed of 24 items that measure stress as a result of the acculturation process in four contexts: social, attitudinal, familial, and environmental acculturative stress (Mena et al., 1987). The original study which reported on the creation of this scale found a Chronbach's alpha of .89. The SAFE inventory was calculated by adding the score that participants reported on the individual questions which ranged from 0 to 5. On the scale, zero meant the participant had not experienced an event that may have caused acculturative stress, and 1 to 5 ranged between "Not at all stressful" and "Extremely stressful," respectively. With a scale of 24 questions, the possible range for the inventory was from 0 to 120. The SAFE inventory scale was found to be reliable in the current study—Chronbach's alpha was .96.

The Stephenson Multigroup Acculturation Scale (SMAS) was also administered. This scale consists of a total of 32 questions that measure the immersion of the participant in their culture of origin (termed Ethnic Society Immersion) and their immersion in the dominant culture, in this case, American culture (termed Dominant Society Immersion; Stephenson, 2000). This scale proposes a multi-dimensional concept of acculturation, where people can express strong or weak immersion in both, one or neither of the dominant and ethnic cultures. Some of the indicators of the SMAS are language knowledge, preferred language use, comfort in speaking the host language rather than the language learned from the country of origin, assimilation with the host society, and the use of food and media adoptions in comparison with the host society. In Stephenson's (2000) study, the overall Chronbach's alpha coefficient was found to be .86, but she also used a principle-components analysis to find a two-factor solution—these factors were termed Ethnic Society Immersion and Dominant Society Immersion and showed alphas of .97 and .90, respectively. The SMAS was calculated in two sub-scales: Dominant Society Immersion (SMAS-DSI, 15 questions) and Ethnic Society Immersion (SMAS-ESI, 17 questions). Participants could endorse various statements about their native society and practices, and about American society and practices on a scale of 1 to 4, ranging from "False" to "Partly false" to "Partly true" and finally "True." Because one of the items in the SMAS-ESI did not apply to this sample of international students (namely, "I have never learned to speak the language of my native country"), this item was not included in the calculation. This item also had a negative point biserial correlation between the endorsement of this item and the total of the sub-scale. The Chronbach's alpha of the ESI sub-scale was .73 and it consisted of 16 items (possible range of 16 to 64).

Data Analysis

Differences between groups were calculated using t-tests and one-way ANOVAs, as appropriate. Type 1 error rate was set to .05. Where there were multiple comparisons, Bonferroni's correction was applied to the Type 1 error rate. An analysis was conducted to determine the relationship between participants' SAFE Acculturative Stress Scale scores and their scores on the SMAS-ESI and SMAS-DSI, respectively, using linear regression.

Results

A total of 253 students completed the questionnaires. Ten participants reported an age below 18 years of age and were removed from the final results, leaving a final sample of 243. Of those, 55.8 percent were women, 74.1 percent were single, and 85.0 percent did not report English as their native language. The average age of participants was M = 23.7 (SD = 4.6), with a median of 23, and a range from 18 to 42. Participants reported 53 unique countries of origin all over the world. These countries were coded for geographical region. The largest proportion of students was from East and Southeast Asia (37.0 percent), followed by the Caribbean (18.5 percent), South Asia (15.6 percent), Europe (14.8 percent), and South America (7.4 percent). The rest of the students reported being born in Africa, the Middle East, and other regions. The primary reason for moving to the United States for most participants was for education (67.9 percent) and because their family migrated (26.2 percent). On average, participants reported living in the United States for M = 3.9 months (SD = 3.4), with a median of 3 months, ranging from 0 to 21 months.

In the current sample, participants reported a mean of M = 64.5 (SD = 28.1) on the SAFE inventory (n = 203). Those participants who

124 *Hardaye R. Hansen et al.*

missed some of the questions on the inventory were marked as missing. Participants who reported their native language as English had a significantly lower score on SAFE (M = 47.4; SD = 5.3) for native English speakers and M = 67.9 (SD = 2.1) for nonnative English speakers, t(198) = −3.83, p = .0001. These participants also reported higher levels of immersion in American society, as measured by SMAS-DSI sub-scale, t(223) = 3.68, p = .0001, M = 47.6 (SD = 1.3) for native English speakers and M = 40.9 (SD = 0.7) for nonnative English speakers. There were no differences on the SMAS-ESI sub-scale.

The mean of SMAS-ESI in the current sample was M = 57.9 (SD = 6.5), with a median of 60, ranging from 33 to 64. The DSI sub-scale was calculated with all the items of the sub-scale and the Chronbach's alpha was 0.89 and it consisted of 15 items (possible range of 15–60). The mean of SMAS-DSI in the current sample was M = 42.1 (SD = 10.2), with a median of 44, ranging from 16 to 59.

Participants who reported their reason for moving to the United States as "education" had a significantly lower score on the SMAS-DSI sub-scale and the SMAS-ESI scale than those whose families migrated to the United States. The mean on SMAS-DSI for those who came to the United States for education was M = 39.9 (SD = 0.8), while those whose families migrated had a mean of M = 47.3 (SD = 1.1), t(209) = −4.95, p = .0001 (here significance level was adjusted using Bonferroni's correction). Similarly, the mean on SMAS-ESI for those who came to the United States for education was M = 56.9 (SD = 0.6), while those whose families migrated had a mean of M = 60.1 (SD = 0.6), t(201) = −3.27, p = .02 (here significance level was adjusted using Bonferroni's correction). There were no differences on the SAFE inventory.

In terms of region of the world, there were some significant differences in acculturative stress and acculturation levels, F(5, 197) = 3.58, p = .004. Participants who reported South Asia as their region of birth reported a higher SAFE mean (M = 78.2, SD = 5.3) compared to those participants who were from Caribbean countries (M = 54.4, SD = 4.8; here significance level was adjusted using Bonferroni's correction). Participants who were born in Europe reported higher levels of SMAS-DSI than those born in East or Southeast Asian countries, M = 45.6 (SD = 1.8) versus M = 39.3 (SD = 1.2) respectively, F (5, 222) = 3.52, p = .004 (here significance level was adjusted using Bonferroni's correction). There were no significant differences on the SMAS-ESI sub-scale.

A linear regression model regressing the SAFE score on the SMAS-DSI and SMAS-ESI sub-scales was run. This model was significant, F (2, 172) = 39.74, p = .0001, and explained 31.6 percent of the variance

Assessing Acculturative Stress 125

Table 8.1 Regression Results (Showing Significant Associations Only)

Model	R^2	Independent variables	B	95% CI of B	β (standardized coefficient)
Model 1—SAFE regressed on SMAS subscales	31.6%	SMAS-DSI	−1.24	[−1.57, −0.90]	−0.46
		SMAS-ESI	1.30	[0.77, 1.83]	0.31
Model 2—SAFE regressed on SMAS subscales, age, sex, native language English, and reason for moving to US	36.2%	SMAS-DSI	−1.25	[−1.62, −0.88]	−0.46
		SMAS-ESI	1.16	[0.6, 1.7]	0.27
		English	−10.39	[−20.42, −0.36]	−0.14

Abbreviations: SAFE = Social, Attitudinal, Familial and Environmental; SMAS = Stephenson Multigroup Acculturation Scale; SMAS-DSI = Dominant Society Immersion; SMAS-ESI = Ethnic Society Immersion.

in SAFE. Both SMAS-DSI and SMAS-ESI were significantly associated with a score on SAFE (Table 8.1). These results mean that for each unit increase in SMAS-DSI, SAFE decreased by 1.24 units. Similarly, for each unit increase in SMAS-ESI, SAFE increased by 1.30. The effect size for this model was calculated using Cohen's f2, which was 0.46 for this model. This effect size is interpreted as large.

Control demographic variables were added to the model—age, sex, native language English, and reason for moving to the United States. Indicator variables were created for this analysis such that male sex, native English speaking, and family migrating to the United States were the reference categories. This model was also significant, $F(7, 167) = 13.55$, p = .0001, and explained 36.2 percent of the variance in SAFE. Both SMAS sub-scales remained significantly associated with the SAFE score in the same direction (see Table 8.1). Additionally, one demographic variable, native language English, was significantly associated with scores on SAFE. This means that nonnative English language was associated with a score on SAFE that was over 10 points lower than those participants who reported English to be their native language. None of the other demographic factors had a significant relationship with the SAFE score. The effect size for this model was Cohen's f2 = 0.57, which is again, a large effect size.

Discussion and Conclusions

The current study assessed the level of cultural immersion and acculturative stress in a sample of international community college students at a large urban 2-year college in New York City. The participants came from most geographic regions of the world, slightly older than traditional US college students (median age 23 list the age range), and, mostly, nonnative English speakers.

The participants' age range (i.e. 18–42 years) may have been a factor in their adaptation success to their new culture. Younger students' acculturation may be observed as part of adaptation since they are surrounded by native culture at home, and may therefore take a more positive approach to both cultures which can result in better outcomes in college. Older students may assume different responsibilities and oftentimes experience separation from other students and marginalization. Separation may cause difficulty in cultivating friendships, focusing on college work, and holding on to one's traditional customs and beliefs. Marginalization can also cause guilt and rebellious attitudes, adding more acculturative stress that leads to unhealthy lifestyles and lack of focus within the college environment (Berry, 2005). The current study did not observe differences in acculturative stress in different age groups, but this may be because of a small sample.

Similar to Zhang and Jung's (2017) findings, this study found lower acculturative stress among international students whose native language was English. Students whose native language was English also showed higher rates of immersion in American culture than those whose native language was something other than English. International students whose native language is not English may require extra academic support from college services and extra social support to combat the higher levels of acculturative stress.

Students from certain regions of the world reported higher levels of acculturative stress and lower levels of dominant culture immersion, particularly those students who came from South and East Asian regions. The current study did not have a large enough sample to examine these differences in depth. Previous studies have found that students' different coping strategies (task-oriented, emotion-oriented, and avoidance-oriented) may mediate the levels of acculturative stress (Ra & Trusty, 2015). Teaching international students coping strategies may be an effective way to lower levels of acculturative stress. This is a needed role for administrative and support services provided to international students.

Like social support and connectedness, this study demonstrates that moving to the United States with one's family, rather than only for academic study, is a factor in dominant culture immersion, which in turn is associated with lower levels of acculturative stress. The current sample may be unusual, since over a quarter of the participants reported moving with their families to the United States which is rare for the broader population of international students. This adds to the uniqueness of the study and shows clear differences in cultural immersion. Indeed, research findings relating to moving are equivocal.

This study did not find a significant direct relationship between reasons for moving to the United States and acculturative stress, whereas separation from family increased acculturative stress. In this study, investigators did not find a direct correlation with acculturative stress, but as mentioned previously there was a correlation with dominant culture immersion. This lack of a significant association may be due to a small sample size. The current study did find that students who moved to the United States for pursuing academic study showed lower immersion in the dominant culture. It may be that students who come to another country for educational reasons feel isolated from the dominant culture. More study is needed in this area. Since there were no differences in acculturative stress of both groups of participants, it is important to note that students who have their families nearby still need support to combat stress levels, similar to their counterparts who moved for education only. One possible reason for the lack of differences may be that the world has become more interconnected with easier access to Internet and mobile technologies, thus allowing students to keep in touch with their families.

The current study found that international students who reported higher immersion in their native cultures experienced higher acculturative stress and that those who reported higher immersion in the US culture experienced lower acculturative stress. It also shows that US culture immersion and speaking English from birth are protective factors against acculturative stress. One possible explanation is that students who partake of US culture and speak English have a smaller acculturative task in front of them which involves learning how to interact with the American educational system, while other students have to learn several new things. They may have an easier time engaging with other students and obtaining social support. Further study is needed to explore health behaviors and risk factors, as well as coping strategies, in international college students.

The current study should be interpreted in light of several limitations. The participants were recruited through a convenience sample from a large urban community college (BMCC). Thus, results may not be generalizable to all international students at other community colleges, such as smaller and/or rural community colleges in the United States. This study was cross-sectional, so no inferences can be made about causality. There was also no direct measure of psychological stress or coping behaviors. Belcastro and Ramsaroop-Hansen (2020) caution that relocation stress is melded in metrics of acculturation stress. There

128   *Hardaye R. Hansen et al.*

may be little need or motivation for an individual or group to adopt the native norms and values so as to live, work, procreate, and practice their faith in residence of the host culture. This would be most true for transient aliens. Thus, inferences of acculturation stress that do not account for relocation stress within its metrics of stress may be compromised.

Future studies should be conducted to explore the relationships between acculturation, acculturative stress, and other psychological stressors. The strengths of the current study include the sample, which was drawn from a highly diverse, urban, community college. This study was unique in its focus on cultural immersion in the native and US cultures when compared with other contemporary research.

Implications

Recommendations for future research include measuring academic achievement and exploring its relationship to the acculturative process. Furthermore, direct measurement of students' reported stress coping behaviors is recommended. A future study should also be conducted to analyze how social environments intensify international students' stress. Professors and staff who work with international students need to be better informed to effectively meet their unique needs. The current study found an association between cultural immersion, family factors, native language, and acculturative stress. Colleges, and especially community colleges with large international student populations, may consider allocating additional resources that directly target acculturative stress for accommodating international students as they undergo the acculturative process. These resources may include staff fluent in a variety of languages, support for English language acquisition, workshops for faculty, students and staff to support international students, and facilitating opportunities for students to socialize with peers encountering similar challenges. Since dominant society immersion seems somewhat protective against acculturative stress, student activities that focus on international students partaking in US culture with other students at the college may be helpful for mitigating stress.

Acknowledgment

With permission from the journal, this chapter is reprinted with some modification which was originally published in the *Journal of International Students*, year (2018), Volume 8, Issue 1. pages. 215–232.

References

Bai, J. (2016). Perceived support as a predictor of acculturative stress among international students in the United States. *Journal of International Students*, 6(1), 93–106.

Belcastro, P. A., & Ramsaroop-Hansen, H. (2020). Acculturation contradictions in the health and sexual behavior of US immigrant populations. In A. Bonsaint (Ed.), *Immigrant students: Perspectives, opportunities and challenges* (pp. 109–127). New York, NY: Nova Science.

Berry, J. W. (2005). Acculturation: Living successfully in two cultures. *International Journal of Intercultural Relations*, 29(6), 697–712. https://doi.org/10.1016/j.ijintrel.2005.07.013

Berry, J. W., Kim, U., Minde, T., & Mok, D. (1987). Comparative studies of acculturative stress. *International Migration Review*, 21(3), 491–511. https://doi.org/10.2307/2546607

BMCC Office of Institutional Research and Assessment. (2016). *Borough of Manhattan Community College-Factsheet Spring 2016*. http://www.bmcc.cuny.edu/iresearch/upload/spring-2016-fact-sheet.pdf

Cho, Y. (2014). Acculturation, psychological and school adjustment of early study-abroad adolescents in terms of stress coping strategy. *Child Studies in Asia-Pacific Contexts*, 4(1), 13–25. https://doi.org/10.5723/csac.2014.4.1.013

Desa, A., Yusooff, F., & Ba'yah Abd Kadir, N. (2012). Acculturative stress among international postgraduate students at UKM. *Procedia-Social and Behavioral Sciences*, 59, 364–369. https://doi.org/10.1016/j.sbspro.2012.09.287

Graves, T. D. (1967). Psychological acculturation in a tri-ethnic community. *Southwestern Journal of Anthropology*, 23(4), 337–350. https://doi.org/10.1086/soutjanth.23.4.3629450

Institute of International Education. (2013). *Open Doors report on international educational exchange*. Retrieved from the Open Doors website: http://www.iie.org/Who-We-Are/News-and-Events/Press-Center/Press-releases/2013/2013-11-11-OpenDoors-Data

Kim, Y. K., & Cronley, C. (2020). Acculturative stress and binge drinking among international students in the United States: Resilience and vulnerability approaches. *Journal of American College Health*, 68(2), 207–218. https://doi.org/10.1080/07448481.2018.1538998

Kuo, B. C. (2014). Coping, acculturation, and psychological adaptation among migrants: A theoretical and empirical review and synthesis of the literature. *Health Psychology and Behavioral Medicine: An Open Access Journal*, 2(1), 16–33. https://doi.org/10.1080/21642850.2013.843459

Lewthwaite, M. (1996). A study of international students' perspectives on cross-cultural adaptation. *International Journal for the Advancement of Counselling*, 19(2), 167–185. https://doi.org/10.1007/BF00114787

Lian, Z., & Wallace, B. C. (2020). Prevalence of past-year mental disorders and its correlates among Chinese international students in US higher education. *Journal of American College Health*, 68(2), 176–184. https://doi.org/10.1080/07448481.2018.1538147

Maeshima, L. S., & Parent, M. C. (2020). Mental health stigma and professional help-seeking behaviors among Asian American and Asian international students. *Journal of American College Health*, 1–7. https://doi.org/10.1080/074 48481.2020.1819820

Matic, D., & Russell, G. M. (2020). How do I go back? Psychotherapy with international students who face stigma upon their return home. *Journal of College Student Psychotherapy*, 34(2), 138–156. https://doi.org/10.1080/87568225.20 19.1574216

Mehta, S. (1998). Relationship between acculturation and mental health for Asian Indian immigrants. *Genetic, Social, and General Psychology Monographs*, 24(1), 61–78.

Mena, F. J., Padilla, A. M., & Maldonado, M. (1987). Acculturative stress and specific coping strategies among immigrant and later generation college students. *Hispanic Journal of Behavioral Sciences*, 9(2), 207–225. https://doi. org/10.1177/07399863870092006

Moon, C. Y., & Larke, P. (2020). Meta-analysis of Asian students' acculturative stress in US higher education. *Journal of Multicultural Affairs*, 5(1), 2–16. https://scholarworks.sfasu.edu/jma/vol5/iss1/3

Ra, Y. A., & Trusty, J. (2015). Coping strategies for managing acculturative stress among Asian international students. *International Journal for the Advancement of Counselling*, 37(4), 319–329. https://doi.org/10.1007/s10447-015-9246-3

Ra, Y. A., & Trusty, J. (2017). Impact of social support and coping on acculturation and acculturative stress of East Asian international students. *Journal of Multicultural Counseling and Development*, 45(4), 276–291. https://doi. org/10.1002/jmcd.12078

Redfield, R., Linton, R., & Herskovits, M. J. (1936). Memorandum for the study of acculturation. *American Anthropologist*, 38(1), 149–152. https://doi. org/10.1525/aa.1936.38.1.02a00330

Smiljanic, I. (2017). The role of attachment, travel experiences and English proficiency in international students' acculturative stress and depressive symptoms. *Journal of International Students*, 7(2), 188–203. https://doi.org/10.32674/jis. v7i2.322

Stephenson, M. (2000). Development and validation of the Stephenson multigroup acculturation scale (SMAS). *Psychological Assessment*, 12(1), 77.

Torres, L., Driscoll, M. W., & Voell, M. (2012). Discrimination, acculturation, acculturative stress, and Latino psychological distress: A moderated mediational model. *Cultural Diversity and Ethnic Minority Psychology*, 18(1), 17. https://doi.org/10.1037/a0026710

Ward, C., & Kennedy, A. (1994). Acculturation strategies, psychological adjustment, and sociocultural competence during cross-cultural transitions. *International Journal of Intercultural Relations*, 18(3), 329–343. https://doi. org/10.1016/0147-1767(94)90036-1

Yakunina, E. S., Weigold, I. K., Weigold, A., Hercegovac, S., & Elsayed, N. (2013). International students' personal and multicultural strengths: Reducing acculturative stress and promoting adjustment. *Journal of Counseling & Development*, 91(2), 216–223. https://doi.org/10.1002/j.1556-6676.2013.00088.x

Zhang, Y., & Jung, E. (2017). Multi-dimensionality of acculturative stress among Chinese international students: What lies behind their struggles? *International Research and Review*, 7(1), 23–43.

Author Bios

Hardaye R. Hansen, EdD, MSW is an Associate Professor at the Borough of Manhattan Community College-City University of New York. Professor Hansen immigrated to the United States and is an alumnus of Borough of Manhattan Community College. Professor Hansen is dedicated to the health education and academic success of community college students. Her research focus concerns emotional well-being throughout the life cycle as well as developing stress intervention strategies for undergraduates and international students in an academic setting. Professor Hansen teaches a range of Health Education courses such as Comprehensive Health, Stress Management, Perspectives of Death and Dying, Principles and Practices of Behavior Change, and Health Counseling. Professor Hansen co-developed the Public Health degree program currently offered in the Health Education Department.

Yuliya Shneyderman, PhD, MA is an associate professor in the Health Education Department of Borough of Manhattan Community College. She is the co-coordinator of the Public Health AS degree and teaches courses in Epidemiology, Biostatistics, Consumer Health, and Health Education. Her research interests include internet health information, sexual and reproductive health, and environmental health. She also lends her knowledge of statistical methods to colleagues and coauthors. She is passionate about educating the future public health workforce of the USA and mentoring students on conducting research.

Gloria McNamara earned a BS degree in dietetics from SUNY Oneonta College and an MS degree in nutrition from CUNY Hunter College. She went on to pursue a doctorate in Educational Psychology, focusing on health education and behaviors, at the Graduate Center of the City University of NY. Dr. Gloria McNamara is currently an associate professor at BMCC for the Health Education Department. She is a registered dietitian and a NYS licensed nutritionist. Dr. McNamara has a well-regarded reputation in public health programs, having served as director of NYCDOH's Project LEAN, NYCDOH's Wellness At Work (WAW) Program, and Maimonides Medical Center's WIC Program. Additionally, she has served as a consultant for the Partnership for the Homeless and NYC's Office of School Food and Nutrition Services. In recent years she has conducted research on health behaviors, specifically diet and exercise, as well as pedagogical practices in educating health care professionals.

Lisa Grace earned her BS in Biology and Sociology from Binghamton University, MPH from Columbia University Mailman School of

Public Health, and EdD in health education from Teachers College, Columbia University. Dr. Grace worked for the New York City Department of Health and Mental Hygiene for over 19 years in a variety of roles, initially as an epidemiologist for the Bureau of Immunization and finally as an Administrative Staff Analyst-M2 before joining the Borough of Manhattan College as a full-time faculty. Dr. Grace currently serves as Deputy Chair of the Health Education Department at the Borough of Manhattan Community College. She teaches courses in Women's Health, Spirituality, Community Health Education, Public Health, Health Communication, and the Social and Behavioral Determinants of Health. Her research interests include adolescent and women health, improving health literacy, and health communication in disadvantaged populations.

9 Frontline Advising for International Students at American Community Colleges

Understanding the Challenges and Policy Issues during the COVID-19 Crisis

Gregory F. Malveaux and Marlon Vallejo

US Government Policies that Impacted International Students Leading up to the COVID-19 Pandemic

In recent years, international students have been facing significant challenges and struggles. In the few years leading up to the COVID-19 pandemic outbreak, their access to US higher education has decreased as increased regulations—a shutting down of the Deferred Action for Children Arrivals (DACA) program and foreign travel restrictions—have been placed on them. The result has been a plunge in higher education enrollment, including at community colleges. In a 2017 survey, administrators at 250 US colleges and universities reported a 40 percent decline in international applications (Redden, 2017). The impact was clearly felt at community colleges where over 91,000 international students were enrolled (Institute of International Education, 2017), making up nearly 7 percent of total student enrollment. Then, a short-term uptick in international student enrollment took place in 2018–2019. Statistical data shows the total number of international students in the United States was 1,095,299, a 0.05 increase from the previous year, despite the different challenges faced (Number of international students, 2019).

COVID-19's Devastating Impact on International Student Enrollment

The onset of the COVID-19 pandemic has not only thwarted the progress of international student access and enrollment at US community colleges, but has sent numbers into an abysmal downward spiral across higher education in the United States and globally. Due to mandated nationwide closures, 1,500 million students are not attending school, which represents almost 90 percent of the world student population (UNESCO, 2020). Post-COVID predictions are dire: the American Council on Education estimates that international enrollment in the

134   *Gregory F. Malveaux and Marlon Vallejo*

United States will decline 25 percent in the next academic year (LeSane 2020). The majority of US colleges and universities have moved to a virtual-only course format. Unique challenges that international students have contended with during this time are increased foreign travel bans, distinct hindrances with course curricula, a digital divide, time zone restrictions, exclusion from federal relief grants, and stoppage of F-1 and other student-issued visas.

Economic Decline at US Community Colleges and the US Economy Due to Loss of Talented Foreign Students

The predicted drop in international student enrollment will prove disastrous for already cash-strapped colleges in the current precarious economy. International students are among the most gifted at community colleges, and their absence is felt. International students have been known to have a hugely positive impact on the US economy; they are the 4th largest exporter and contribute 45 billion to the US economy (Lu, 2020). Also, about 328K jobs are connected to International Education (Number of International students, 2019). Many successful companies, such as WeWork, Moderna, SpaceX, and Unshackled Ventures, were either started by former international students or owe their growth and success to students who came to the United States from abroad. Nearly one-quarter (21 of 91) of US billion-dollar startup companies had a founder who first came to America as an international student (Anderson, 2018). Furthermore, international students add to the cultural diversity of US college and university campuses.

Upon completion at US community colleges, talented international students contribute important work development skills that benefit the American economy. Riti Karki, an international student who attended Montgomery College (MC), serves as a prime example of one "making good on" her education. Born and raised in Asia, Riti came in the fall of 2001 to the United States to pursue her studies at MC; she left a society where women's rights and opportunities, at the very best, were minimal (Karki, personal communication, July 7, 2020). Riti was expected to accept an undesired, arranged marriage at the early age of 18, and to forgo the same educational opportunities as a US resident. Against her parents' wishes, she decided to stay in the United States as a student visa holder (Karki, personal communication, July 7, 2020). With a lot of work and support from friends, Riti successfully changed her visa status to F-1 with the help from the MC International Student Advising office, and her American journey began (Karki, personal communication, July 7, 2020). After very challenging years, and a lot of commitment and hard work, she successfully completed an Associate's Degree at MC (Karki, personal communication, July 7, 2020). She then transferred to the University of Maryland where she obtained a Bachelor's Degree, after which she went on to earn a Master's Degree at Johns Hopkins University (Karki, personal communication, July 7, 2020). When last spoken to in July of 2020, Riti Karki expressed her gratitude to MC for helping her achieve a better life (Karki, personal communication, July 7, 2020). She is proud to share that "I work at the World Bank as a Financial Analyst and have become a United States citizen" (Karki, personal communication, July 7, 2020). Community colleges, like MC, play a vital role in enhancing the lives of international students, who in turn, meaningfully contribute to the college and the country. MC is an example of a community college that contributed to helping a global citizen become a local citizen who first paid her way through college and now pays US taxes, significantly aiding the US economy (Karki, personal communication, July 7, 2020).

In the past, international students have been healthy participants of various educational components in US higher education, including study abroad. Similar to other college programs, their enrollment in study abroad has immensely declined due to US governmental policies and the onset of the COVID-19 pandemic.

Decreased Study Abroad Participation

Students choose to study abroad to experience, beyond obvious academic advantages, cultural and cross-cultural aspects of the environment they are in, either on campus or in the community (J. Cheng-Levine, personal communication, November 25, 2020). "Today's Millennials (born between 1980 and 2000) and Boomlets (born after 2001) ... have brought expanded objectives to overseas education and training... For these career-minded students, workforce development opportunities in their academic field serve as the driving force for overseas program choices. Often these are STEM (science, technology, engineering, and mathematics) students" (Malveaux, 2016, p. 2). Yet, the few years prior to the worldwide spread of COVID-19, international student enrollment in study abroad was already on the decline. MC illustrates a community college where international students have been a hallmark for active participation in study abroad. This student population represents over 160 nations at our college, and 10 percent of all MC study abroad participants are international students (Montgomery College, 2019). However, this is a 50 percent decrease from the previous year, with international student participation dipping from 20 percent to 10 percent of our total study abroad population (Malveaux, 2019). With current global travel restrictions and study abroad restrictions due to the COVID-19 virus, the drop is expected to continue.

The downward spiral in traditional study abroad participation is a national phenomenon. In a 2019–2020 Institute for International Education (IEE) Open Doors survey involving 520 institutes of higher education, including MC, findings revealed that over 79 percent of colleges and universities expect a substantial decline in study abroad numbers for the 2020–2021 academic year, while 18 percent expect some decline (Kennedy, 2020). This has proven to be true. For example, at the College of Canyons in California, 40 percent of study abroad students decided to take a leave of absence (Cheng-Levine, personal communication, November 25, 2020). The good news is that Study abroad administrators and staff have proven to be highly adaptable and resilient. Despite a significant decline in study abroad enrollment since fall 2020, 84 percent of institutions said they continue to plan study abroad programs to some extent for future semesters (Kennedy, 2020). While traditional study abroad programs are canceled, alternative options such as virtual study abroad, global internships, and scholarship opportunities are being offered to students, including international students. It is paramount for college advisers to keep themselves updated on academic programs that remain available to international students who hope to gain access and support at their institutions.

Administrative Roles for Servicing International Students

Informed counseling must come from international student advisers and administrators since their students face unprecedented challenges that include DACA policy blockage, travel restrictions and detainment, exclusion from federal grants during the economic crisis driven by COVID-19, and F-1 student visa obstruction. These frontline advisers, often the first in line to guide international students, include International Education Administrators (IEA), Study Abroad Coordinators, and Principal Designated School Officials (PDSOs). They must remain aware of ongoing policies and regulations issued by the current Trump administration that impact international students. Deportation, airport detainment, lost citizenship or visa use, and loss of education and finances are all negative impacts that may result from not heeding ongoing regulations. IEA, Study Abroad Coordinators, and PDSOs take on defining roles to best assist international students. International Education aids studying students, in which the study is often abroad, to become part of a genuine and dynamic international community, where they have invaluable access to a wide range of cultures, languages, faiths, and perspectives (Lukins, 2019). International Education administrators go beyond the academic environment that they are teaching to encourage diversity and inclusivity among students where culture and language may once have been obstacles (Lukins, 2019); and the obstacles that current International students contend with are significant. Within the umbrella of International Education is Study Abroad. Study Abroad Coordinators are leaders of study abroad, the educational approach for students to study outside of the traditional university classroom setting through programs and curriculum that combine travel with a recognized, legitimate form of study likely to count toward a degree (Kuh et al., 2005). International students often make up a large part of the overall International Education and Study Abroad student population, especially at highly diverse community colleges like MC, which represents over 160 countries (Montgomery College, 2019) and with 10 percent of MC study abroad participants being international students (Malveaux, 2019). Again, proper counseling and educational support for international students by frontline advisers and administrators is paramount due to a high stakes environment created by the COVID-19 restrictions and Trump Administration regulations. Those restrictions and regulations will be further detailed in this study.

Similar to an International Education administrator, a PDSO's work has become more challenging as it requires PDSOs to keep in compliance with federal regulations on behalf of the college, as well as in advocating for students and assisting them with everyday life issues. A PDSO serves as a student adviser and is a dedicated employee of the school to aid in overseeing the enrollment of F-1 students, and enable the institution to be Student and Exchange Visitor Program (SEVP)-certified (Study in the states, 2020).

More than ever, the presence of frontline advisers is paramount for the present and the future, International student enrolment has nose-dived due to the global pandemic and instructors are facing increased layoffs as institutions attempt to offset millions of dollars in lost revenue (DeRosa, 2020). One will have to wait to know the ultimate impact of the COVID-19 pandemic on international students and US community colleges, but increased strains placed on international students, and their advisers, does not bode well.

Obstacles for International Students at Community Colleges

DACA Program Stoppage by Trump Administration and Beyond

In the past few years, there has been a fierce debate surrounding the acceptance of students in the DACA program. It was made clear early in the Trump administration tenure the intention to accept no new applicants and to dissolve the DACA program, which protects 800,000 young undocumented immigrants from deportation. Community college advisers and administrators have heard a large outcry from these students. Nathan Jensen, Associate Dean of Global Engagement, and his team of international student advisers at Orange Coast College in California have encountered "a great deal of worry from this population because they really have no options if DACA is stopped" (Jensen

138　*Gregory F. Malveaux and Marlon Vallejo*

Interview, personal communication, November 18, 2020). Perhaps in an attempt to alleviate some burdens experienced by international students during the COVID-19 pandemic period, in June and July of 2020, both Federal and Supreme Courts ruled that the Trump Administration must operate the DACA program again (Durkee, 2020). In response, the administration "dug in its heals" and declared continued rejection of new applications for the DACA program despite the federal judge's order (Aguilar, 2020). All the while, DACA students contend with less access to US higher education.

Foreign Travel Bans

The recent US travel bans of 2017 impeded mobility, extending the social distance between countries and bringing fresh anxieties for international students studying in the United States. A major concern for international students is inability to reenter the United States and their college of study if they visit home for a hiatus. Starting in 2017, the Supreme Court backed the Trump Administration's set travel restrictions on eight countries—Chad, Iran, Libya, North Korea, Somalia, Syria, Venezuela and Yemen (Cameron, 2017). Students from these countries are aware that they must remain in the United States, and not return home, if they intend to earn their degrees. What is unfortunate is that international students who are not from the list of restricted countries, with legal visas, must also be wary of leaving the United States to visit home; they too may be detained at the airport and/or being blocked from reentering the United States (Malveaux et al., 2019). As a counselor for such students, it is essential to communicate this risk. For example, I recently had an Egyptian student deregister from study abroad in London because I could not guarantee she would not be detained or kept from reentering the United States. With increased frequency, students from countries where the citizens are predominantly Muslim are foregoing study abroad or visiting home. The travel ban, fueled by the Trump Administration, has increased international student anxieties, and contributed to decreased enrollment numbers by these students.

It is worth noting that 2020 COVID-19 travel restrictions have, to say the least, further impeded foreign student mobility and enrollment. For some community colleges, such as Kirkwood Community College in Iowa, travel bans are considered a top deterrent for international students who want to remain enrolled (Ingleby, personal communication, December 2, 2020). At present, the US Centers for Disease Control and Prevention (CDC) has declared that only with specific exceptions, "travelers [are] prohibited from entry into the United States" and have listed 179 countries where US citizens should avoid all travel (Coronavirus disease 2019, 2020). International Student Adviser and PDSO, Shannon

Frontline Advising for International Students 139

Ingleby, at Kirkwood Community College, discovered that as a result of travel bans, "some [international students] have continued their studies from home and remain in active status, [while] others were unable to continue and unable to return" (Ingleby, personal communication, December 2, 2020).

Challenges for International Students Resulting from the COVID-19 Pandemic

Trials with Changing Educational Format for International Students Who Remained in the United States to Study

International students, with minimal resources, who have remained in the United States to continue their education during the COVID-19 crisis, have significant concerns about contracting the virus. Data shows that international students are one of the most vulnerable groups during this pandemic, not only for financial reasons, but also for mental health reasons as these students are far from home and often isolated (Ingleby, personal communication, December 2, 2020). College of the Canyons' Dean of International Affairs and Global Engagement, Jia-Yi Cheng-Levine, asserts:

> The US' inability to control the spread of the virus further hampers students' sense of safety. No one wants to study in an environment when they cannot go out of their apartment or even feel safe to do grocery shopping ... Most of them don't have a car, which makes it even more challenging to conduct necessary routines, as they don't feel safe taking public transportation. I have students who were in their apartments for more than 3 months without setting foot outside their apartment. They are isolated and they are fearful.
> (Cheng-Levine, personal communication, November 25, 2020)

As a student group, international students may be the most impacted by the loss of physical classroom meetings, particularly at US community colleges. According to MC International Student Adviser, Heidi Russell-Kalkofen, "classes for two year undergraduate AAS (Associate of Applied Science) and AA (Associate of Arts) degrees are more hands-on than lecture-based university classes" (Russell-Kalkofen, personal communication, November 18, 2020). The move to online-only instruction is a greater barrier and detriment for international students because online learning reduces a large part of the nonverbal (body language and gestures) portion of communication and reduces group discussion—two ways in which international students gather valuable context and additional information in class settings (Russell-Kalkofen, personal communication, November 18, 2020). In juxtaposition, the

140   *Gregory F. Malveaux and Marlon Vallejo*

few students who still take some face-to-face classes feel trepidation amid our current COVID-19 pandemic environment. According to Kirkwood Community College's PDSO, Ingleby, "although Kirkwood is operating in a hybrid model, students email me daily asking if they are able to take more than one online class for fear of being exposed to COVID. Uncertainty is a constant worry for them and, as advisers, it is difficult to advise when we also have uncertainty" (Ingleby, personal communication, December 2, 2020). As international students attempt to keep up with coursework in hybrid or all-virtual models, they have also had to contend with a digital divide and time zone differences.

Impacts of Digital Divide and Time Zone Issues with All-Virtual Course Offerings

Digital Divide

Massive college closures due to the COVID-19 pandemic increased a digital divide among students; this and time zone constraints have plagued international students who have taken on an all-virtual course schedule while pursuing their education here or at home. Having depended on college campus technology, many do not have Internet access, or simply cannot afford to purchase a computer, laptop, or notebook to sustain their education. For example, at College of the Canyons, some students who remained in the United States to study have had to drive to the college's parking lot to use strong WiFi when they submit homework or take an exam (Cheng-Levine, personal communication, November 25, 2020). The PDSO at Kirkwood Community College "has had several reports from Chinese students of not being able to access Talon, [their] online course delivery platform, in order to submit assignments, watch recordings, [and so forth]. Those students have been forced to drop their classes mid-semester" (Ingleby, Interview, December 2, 2020). Similarly, when Everett Community College moved to online courses, restricted Internet access and the inability to find required class textbooks were major impediments for international students (Liang, 2020). At MC, international students have voiced a range of struggles with online learning—stress, distraction (due to family member who expect interaction while at home), Internet connectability, time zone differences, or just the remote experience overall (Russell-Kalkofen, personal communication, November 18, 2020). Data shows that international students are one of the most vulnerable groups during this pandemic, not only for financial reasons, but also for mental health reasons as these students are far from home and often isolated (Ingleby, personal communication, December 2, 2020).

Frontline Advising for International Students   141

This is a very serious matter. Tragically, it was recently reported that a 19-year-old student in India, Aishwarya Reddy, ended her life at her Hyderabad home because her parents could not afford to give her a laptop or a smartphone to take online classes; apparently, worries over fees and her scholarship had mounted (COVID-19: Digital divide deepens, 2020). Though not an international student, Aishwarya's suicide reveals the immense anxiety that some students, including international students, are feeling without campus programs and support systems in place for aid. Since COVID-19 restrictions, "community college support systems (campus life or health services) are less robust. For international students with less cultural knowledge and with most family support outside of the United States, this leaves them more vulnerable because they cannot access mental and physical health support and make or create connections" (Russell-Kalkofen, personal communication, November 18, 2020). This experience is shared at College of the Canyons. The Dean of International Affairs and Global Engagement relates that "we have seen real academic and psychological challenges faced [by international students and] it is hard for us to fathom the lasting impact on the students" (Cheng-Levine, personal communication, November 25, 2020).

Time-Zone Impacts

In addition, with only virtual classes made available, international students have to work through problematic time zone differences between their home country and the host institution. College of the Canyons advisers discovered for international students "who have returned home that are taking online classes, time zone differences are a real challenge for online live classes. Students in China have issues accessing some course content" (Cheng-Levine, personal communication, November 25, 2020). Kirkwood Community College advisers agree with the concern "that students who have returned home may have to participate in synchronous classes at inconvenient times—sometimes in the middle of the night" (Ingleby, personal communication, December 2, 2020). Soyeong Cha, an international student at Everett Community College (EVCC) in Washington State, details that "since South Korea is 16 hours ahead of the United States, my classes' meetings mostly are scheduled at midnight, or very early morning" (Liang, 2020). Similarly, at Orange Coast College in California, administrators and advisers are finding that international students "want to try to study even if the class is in the middle of the night for them, but it gets to be too much for some" (Jensen Interview, personal communication, November 18, 2020). To their credit, international students "rarely complain about the time difference explicitly... [It is] some faculty [who] have noted that students overseas would miss deadlines or miss class and noted the time difference as a

142 *Gregory F. Malveaux and Marlon Vallejo*

factor" (Russell-Kalkofen, personal communication, November 18, 2020). Without access to federal emergency grant assistance, coupled with existing logistical issues (a digital divide and time zone differences), it has become difficult for international students to resume their studies at US community colleges and in US higher education as a whole.

Exclusion from Federal Emergency Stimulus Grants

International students are denied equal access to the financial benefits that other students are receiving during the COVID-19 crisis. While most higher education students are able to apply for the federal $2.2 trillion Coronavirus Aid, Relief, & Economical Security (CARES) Act stimulus package, undocumented students have been deemed ineligible to apply by the Education Department (Murakami; No emergency aid, 2020). Only students who are US citizens are eligible to file a "Free Application for Federal Student Aid" form to apply for the CARES Act grants (Knudson, 2020). This means that international students, as well as undocumented and DACA students, are not eligible. Not being provided federal relief is another disappointment that these students face as the rhetoric continually tells them they are not valued in the United States (Ingleby, personal communication, December 2, 2020).

Dasha Semisynova, an international student from Russia who attends St. John's University, serves as a prime example. With the closure of her college due to the pandemic, she finds herself in a precarious position while she continues her studies through online classes (Knudson, 2020). "As of right now, I can't go back because the flights are canceled—so basically I'm literally stuck here. The lockdown keeps postponing, and I don't know how long I'm going to be here or even allowed to go back [to Russia] any time soon" (Knudson, 2020). Without the ability to live in her dormitory or use campus technology, her current housing situation and lack of computer access has caused serious financial strain. Dasha desires assistance through the CARES Act, and due to her international student status, she was disqualified for funding through the relief package (Knudson, 2020).

Ironically, the challenges that Dasha Semisynova and international students are contending with mirror the same obstacles that the CARES Act was meant to aid—$6 billion of the CARES Act funds are designed to go to students through emergency grants to help them pay for a variety of needs, ranging from buying tickets home after their campuses were closed to getting needed computers as courses have moved online (Murakami; No emergency aid, 2020). It is worth noting that not only International students, but community college students on a whole have less access to funds than students at 4-year institutions due to Congress' unequal structuring of the stimulus package. The

CARES Act funding is based on the number of full-time-equivalent students colleges enroll, which worked against those with large numbers of part-time students, or community colleges (Murakami; Community colleges, 2020). As a result, while community colleges educate almost 40 percent of students, they only received about 27 percent of the CARES Act funds; had the package based funding on the total number of students, public colleges of two years or fewer would have received 39 percent of the funding (Murakami; Community colleges, 2020). Overall, community college students, and staff members, are hamstrung with having less CARES Act funding to assist struggling students in contrast with those at four-year institutions.

Though well-intentioned, higher education institutions that are forming their own student emergency funds, created and funded by donor gifts, often follow the same unequal policies placed by federal grants that exclude international students. The type of emergency and size of awards will likely vary, but the common thread will be an ability to demonstrate that need stems, in some way, from impacts of the coronavirus (Helhoski, 2020). However, what seems to be overlooked is the mention of who is eligible. Only students eligible to receive federal financial aid can receive the funding, which leaves those in the Deferred Action for Childhood Arrivals program and international students unable to tap this resource (Helhoski, 2020).

Community college officials' initiative to find private aid that helps some international students has taken the place of federal funding that would assist many. As the Dean of International Affairs and Global Engagement at College of the Canyons notes, "we were able to obtain some funding to help a couple of students, [but] many are struggling financially. Our college gathers food bags, and my office staff delivered them to students' places" (Cheng-Levine, personal communication, November 25, 2020). According to PDSO Ingleby, COVID-19-related campus closures and segregation from federal grants have also displaced beneficial resources at community colleges:

> Exclusion from federal relief funds comes right alongside fewer on campus job opportunities for international students (the only place they can work). At Kirkwood Community College we are fortunate to have a 4 diamond Hotel on campus which is also a learning facility for our Hospitality and Culinary Arts programs. Since this is an on campus facility, international students are able to work there. However, with the pandemic, hotels have closed or furloughed employees and the abundance of on campus jobs that used to be available are no longer there.
>
> (Ingleby, personal communication,
> December 2, 2020)

144 *Gregory F. Malveaux and Marlon Vallejo*

Lost opportunities and exclusion from federal relief funds, once again, send the unfortunate message that international students are not welcome to study at US community colleges (Jensen Interview, personal communication, November 18, 2020).

Current Mechanisms in Place for F-1 Student Processing

Ever since the fateful day of September 11, 2001, the world of international education and foreign student visas in the United States changed. The F-1 student visa program became a political and national security issue. New regulations were implemented to create a system in which every international student under a student visa needed to be accounted for. Under the newly created Department of Homeland Security (DHS), the international student visa and exchange program became a responsibility of Immigration and Customs Enforcement (ICE), which in part created the Student Exchange Visitor Program (SEVP) office to handle all aspects of student visa monitoring and school certification. As a result, SEVP formed the Student Exchange Visitor Information System (SEVIS). SEVIS is a web-based system for maintaining information on international nonimmigrant students and exchange visitors in the United States. SEVIS was set up to enforce Section 641 of the Illegal Immigration Reform and Immigrant Responsibility Act of 1996, which requires DHS to continually collect current information from nonimmigrant students and exchange visitors during the course of their stay in the United States (Student and exchange visitor program, 2020).

F-1 Student Restrictions and the Power of Collective Advocacy

International students, including F-1 students, have had to face recent opposition with entering US community colleges and four-year institutions. On July 6, 2020, SEVP notified colleges and universities with F-1 students to instruct those students that they would be banned from attending schools operating entirely online during the COVID-19 crisis and that those students would either have to leave the United States or transfer to schools that offer in-person classes. This new directive sent a shockwave throughout the international student community. College of the Canyon administrators agrees that "students and institutions were not given enough notice to make sound decisions or alternative plans" (Cheng-Levine, personal communication, November 25, 2020); and the Associate Dean of Global Engagement at Orange Coast College maintains "this created a great deal of stress and a feeling amongst our students that they are not welcome in the US" (Jensen Interview, personal communication, November 18, 2020).

Frontline Advising for International Students   145

There was collective concern about implementing the new SEVP guidance from staff members at colleges, universities, and English language schools throughout the country. College administrators and staff, including those at MC, began to hold a series of meetings to address this issue, as well as figure out how to best assure international students that they are welcome on MC campuses. MC leadership became very supportive of F-1 student visa holders, and MC's President, Dr. DeRionne Pollard, immediately called for a Senior Administrative Leadership Team (SALT) meeting to find options to assist F-1 students. She expressed that "MC values the cultural and intellectual contributions that these students make to the educational processes at our institution, bringing their knowledge of history, politics, and languages from their home countries" (Statement from Dr. DeRionne P. Pollard, 2020).

The Massachusetts Institute of Technology (MIT), Harvard, Johns Hopkins University (JHU), and other universities filed a lawsuit against DHS/ICE on July 8, 2020. A preliminary hearing was heard on July 14, 2020, which resulted in the finding that "DHS/ICE has agreed to rescind the 7/6 guidance document and will not enforce on a nationwide basis" (Rescinded fall 2020 SEVP, 2020).

Lauding the decision, the Director and CEO of NAFSA: Association of International Educators, Dr. Esther D. Brimmer, announced:

> Today's decision is a victory for campuses and communities across the nation. The July 6 guidance dangerously linked international students' legal status to their institution's decision-making on how best to navigate keeping their campus community safe during a highly unpredictable pandemic. It put university administrators in the position of weighing the deportation of valued members of their campus community against the public health risks of holding in-person classes. We are heartened to see the guidance put to rest. While this is a positive outcome, we cannot ignore the damage inflicted by the perception of the July 6 guidance. The COVID-19 pandemic in the United States remains unpredictable and institutions must be trusted and be given the authority to make decisions that are right for their campuses based on their local circumstances and the safety and well-being of all involved. We will continue to work with our coalition partners and take every avenue available to us to advocate for international students.
>
> (NAFSA applauds decision, 2020)

As a follow up to the July 14 court ruling, the DHS changed course and sent out a new guidance allowing current international students to engage in online classes without having to lose their visa statuses or having to leave the United States (Read an update, 2020). The collective

146 *Gregory F. Malveaux and Marlon Vallejo*

advocacy for International students by organizations such as NAFSA, and the leadership at MIT, Harvard, JHU, and MC, proved to be highly effective. Protections for international students were a success.

However, the short term ban on international students attending schools with classes operating entirely online has left a negative, residual effect:

> This attempt from June 2020, quickly rescinded a week later, on the outside appears "resolved"; however that week led to turmoil for international students as they panicked about what to do and how to get home. Those who were able to get immediate flights home may not have returned due to lack of flights and travel bans. Those who stayed were again left feeling that the system was not set up to help them succeed. I believe that those fears of instant change linger with students and it is hard for them to trust that they will be able to stay in the US to complete their studies.
>
> (Ingleby, personal communication, December 2, 2020)

Community college administrators and advisers throughout the country concur that "the prosed rules in July, later rescinded, generated a strong sense of unease and uncertainty" (Cheng-Levine, personal communication, November 25, 2020) and "gave the perception that international students are 'unwelcome'" (Russell-Kalkofen, personal communication, November 18, 2020). This created an "unwelcoming political climate that would only [serve to] further discourage international students from wanting to study in the US" (Cheng-Levine, personal communication, November 25, 2020). "Many students [who] planned to study from home, or postpone [coursework until] the beginning of study in the US, wanted to make that decision themselves" (Russell-Kalkofen, personal communication, November 18, 2020).

Expected Visa Processing Problems within the COVID-19 Period and into the Future

Visa Processing Back Up

Again, amidst the COVID-19 global health emergency, foreign travelers coming into the United States are facing trials in getting US visas and finding flights into the country. The visas in consideration are F-1, M-1, and J-1 visas because they are all student visas of impact within US community colleges (H. Russell-Kalkofen, personal communication, November 18, 2020). F-1 is a study visa, M-1 a vocational visa, and J-1 an exchange visitor visa. If the consulate is operational, these visa types are supposed to get priority (H. Russell-Kalkofen, personal communication, November 25, 2020).

US embassies are temporarily closing down and thus not allowing interviews for new international student visas. The impact for new international students will be to sit out the 2020 fall semester and wait until next spring 2021 semester, or after. Those seeking change of status inside the United States via United States Citizenship and Immigration Services (USCIS) processing, may also take longer due to the global pandemic. Based on the USCIS' latest information, adjudication for change of visa status takes on average between 5.5 to 7.5 months (US Citizenship and Immigration Services, 2020).

There is uncertainty among international students and their advisers as to how long it will take to have a student visa issued, if at all. Visa stoppage depends on the country; different consulates have different approaches, and waiting periods vary. There is not a consistent approach. The US State Department provides a baseline of information and advice, and each country's consulate gives specific procedures, often driven by its local government (Russell-Kalkofen, personal communication, November 25, 2020). For MC International Student Adviser, Russell-Kalkofen, "processing itself is not slower than it has often been at other times. The current issue is availability of visa appointments at all. Many US consulates are officially still closed or processing 'emergencies only.' The perception of slowdowns and unpredictability has been the biggest stressor. Of course, there is likely a backlog of demand so that may stretch appointment wait times" (Russell-Kalkofen, personal communication, November 25, 2020). Consulate closures have been Dean Cheng-Levine's chief experience at College of the Canyons: "It's not slowdown; it's stoppage. New Chinese students cannot come because they can't get the visa; students from Iran, even when they finally got an appointment, are rejected a visa. Embassy closures have completely negated decades of recruitment efforts" (Cheng-Levine, personal communication, November 25, 2020).

Many students would like to come to US community colleges and universities for study, but have not been able to do so because of the visa processing (Jensen Interview, personal communication, November 18, 2020); and the issue is more dire at community colleges than universities. "Community colleges are already facing increased visa denials—more so than our university partners. As the processing of visas or visa appointments slow down, students are less likely to have time to go for a second interview if their visa is denied the first time. This means deferrals and loss of potential students in the process" (Ingleby, personal communication, December 2, 2020). Future international student enrollment at US community colleges does not look promising. According to projections by the National Foundation for American Policy, due to COVID-19-related delays in visa processing, the enrollment of new international students in the upcoming academic year will decline 63 percent to 98 percent from its level in 2018–19 (Treisman, 2020).

Concluding Thoughts

Regulations set by the Trump administration, followed by the outbreak of the worldwide COVID-19 pandemic, have put immense obstacles in the path of international students who are pursuing higher education in the United States. The pitfalls that these students endure include the closure of the DACA program, travel restrictions, lost campus resources, an increased digital divide, time zone restrictions, disqualification from federal relief funds, and delayed visa issuance. International students are a resilient group, yet the strain being placed on them is taking its toll on their enrollment at US community colleges and other institutions of higher education. Again, the American Council on Education estimates that international enrollment in the United States will decline 25 percent in the next academic year (LeSane 2020). It is paramount that these students' advisers, whether International Education administrators, Study Abroad coordinators, or PDSOs, be informed about current US governmental policies and new COVID-19 restrictions that impact international student access and retention in US community colleges and institutions of higher education.

Future Research Directions

US community college advisers, educators, and administrators should engage in further advocacy efforts on behalf of F-1 visa holders and international students, like MC student Riti Karki, because reducing their enrollment damages colleges and the economy at large. In order to do so, further research is needed to gauge the impacts resulting from the COVID-19 pandemic as well as federal regulations to F-1 and international student enrollment. In addition, further research needs to be done in an effort to safeguard the future of this student population at US community colleges.

References

Aguilar, J. (2020). Trump administration says it will reject new DACA applications while weighing future of the program. *The Texas Tribune.* https://www.texastribune.org/2020/07/28/daca-trump-texas/

Anderson, S. (2018). International students are founding America's great start ups. *Forbes Magazine.* https://www.forbes.com/sites/stuartanderson/2018/11/05/international-students-are-founding-americas-great-startups/#292bc13d5568

Cameron, D. (2017, January 19). The eight countries in Trump's new travel ban. *The Washington Post.* https://www.washingtonpost.com/graphics/2017/national/permanent-travel-ban/

Cheng-Levine, J. (November 25, 2020). Personal interview [Personal interview].

Coronavirus disease 2019. (2020, November 21). COVID-19 travel recommendations by destination. *Centers for Disease Control and Prevention*. https://www.cdc.gov/coronavirus/2019-ncov/travelers/map-and-travel-notices.html

COVID-19: Digital divide deepens, so does student despair. (2020, November 17). *Deccan Chronicle*. https://www.deccanchronicle.com/lifestyle/culture-and-society/171120/covid-19-digital-divide-deepens-and-so-does-student-despair.html

DeRosa, K. (2020, May 6). International-student enrolment plunges, teachers facing layoffs. *Times Colonist*. https://www.timescolonist.com/news/local/international-student-enrolment-plunges-teachers-facing-layoffs-1.24130292

Durkee, A. (2020). Federal court orders Trump administration to comply with Supreme Court's DACA ruling, start accepting applications. *Forbes Magazine*. https://www.forbes.com/sites/alisondurkee/2020/07/17/federal-court-orders-trump-administration-to-comply-with-supreme-courts-daca-ruling-start-accepting-applications/#7d6733d26336

Helhoski, A. (2020, April 23). College students can get more aid during the coronavirus crisis. *NerdWallet*. https://www.msn.com/en-us/money/careersandeducation/college-students-can-get-more-aid-during-the-coronavirus-crisis/ar-BB136GoS

Ingleby, S. (December 2, 2020). Personal interview [Personal interview].

Institute of International Education. (2017). *Open Doors*. Institute of International Education.

Jensen, N. (November 18, 2020). Personal interview [Personal interview].

Karki, R. R. (July 7, 2020). Personal interview [Personal interview].

Kennedy, K. (2020). US: Half of HEIs see drop in applications, 18% see substantial decline. *The PIE News*. https://thepienews.com/news/us-half-heis-see-drop-applications-18-see-substantial-decline/

Knudson, A. (2020). International student struggles amid Coronavirus: "I'm literally stuck here." *SILive.com*. https://www.silive.com/coronavirus/2020/05/international-student-struggles-amid-coronavirus-im-literally-stuck-here.html

Kuh, G. D., Kinzie, J., Schuh, J. H., & Whitt, E. J. (2005). *Student success in college: Creating conditions that matter*. Jossey-Bass.

Liang, D. (2020, May 5). Deciding to stay or leave during a pandemic: International student's perspective. *The Clippper*. https://everettclipper.com/12749/culture/deciding-to-stay-or-leave-during-a-pandemic-international-students-perspective/

LeSane, C. B. (2020, September). Essay "Enrollment" featured in *the post-pandemic college. The Chronicle of Higher Education*, 46–52.

Lu, M. (2020). The impact of international students on the US economy. *Visual Capitalist*. https://www.visualcapitalist.com/international-students-impact-u-s-economy/

Lukins, S. (2019). What is international education and why is it important for you? *TopUniversities*. https://www.topuniversities.com/student-info/studying-abroad/what-international-education-why-it-important-you

Malveaux, G. F., Rhodes, G., & Raby, R. (2019). Community college education abroad health and safety concerns: Standards needed to meet the challenges. *Study abroad opportunities for community college students and strategies for global learning*. IGI-Global.

150   *Gregory F. Malveaux and Marlon Vallejo*

Malveaux, G. F. (2016). *Look before leaping: Risks, liabilities, and repair of study abroad in higher education.* Rowman & Littlefield.

Malveaux, G. F. (2019). How to survive and thrive as a community college consortium: A case study of the Maryland community college International Education Consortium. *Study abroad opportunities for community college students and strategies for global learning.* IGI-Global.

Murakami, K. (2020a). No emergency aid for DACA students. *Inside Higher Education.* https://www.insidehighered.com/news/2020/04/22/daca-students-excluded-emergency-stimulus-grants

Murakami, K. (2020b). Community colleges got disproportionately less in CARES Act. *Inside Higher Education.* https://www.insidehighered.com/quicktakes/2020/05/12/community-colleges-got-disproportionately-less-cares-act

Montgomery College. (2019). Admissions and records: resources for International students. http://cms.montgomerycollege.edu/edu/department2.aspx?id=10078

NAFSA applauds decision to rescind ICE guidance threatening International students with deportation. (2020). *NAFSA: Association of International Educators.* https://www.nafsa.org/about/about-nafsa/nafsa-applauds-decision-rescind-ice-guidance-threatening-international-students

Number of international students in United States hits all-time high. (2019). IIE/Open Doors. https://www.iie.org/Why-IIE/Announcements/2019/11/Number-of-International-Students-in-the-United-States-Hits-All-Time-High

Read an update on federal guidance for the fall semester. (2020). Study in the States. *US Homeland Security.* https://studyinthestates.dhs.gov/2020/07/read-an-update-on-federal-guidance-for-the-fall-semester

Redden, E. (2017, 13 March). Will international students stay away? *Inside Higher Education.* https://www.insidehighered.com/news/2017/03/13/nearly-4-10-universities-report-drops-international-student-applications

Rescinded fall 2020 SEVP COVID-19 guidance. (2020). NAFSA: Association of International Educators. Retrieved from: https://www.nafsa.org/regulatory-information/rescinded-fall-2020-sevp-covid-19-guidance

Russell-Kalkofen, H. (November 18, 2020). Personal interview [Personal interview].

Russell-Kalkofen, H. (November 25, 2020). Personal interview [Personal interview].

Statement from Dr. DeRionne P. Pollard, President of Montgomery College: ICE restrictions on F1 visa college students threaten their health and slows economic recovery. (2020). *MC News.* Montgomery College. http://mcnews.montgomerycollege.edu/2020/07/statement-from-dr-derionne-p-pollard-president-of-montgomery-college-ice-restrictions-on-f1-visa-college-students-threatens-their-health-and-slows-economic-recovery/

Student and exchange visitor program. (2020). US Immigration and Customs Enforcement. https://www.ice.gov/sevis

Study in the states. (2020). Homeland Security. https://studyinthestates.dhs.gov/schools/get-started/designated-school-official

Treisman, R. (2020). ICE confirms new foreign students can't take online-only course loads in the US National Public Radio (NPR). https://www.npr.org/sections/coronavirus-live-updates/2020/07/24/895223219/ice-confirms-new-foreign-students-cant-take-online-only-course-loads-in-the-u-s

UNESCO. (2020, March). COVID-19 educational disruption and response. *UNESCO Institute for Statistics data.* https://en.unesco.org/covid19/educationresponse [Accessed 30 March 2020].

US Citizenship and Immigration Services. (2020). https://egov.uscis.gov/processing-times/

Authors Bios

Gregory F. Malveaux, PhD, is a professor of English at Montgomery College, has been a study abroad coordinator and international education coordinator in higher education for two decades, is co-Chairperson of the Maryland Community College International Education Consortium, and serves on the board for the College Consortium for International Studies. In addition, he is an accomplished writer; most recently, he coedited, *Study Abroad Opportunities for Community College Students and Strategies for Global Learning* (IGI-Global, 2019) and wrote the book, *Look Before Leaping: Risks, Liabilities and Repair of Study Abroad in Higher Education* (Rowman & Littlefield Press, 2016). He has traversed more than 60 countries and has led student, faculty, and community-based study abroad programs to Africa, Asia, Central America, South America, and Europe. His passion to be a global citizen led him to pursue overseas studies in Africa, teach ESOL throughout Southeast Asia, Chair the English and US Business Department at Nation University in Thailand, and serve as a Global Studies specialist in American higher education. He is dedicated to cultivating current and responsible advising for study abroad and international students in higher education.

Marlon K. Vallejo is an International Coordinator and a Principal Designated School Official (PDSO) at Montgomery College. For over 25 years he has worked in the international education field as a PDSO. As an international educator and NAFSA member, he has had the privilege of meeting and helping students from over 160 nations. Also, he has volunteered in his local community as a member of the Montgomery County Hispanic Chamber of Commerce and the Latin American Advisory Committee.

Part III

Promoting Diversity and International Education at Community Colleges

10 Community College as a Gateway to Baccalaureate Success for International Students

Veronika Rozhenkova and Elizabeth S. Park

Introduction

Over 1 million international students currently attend US higher education institutions (Open Doors, 2020b). While most international students who pursue higher education in the United States, enroll in a degree-granting program at a 4-year institution, 7.4 percent of international students choose an alternative path and attend community colleges (Open Doors, 2020a). International students who first enroll in community colleges and later transfer to a 4-year institution are identified as international transfer students. The experiences of international students who are taking this less traditional path remain largely unstudied. Once they transfer to a 4-year institution, they become a part of the campus's existing international student population and are often not recognized as a potentially different group of students with their own academic characteristics, challenges, and needs. Although the community college experience can make them more capable of navigating college life, they may still be experiencing additional difficulties adjusting to college similarly to other transfer students. These challenges may include adjusting to a new departmental and institutional environment, new class settings (e.g. larger classes), and faster university pace. Unable to fully accommodate these differences, 4-year institutions provide the same support services and resources for all international students instead of tailoring them to specific student subgroups. This chapter aims to help narrow the identified gap in the literature and add to the discourse on international transfer students. We take a closer look at these students by comparing their demographic profiles and academic characteristics with those of traditional international students, while examining the case of a major research university located in California, one of the states that attract the largest number of international students. Additionally, the goal of this work is to identify potential ways of providing more adequate support services for international transfer students throughout their American college experiences.

International Students in the US

In the last few decades, the internationalization of higher education has affected numerous institutions across the globe having brought significant changes to their student demographics. With increased student mobility, the United States has witnessed an even larger inflow of international students and has become the country that hosts the largest numbers of students coming from abroad for short- and long-term programs. According to the Open Doors report of 2019–2020, in the last decade, the number of international students rose from 690,923 in 2009/2010 to 1,075,496 in 2020, making up 5.5 percent of the total US higher education student population (Open Doors, 2020b). The US Department of State's Bureau of Educational and Cultural Affairs constantly highlights the continued competitiveness of the United States as the primary destination for international students. The top five countries that are sending students to the United States include China, India, South Korea, Saudi Arabia, and Canada. New York, Massachusetts, and California are among the states that receive the largest proportion of international students with New York University, North Eastern University, and University of Southern California being at the top of the list (Open Doors, 2020b). With the number of international students reaching an all-time high in 2019, China has remained the country sending the most students to study in the United States for the tenth consecutive year. From the previous year, the numbers of students coming from China and India have increased by 1.7 percent and 2.9 percent accordingly, while those numbers dropped for South Korea and Saudi Arabia by 4.2 percent and 16.5 percent (IIE, 2019). Emerging market countries demonstrated some of the strongest growth in the outward student mobility in 2018–2019. For example, the number of students coming from Bangladesh increased by 10 percent, from Brazil—by 9.8 percent and Nigeria—by 5.8 percent (IIE, 2019). A global pandemic of 2019–2020 has caused a slight decrease in the overall number of newly enrolled international students in the US higher education institutions by 0.6 percent (Open Doors, 2020b).

Some of the most attractive majors for international students include Engineering, Math and Computer Science, and Business and Management, while Agriculture, Education, and Legal Studies and Law Enforcement attract the least number of students (Open Doors, 2020b). Out of the top three fields of study, Math and Computer Science saw a considerable growth of enrolled students by 9.4 percent from 2018 to 2019, surpassing Business and Management that experienced a noticeable drop of 7.1 percent from the previous year. In 2020, both of these majors experienced a decrease in enrollment: by 0.9 percent in Math and Computer Science, and a larger drop by 4.2 percent in Business and Management. Engineering has remained the largest academic field for international students in the same period, containing 20.5 percent of all international students (Open Doors, 2020b). It appears that international students tend to choose Science, Technology, Engineering, and Mathematics (STEM) disciplines over Humanities or Social Sciences (Hunt & Gauthier-Loiselle, 2010). The main reason is that a STEM degree generally provides better internship and job opportunities, while also creating an additional advantage in obtaining Optional Practical Training (OPT) upon degree completion. OPT is temporary employment that is available to F1 (student visa) holders and should be directly related to a student's major (USCIS, 2020). All F1 students can apply to receive up to 12 months of employment authorization both before and after completion of their studies; however, those majoring in STEM disciplines are eligible to apply for an additional 24-month extension. In 2018–2019, the number of students in the OPT programs increased by 9.6 percent and in 2020—by only 0.2 percent to 223,539 students (Open Doors, 2020b). The combined 36-month postgraduate period provides an opportunity for international students to obtain work experience before heading back to their home countries or to secure further employment and stay in the United States, which, along with other reasons, such as positive career outlook, makes STEM majors even more appealing (Lu, 2019).

International students play an important role in the higher education systems of host countries. First of all, these students bring greater diversity, global fluency, and cultural awareness to their classrooms, campuses, and communities. They contribute their own views and perspectives in the classroom, enhancing understanding and appreciation of the differences found around the world. Additionally, enrolling international students provides an opportunity for faculty and students of host countries to experience different languages, cultures, and traditions. These opportunities help faculty and students further develop cultural sensitivity and provide experiences of working with individuals coming from diverse backgrounds (Wu, Garza, & Guzman, 2015). These aspects are particularly valuable at a time when ethnic, racial, and cultural relations are most needed, allowing these students to provide an additional opportunity for "just in time lessons in humanity and diversity" (Hagedorn, 2020, p. 6). Another frequently discussed benefit that international students bring to their host institutions and the host country is financial benefits. Most international students pay full tuition while frequently being ineligible for institutional, state, and federal financial aid. Therefore, attracting more international students means increased revenue for the institutions that they are enrolled in. Furthermore, international students contribute to the country's economy on an even larger scale. According to NAFSA (2019), more than one million international students enrolled in all types of postsecondary institutions during the 2018–2019 academic year, contributed nearly

158 *Veronika Rozhenkova and Elizabeth S. Park*

$41 billion to the US economy and supported 458,290 jobs. This represents a 3.8 percent increase in dollars contributed to the economy from the previous academic year.

In the context of international students' experiences, entering universities abroad can be an overwhelming life event and a stressful transition. According to a study that involved 900 international students in Australia, 41 percent of students experienced a substantial amount of stress that affected various spheres of their academic experience (Russell, Rosenthal, & Thomson, 2010). International students may experience a range of challenges: academic, social, emotional, administrative, and financial. Some of these difficulties may include but are not limited to the language barrier, homesickness, discrimination, and loneliness leading to stress, anxiety, and social interaction issues (Heikinheimo & Shute, 1986; Sun & Chen, 1997). Sun and Chen (1997) identified several issues that lead to miscommunication and create communication problems among international students and their native peers, including the language barrier and unfamiliar communication rules or intergroup expectations. These issues present additional barriers for the process of intercultural interaction and may thwart effective communication.

Another often-cited problem that international students may experience is culture shock. When moving to another country with an unfamiliar culture, individuals may feel uncertainty, confusion, anxiety or a spectrum of other unsettling feelings that may affect their wellbeing. Acculturation, which is a component of culture shock, is the process of adjusting to a host culture and gradual assimilation in that foreign culture. This phenomenon is often referred to as a "sojourner experience" (sojourner—a temporary between-society traveler), which embodies a wide range of affective, behavioral, and cognitive changes that individuals experience when they come in contact with the host culture (Fülöp & Sebestyén, 2012; Roskell, 2013). Adjustment to the new culture and environment involves both psychological and socio-cultural adjustments. The success of psychological adjustment is defined by the extent to which individuals can feel comfortable in a new environment and cope with the stress associated with that transition. Socio-cultural adjustment involves acquiring social skills, which enables individuals to efficiently interact and coexist with the representatives of the host culture (Laanan, 2007). Once sojourners successfully adjust and assimilate, they acquire intercultural competence and become noticeably more comfortable in the new environment; however, this process might take time, as it requires a shift in beliefs, values, morals, and standpoints (Kim, 2009).

International Students at Community Colleges

Traditionally, international students enroll in 4-year colleges and universities; however, from the 1960s to the 1970s, they slowly began to discover community colleges as a path to higher education (Bevis & Lucas, 2007).

According to the 2020 Open Doors data report, the number of international students attending community colleges reached 79,187, representing approximately 7.4 percent of the total international enrollment in degree-granting US higher education institutions (Open Doors, 2020b). China remains the leader in the list of sending countries (18.6 percent), followed by Vietnam (10 percent), Japan (6 percent), South Korea (5.7 percent), and Brazil (4.3 percent) (Open Doors, 2020b). Similar to the traditional international student enrollment patterns, STEM disciplines top the list with Physical and Life Sciences, Health Professions, and Engineering serving as the most attractive areas of study. Business and Management, and Social Sciences continue to top the list of the majors that international community college students tend to enroll in. The least attractive areas of study include Legal Studies and Law Enforcement, Humanities, and Education (Open Doors, 2019a).

International students choose to begin higher education in a community college for various reasons, such as less stringent admissions requirements, affordable application fees and tuition costs, English as a second language (ESL) support, an opportunity to adjust to a foreign academic environment with smaller class sizes, and a chance to better prepare for and transfer to a 4-year institution (Durrani, 2019; McIntyre, 2019; Hagedorn, 2020). Additionally, the English language proficiency requirement is usually not as rigid at a community college as at most 4-year institutions where higher TOEFL or IELTS scores may be required for admission. This might be one of the most important factors, since the English language proficiency is typically one of the most eminent barriers to enrolling in American universities for international students (Hagedorn & Li, 2017; Sherry, Thomas, & Chui, 2010). High admission requirements on the Test of English as a Foreign Language (TOEFL), the International English Language Testing System (IELTS), and American College Testing (ACT)/Scholastic Aptitude Test (SAT) scores may leave many international students with very limited postsecondary education options. Language proficiency at community colleges, however, can be demonstrated via other ways ranging from taking language placement tests and ESL classes to obtaining instruction primarily in English in high school. Affordability appears to be another major factor attracting international students to community colleges. To put cost into perspective, the average tuition and fees for a community college can be as little as $3,500 compared to roughly $35,000 for out-of-state students at a 4-year public university (NSHSS, 2019). Another reason why international students may choose to enroll in a community college is the career and technical programs that are uniquely offered there. Many countries do not have a well-developed vocational education sector and/or technical programs at that level, which makes American community colleges even more attractive. For example, in a US community college, one can get an associate degree or a certificate in such areas as Engineering Technology, a field that is

160 Veronika Rozhenkova and Elizabeth S. Park

frequently sought-after by high-tech companies all over the world (Krigman, 2014). Additional examples of the degrees that are offered at the community college level and are very attractive to international students may include but are not limited to: Radiation Technology, Nuclear Medicine Technology, and Medical Sonography.

Transfer Experience at 4-Year Institutions

International students who transfer from a community college to a 4-year institution encounter a number of challenges in the new learning environment. Transfer shock, defined as an initial drop in academic performance immediately following the transfer experience (normally within the first semester or quarter) is a common difficulty among transfer students (Ishitani, 2008; Poisel & Joseph, 2011). Transfer shock influences not only the academic aspect of students' college experiences but also their social experience. According to Poisel and Joseph (2011), transfer students are generally less engaged in research projects with faculty members, student organizations, service-learning, and other on-campus activities, which constitute student involvement.

Not surprisingly, students' level of satisfaction and their perception of the new learning and living environment largely depends on how efficiently their inter-institutional transition goes. Transfer students discuss several challenges like feeling a lack of connection with faculty and difficulty making connections with peers (Townsend & Wilson, 2006). Students report feeling "old and out of place" in certain social settings as they enter 4-year institutions with third-year academic standing while traditional students enter college as freshmen (p. 448). In addition, transfer students report having difficulty making personal connections with faculty given larger class sizes and feeling intimidated by university professors. Furthermore, students mention feeling "like a number" and report minimal opportunities for faculty-student interactions relative to their experiences at community colleges (Townsend & Wilson, 2006, p. 446). At 4-year institutions that mostly cater to traditional-aged first-year students, transfer students often feel a reduced sense of belonging as compared to their experiences at community colleges.

Finally, international transfer students might experience similar additional academic difficulties as domestic transfer students. In general, community college students who transfer tend to experience a drop in GPA during the first semester after transfer and are prone to psychological stress associated with having to adjust to a new environment (Laanan, 2001). Additionally, since they enter college or university as third-year students, they have considerably less flexibility in switching majors unless they do that at the expense of extending their time to degree. Besides, articulation issues that may arise between institutions frequently lead to the necessity for transfer students to retake or take more classes after they transfer. Moreover, international students who transfer to large, public institutions may have to adjust to larger enrollment sizes or navigate the system with minimal counseling support.

Because transfer students tend to be categorized as a subpopulation of the broader undergraduate student body, there is a variation in whether and to what extent transfer students are included in typical programmatic and retention efforts (Herman & Lewis, 2004). Orientation and transition programs are aimed at acclimating students to college academic expectations and expose students to various social and extracurricular opportunities. Transfer students likely need more tailored information on what they can expect given their experiences with the community college system in order to be situated for success in a new academic environment. Yet, it is unclear to what extent institutions provide adequate support for this unique group of students.

International Transfer Students—Case of a Major Research University

While there has been considerable research examining the higher education experience for both international student and transfer student populations independently, there is little work on the intersection of these two subpopulations: international transfer students. To better understand the demographic profile and academic characteristics of international transfer students compared to traditional international students, we focus on a population of international students attending one large 4-year institution in California. About 16 percent of the undergraduate student population at this institution are international students. We obtained international students' administrative records of those who matriculated in fall 2015, with outcomes observable up to summer 2020.

Table 10.1 shows the demographic and academic characteristics of the 1,646 international students who first entered the institution in fall 2015. Almost 20 percent of those students are transfer students (n = 322) while 80 percent of the students are traditional international students. We see that international transfer students are more ethnically and socio-economically diverse than traditional international students. Among the traditional international students, 75 percent of them identify as Chinese compared to 53 percent of international transfer students. Additionally, 22 percent of transfer students identify as racially minoritized students, defined as Black, Latinx, Native American, Pacific Islander, and Southeast Asian, compared to 12 percent of traditional international students, indicating greater racial and ethnic diversity among international transfer students. Furthermore, a greater

162   *Veronika Rozhenkova and Elizabeth S. Park*

Table 10.1 Demographic Breakdown by Transfer and Traditional International Students

	Transfer International Students		Traditional International Students	
	Mean or %	N	Mean or %	N
Black	2%	322	0%	1324
Chicano	6%	322	7%	1324
Chinese	53%	322	75%	1324
Decline to State	2%	322	5%	1324
East Indian	1%	322	3%	1324
Japanese	3%	322	0%	1324
Korean	16%	322	4%	1324
Latino	2%	322	1%	1324
Filipino	1%	322	1%	1324
Thai/Other Asian	7%	322	2%	1324
Vietnamese	5%	322	1%	1324
White	3%	322	2%	1324
Women	44%	322	50%	1324
Low-Income	7%	322	4%	1324
First-Generation	45%	303	32%	1226
SAT Math	619.35	31	691.98	1324
SAT Verbal	475.48	31	497.82	1324
HS GPA Weighted	3.44	322	3.85	1324
TOEFL Score	93.73	26	90.80	1058

Note: There were 1,646 international students at this institution in fall 2015, of whom 322 were international transfer students.

proportion of transfer students are first-generation college students and are categorized as low-income students relative to traditional international students. These numbers indicate that community colleges offer an additional pathway for racially minoritized students and to those coming from more disadvantaged backgrounds.

In terms of prior academic preparation, we note that traditional international students have slightly stronger academic achievements based on their reported high school GPA. While examining their SAT scores, we see that all traditional international students reported their SAT scores whereas only 10 percent of transfer students did the same. This is likely because community colleges do not require SAT scores for admissions, rendering the test unnecessary for transfer students who started their college trajectory at a community college. In addition, while international transfer students' high school GPA is lower than that of the traditional international students, their TOEFL score is higher. However, only 26 out of 332 students have taken the TOEFL test and therefore the higher score may be driven by higher-achieving international transfer students who opted to take this test for admissions.

Community College as a Gateway 163

Table 10.2 Visa Status by Transfer and Traditional International Students

	Transfer International Students	Traditional International Students	All
F1	85%	30%	40%
Unknown	11%	64%	53%
Other	4%	7%	6%
Total	322	1,324	1,646

Note: "Unknown" visa status: if a student did not submit the materials needed to make a determination, the student is identified with an "unknown". The "Other" category includes visas like A1 = foreign government diplomats and officials and their immediate family members; B2 = temporary visit or tourism; E1 and E2 = international trade or to start a business; J1 = research scholar or exchange visitors, and others.

We next turn to the types of visas that are held by international students at this university and disaggregate these types by traditional and transfer students. Table 10.2 indicates that the majority of international transfer students (85 percent) hold an F1 visa, a student visa that allows foreign individuals to pursue education in the United States. Very few international students, both transfer and traditional, have visas that are granted for spouses and children of those visa holders that come to the United States for work on a temporary basis, whether they are sponsored by government or businesses. These types of visas usually allow individuals to take classes at the college level. The other category that is prevalent particularly among traditional international students at this institution is the Unknown categorization. "Unknown" means that the applicant has not indicated their visa status at the time of application and thus the actual categorization is pending upon approval of additional documents.

Next, we examine major selection and degree completion status for international students as of summer 2020. We aggregated the different majors to broader categories for the ease of interpretation. For example, "other social sciences" include anthropology, psychology, sociology and so forth. Similarly, "biology/health" includes biology, molecular biology, biochemistry, medicine, and so forth. We decided to include business/economics as a separate category instead of including it with social sciences given that a significant number of international students identified business/economics as their major, confirming national trends. The initial major is the major that students declared in their admissions application whereas the final major is the recorded major associated with their degree receipt.

Table 10.3 shows the seven aggregated major categories at the start of college in fall 2015 and their final major as of summer 2020. The top panel shows the percentages for the 322 international transfer students and the bottom panel shows the percentages for the 1,324

Table 10.3 Switch Out Patterns by Initial Major among Transfer and Traditional International Students, Row Percentages

				Final Major						
Initial Major	Drop out	Business/ Econ	Engineering/ Comp Sci	Bio/Health	Humanities	Chemistry	Math/Stats	Other Social Science	Physics	N
Transfer International Students										
Undeclared	0%	100%	0%	0%	0%	0%	0%	0%	0%	1
Business/Econ	1%	98%	0%	0%	1%	0%	0%	0%	0%	80
Engineering/ Comp Science	6%	2%	88%	2%	0%	0%	0%	2%	0%	48
Bio/Health	7%	0%	0%	86%	7%	0%	0%	0%	0%	14
Humanities	23%	8%	0%	2%	56%	0%	0%	12%	0%	52
Chemistry	22%	0%	0%	0%	0%	67%	0%	11%	0%	9
Math/Stats	16%	16%	0%	0%	0%	0%	68%	0%	0%	19
Other Social Science	8%	18%	0%	1%	1%	0%	0%	72%	0%	97
Physics	0%	0%	0%	0%	0%	0%	0%	0%	100%	2
Total	9%	32%	13%	5%	10%	2%	4%	24%	1%	322
Traditional International Students										
Undeclared	27%	27%	19%	4%	3%	2%	3%	14%	1%	360
Business/Econ	17%	76%	2%	1%	1%	0%	1%	3%	0%	321

Engineering/ Comp Science	22%	11%	60%	2%	2%	0%	0%	2%	0%	123
Bio/Health	22%	6%	4%	56%	1%	0%	1%	10%	0%	116
Humanities	8%	13%	5%	0%	53%	0%	3%	18%	0%	38
Chemistry	27%	3%	3%	7%	3%	43%	0%	13%	0%	30
Math/Stats	18%	31%	16%	1%	2%	0%	29%	2%	1%	170
Other Social Science	21%	7%	1%	2%	2%	0%	1%	67%	0%	128
Physics	40%	8%	11%	0%	0%	0%	8%	0%	34%	38
Total	22%	33%	14%	7%	3%	1%	5%	13%	1%	1324

traditional international students. Overall, we note that about a quarter of all international students entered the university declaring business/economics as their major. In addition, while 27 percent of traditional international students entered undeclared, only one transfer student entered undeclared. This pattern is expected as transfer students are typically admitted to a particular department of the university with junior standing while traditional international students enter the university with freshman standing. Finally, we find that traditional international students switch majors more than international transfer students, which is not surprising since transfer students have less flexibility in switching majors due to the limited time left to degree completion

Despite certain similarities, we note several differences among transfer and traditional international students. First, we find high retention rates among international transfer students in the fields of business/economics, biology/health, engineering, physics, and other social sciences. Specifically, 25 percent of international transfer students entered the university as a business/economics major and nearly all of them graduated with that same major. While there is a high retention rate in business/economics among transfer students, the retention rate is much lower in humanities, chemistry, and math. Among the 52 students who started college as humanities majors, only about half of them graduated with a humanities degree while some dropped out and others switched to either business/economics or other social sciences. Similarly, among the 28 students who entered the university as a chemistry or math major, some either dropped out or switched to business/economics.

Similarly to international transfer students, we find that traditional international students who started university as a business/economics, engineering, and social sciences major tend to graduate with that major. Unlike transfer students in biology/health and physics, however, the retention rate is lower among traditional international students in those majors. 56 percent of the 116 traditional international students who started as a biology/health major graduated within the same discipline. 22 percent of them dropped out and the remaining students switched to business/economics or engineering/computer science. In physics, only 34 percent of the 38 traditional international students graduated with a physics degree with 40 percent of the students dropping out and the remaining students switching to business/economics, math, or engineering/computer science. Lastly, it appears that traditional international students who entered undeclared, as a chemistry major or a physics major tend to drop out by summer 2020.

Finally, we examine international transfer students' and traditional international students' time to degree. Table 10.4 shows the proportion of students who spent said amount of time out of the total number of international transfer students (and correspondingly traditional international students). As such, "less than a year" is the minimum amount of

Community College as a Gateway   167

Table 10.4 Proportion of International Students that Graduated within Each Time Frame

	Transfer International Student	Traditional International Student	All
Dropped out	9%	22%	19%
Less than a year	2%	0%	0%
1 yr	8%	0%	2%
1 yr 1 qtr	15%	0%	3%
1 yr 2 qtrs	28%	0%	6%
1 yr 3 qtrs	12%	0%	2%
2 yrs	7%	0%	2%
2 yrs 1 qtr	4%	1%	2%
2 yrs 2 qtrs	11%	5%	6%
2 yrs 3 qtrs	2%	6%	6%
3 yrs	0%	7%	6%
3 yrs 1 qtr	0%	13%	11%
3 yrs 2 qtrs	0%	31%	25%
3 yrs 3 qtrs	1%	8%	6%
4 yrs	0%	3%	3%
4 yrs 1 qtr	0%	2%	2%
4 yrs 2 qtrs	0%	2%	1%
4 yrs 3 qtrs	0%	0%	0%
N	322	1,324	1,646

Note: yr = years; qtr = quarters.

time students took to graduate whereas "4 years and 3 quarters" is the maximum amount of time. Out of the 322 international transfer students, 72 percent of them graduated within 2 years, 9 percent of students dropped out entirely, whereas another 19 percent of them took longer than 2 years. Among the traditional international students, we see that 66 percent of them took three or more years to graduate, 22 percent of them dropped out and 12 percent graduated in under 3 years.

Support for International Transfer Students

Traditional international students and those who transferred from community colleges bring cultural and ethnic diversity as well as financial benefits to their host institutions. It is important to remember that international students, including those who transfer from community colleges, arrive at 4-year institutions, with their unique academic and social needs. If universities want to embrace international students on their campuses, these needs should be addressed and accommodated. Previous studies on support services available to international students suggest a number of ways to assist this student population. First, students need to be supported from the very moment they arrive at the institution. General orientation for new incoming students will not be sufficient for international students, especially those who transferred from community colleges. Robertson et al. (2011) suggest redesigning traditional orientation sessions by providing more one-on-one attention to incoming transfer and international transfer students. Based on a case of a major research university, introducing this new form of orientation, together with a new student seminar course that was specifically designed for transfer students, yielded positive results in relation to students' connection to campus and satisfaction with orientation and advising (Robertson et al, 2011). Additionally, they saw improvements in the GPA and first-semester retention for the students enrolled in that course. Frequently, such courses are offered for credit, so that they do not add burden to the students' existing workload and do not thwart students' academic progress. Hagedorn (2020) further emphasizes the importance of additional advising for international students and, potentially, exploring the option of having specially trained academic counselors and advisors who work solely with international students. More research should be done in order to learn how instructors and academic counselors can be trained to better assist international transfer students on their path to obtaining a university degree. Moreover, faculty would also likely benefit from training that illuminates the international student perspective. Many of the previously described issues that international students face can lead to misaligned expectations between instructors and international students and can be averted if faculty had a better understanding of the cultural differences that these students bring to the classroom.

Furthermore, building a strong community of international students on campus is crucial for their academic success. Many 4-year institutions already create special services for international students; however, in order to avoid isolation, including additional activities and events that integrate international students with their domestic counterparts should be considered. To help students go through the process of acculturation faster and more smoothly, higher education institutions should facilitate students' continuous engagement in various on-campus events while helping them form new social networks with their peers, mentors, and faculty. It is important that these events and activities involve not only international students but also their domestic peers. This tends to help international students overcome the aforementioned issues of misunderstanding and alienation from other students.

Other suggestions aiming to improve international transfer students' experiences, include implementing more efficient and productive programming, such as peer mentoring, and addressing the high cost of college attendance with increased financial aid opportunities (McIntyre, 2019). Peer mentoring programs are one of the most frequently utilized means of support for students, especially during their first year of college. Such a peer support program has been introduced on the study campus with the goal of creating a strong academic and

Community College as a Gateway 169

social support system for the first-year international students. The program matches students with trained peer mentors who provide individual coaching and counseling for students and help them better navigate the college system. Program participants in their 2nd to 5th year are also offered research opportunities through collaborative projects with other students and faculty. The major drawback of such support programs, as well as of new student orientations and on-boarding events, however, is that they primarily target first-year students, which means that international transfer students who arrive at the institution as third-year students will not be able to benefit from those opportunities. Furthermore, most peer mentoring programs match students with mentors based on their major and/or nationality/country of origin while not taking into consideration individuals' intersectional identities, such as transfer student identity and international student status. These students may experience additional challenges in finding community and safe spaces on campus, and, therefore, may require extra support. Failing to address the intersectionality of international students' identities may affect their sense of belonging in the institution, and, consequently, increase attrition. One way to address this issue is to leverage peer mentors who share similar identities with the incoming international students in order to successfully usher in the new cohorts of international transfer students.

Finally, it is crucial for international transfer students to be aware of available resources in case they need help and assistance with the issues that they are unable to deal with alone, including mental health services or discrimination and harassment. International students are an important part of the university community, and they can and are willing to benefit from American college experiences. However, in order to maximize their success and enable them to leave their institution as international ambassadors, they must be supported.

Conclusion

Based on the case of a major US university, this study aimed to take a closer look at international transfer students, a subgroup of a broader international student population. The demographic data shows that international transfer students come from a wider, more diverse range of ethnic, racial and socio-economic backgrounds in comparison with traditional international students. Additionally, there are more first-generation college students among international transfers as well as more students who are categorized as low-income individuals. As for their academic profile, international transfer students tend to be on a shorter timeline to graduate that spans about 2 years. In line with this finding, international transfer students do not often deviate from their initially declared majors. The data further shows higher retention rates

170 *Veronika Rozhenkova and Elizabeth S. Park*

among international transfer students in comparison with traditional international students.

While a growing number of international students are discovering community colleges as pathways to higher education in the United States, their specific experiences frequently get overlooked and are combined with those of traditional international students or native transfer students. Previous studies have identified various ways of supporting international students; however, more research needs to be done in order to better understand the intersecting identities of international transfer students. This understanding should help inform support services that can be provided for this specific student population group. To better address the international transfer students' unique challenges, higher education institutions should proactively reach out to these students and develop more targeted support. Universities should recognize and validate the specific needs of individual student groups, leveraging their unique characteristics in order to increase their visibility and to help create a more diverse student body.

References

Bevis, T. B., & Lucas, C. (2007). *International students in American colleges and universities: A history.* Palgrave Macmillan.

Durrani, A. (2019, July 9). *What international students should know about community college admissions?* U.S. News and World Report. https://www.usnews.com/education/community-colleges/articles/2019-07-09/what-international-students-should-know-about-community-college-admissions

Fülöp, M., & Sebestyén, N. (2012). Being a student abroad. The sojourner experience: USA meets Hungary. In S. Goncalves & M. Carpenter (Eds.), *Intercultural policies and education* (pp. 141–171). Peter Lang.

Hagedorn, L. S. (2020). *International students in community colleges: An unplanned diversity.* American Council on Education.

Hagedorn, L. S., & Li, R. (2017). English instruction at community colleges: The language bridge to the U.S. In L. T. Tran & K. Dempsey (Eds.), *Internationalization in vocational education and training: Transnational perspectives* (pp. 229–244). Springer.

Heikinheimo, P. S., & Shute, J. C. M. (1986). The adaptation of foreign students: Student views and institutional implications. *Journal of College Student Personnel, 27*(5), 399–406.

Herman, L., & Lewis, R. (2004). Transfer transition and orientation programs. In T. J. Kerr, M. C. King, & T. J. Grites (Eds.), *Advising transfer students: Issues and strategies* (pp. 57–64). National Academic Advising Association.

Hunt, J., & Gauthier-Loiselle, M. (2010). How much does immigration boost innovation? *American Economic Journal: Macroeconomics, 2*(2), 31–56.

Institute of International Education (IIE). (2019). *Number of international students in the United States hits all-time high.* https://www.iie.org/Why-IIE/Announcements/2019/11/Number-of-International-Students-in-the-United-States-Hits-All-Time-High

Ishitani, T. T. (2008). How do transfers survive after ⎯transfer shock? A longitudinal study of transfer student departure at a four-year institution. *Research in Higher Education*, *49*, 403–419.

Kim, Y. Y. (2009). Cross-cultural adaptation theory. In S. W. Littlejohn & K. A. Foss (Eds.), *Encyclopedia of communication theory* (Vol. 2, pp. 244–247). SAGE Publications Ltd.

Krigman, E. (2014, August 19). *New study shows gap in specific STEM skills*. U.S. News & World Report. https://www.usnews.com/news/stem-solutions/articles/2014/08/19/new-study-shows-gap-in-specific-stem-skills

Laanan, F. S. (2007). Studying transfer students: part II: Dimensions of transfer students' adjustment. *Community College Journal of Research and Practice*, *31*, 37–59.

Laanan, F. S. (2001). Transfer student adjustment. *New Directions for Community Colleges*, *2001*(114), 5–13.

Lu, X. (2019, July 25). *What are the most popular majors for international students in the U.S. World Education Services?* https://www.wes.org/advisor-blog/popular-majors-international-students/

McIntyre, N. (2019). *Unfamiliar territory: a preliminary exploration of the experiences of international junior transfer students* (Publication No. 1269). [Master's Theses, University of San Francisco]. Scholarship repository.

NAFSA. (2019). *NAFSA international student economic value tool*. https://www.nafsa.org/policy-and-advocacy/policy-resources/nafsa-international-student-economic-value-tool-v2

National Society of High School Scholars (NSHSS). (2019). *Community college vs university: Pros and cons of cost, class size and student experience*. https://www.nshss.org/blog/community-college-vs-university-pros-and-cons-of-cost-class-size-and-student-experience/

Open Doors. (2019a). *Community college student characteristics*. [Data set]. Institute of International Education. https://opendoorsdata.org/data/us-study-abroad/community-college-student-characteristics/

Open Doors. (2020a). *International students. Enrollment by institutional type*. [Data set]. Institute of International Education. https://opendoorsdata.org/data/international-students/enrollment-by-institutional-type/

Open Doors. (2020b). *Enrollment trends*. [Data set]. Institute of International Education. https://opendoorsdata.org/data/international-students/enrollment-trends/

Poisel, M. A., & Joseph, S. (2011). *Transfer students in higher education: Building foundations for policies, programs, and services that foster student success*. University of South Carolina.

Robertson, H., Trapani, S., & Hopkins, E. (2011). Advising and orienting transfer students: A two-pronged approach to improving transitions. *Journal of College Orientation and Transition*, *19*(1), 103–112.

Roskell, D. (2013). Cross-cultural transition: International teachers' experience of "culture shock." *Journal of Research in International Education*, *12*(2), 155–172.

Russell, J., Rosenthal, D., & Thomson, G. (2010). The international student experience: Three styles of adaptation. *Higher education*, *60*(2), 235–249.

Sherry, M., Thomas, P., & Chui, W. H. (2010). International students: A vulnerable student population. *Higher Education*, *60*(1), 33–46.

172   *Veronika Rozhenkova and Elizabeth S. Park*

Sun, W., & Chen, G. M. (1997, March). Dimensions of difficulties mainland Chinese students encounter in the United States (Conference presentation). *International Conference in Cross-cultural Communication.* Tempe, AZ, United States.

Townsend, B. K., & Wilson, K. (2006). "A hand hold for a little bit": Factors facilitating the success of community college transfer students to a large research university. *Journal of College Student Development, 47*(4), 439–456.

U.S. Citizenship and Immigration Services (USCIS). (2020, April 4). *Optional Practical Training (OPT) for F-1 students.* https://www.uscis.gov/working-in-the-united-states/students-and-exchange-visitors/optional-practical-training-opt-for-f-1-students

Wu, H., Garza, E., & Guzman, N. (2015). International students' challenges and adjustment to college. *Education Research International, 20,* 1–9.

Authors Bios

Veronika Rozhenkova is a Postdoctoral Scholar at the University of California, Irvine in the Office of the Vice Provost for Teaching and Learning. She is conducting research in higher education for the Education Research Initiative (ERI), specifically focusing on STEM student success and retention. Veronika received her PhD in Social Sciences and Comparative Education from UCLA, where she held a fellowship as a Conrad N. Hilton Scholar with the WORLD Policy Analysis Center, conducting research measuring various aspects of public policy internationally. Prior to her doctoral studies, Veronika received a Master's degree in International Education Policy from Harvard University, a Diploma in Philology from Yaroslavl State Pedagogical University, and worked as a university faculty member in Russia. Her research interests are in international comparative education, higher education policy and reform, and STEM education.

Elizabeth S. Park is a Postdoctoral Scholar at the University of California, Irvine, Office of the Vice Provost for Teaching and Learning. Her research interests include improving retention and success rates of underrepresented college students in STEM fields, studying access and success of community college students, and improving the K-16 pipeline. She uses large-scale datasets and advanced quantitative methods to answer her research questions. She received her Ph.D. in Urban Education Policy from University of Southern California, a Master's degree from University of Pennsylvania and a Bachelor's degree from University of California, Los Angeles.

11 From Oppression to Global Social Justice

Practitioners' Responsibility to International Students in the US Community College

Tiffany Viggiano, Evelyn Vázquez, and Ariadna I. López Damián

Introduction

Global events and internationalization processes are not apolitical (Yao & Viggiano, 2019). In response to international issues, policy pieces such as the recent US Travel Bans of 2017 and COVID Visa/Travel Restrictions of 2020 impeded mobility, these impediments are not experienced as neutral. Higher education scholars have responded to these events: Blanco (2020) described the executive proclamation suspending entry of immigrants in response to the COVID pandemic as "hostage taking" and Lee (2020) highlighted the way in which international students were being used as "political pawns". Weimer and Barlete (2020) link the discourse of the Trump administration to "othering" of international students. Current discourse largely links current international student turmoil to the recent federal administration that began in 2016.

But toxic and exploitative internationalization at community colleges is not new and it did not begin in 2016. If we conceptualize these events as rare symptoms of a particular political regime, we continue to ignore the substantive problems that are deeply ingrained in institutional and US culture. We return to our analysis of data collected in 2014 to highlight that current events merely exacerbated already existing ideological deficiencies in the ways in which US citizens conceptualize their cultural commitment to international student constituents at the community college. To ground the implications of current events, we take a more critical look at our conclusions about the ways in which community college decision makers were conceptualizing international students. How are the rationales we identified amongst practitioners in "Others" expressed on the national stage? How might these rationales exacerbate oppressive conditions?

International Students at US Community Colleges

Our initial investigation explored how decision makers justified the recruitment, enrollment, and treatment of international students at three community colleges in the Pacific region of the United States (Viggiano et al., 2018). We called those with power to influence policy "decision makers" and included chancellors, senior administrators, deans, faculty chairs, and faculty on relevant committees—those paramount to forming a shared vision (Kouzes & Posner, 2007). We found that international students were welcomed at the community college only because of their transactional benefits (i.e. as sources of tuition revenue and sources from which domestic students could extract diversity skills). From these transactional rationales, we identified the existence of the international access paradox: the decision makers in our study first crafted a class of economically privileged international students, then justified economic discrimination of all potential international students on the basis of this manufactured economic privilege. In this chapter, we revisit the international access paradox and observe the ways in which this logic has permeated the national stage.

Around the time the original interviews were conducted, 41 percent of participants representing associate granting institutions in an American Council on Education (ACE) survey had indicated that increasing the number of students that study abroad was their primary internationalization goal (ACE, 2016). Roughly 72 percent indicated that internationalization had accelerated at, at least a moderate rate between the years of 2011 to 2015 (ACE, 2016). As such, many community colleges were well-established internationalized institutions. Those in our study had been actively involved in internationalization since the turn of the century (Levin, 2001).

Our initial interest in this topic was born from four characteristics of the US community colleges and the literature on them: (1) there was an increase in the recruitment of international students at community colleges; (2) the primary discourse for the inclusion of these students focused on transactional arguments, that is, the benefits that their presence brought to domestic students—or to community colleges—with a limited critical perspective on the forms of this inclusion or its consequences; (3) there seemed to be a contradiction between the traditional open-access mission of community colleges and the primary recruitment of affluent international students in these institutions; and (4) the majority of research had focused on the students' experiences, leaving unattended the study of those with authority to shape those experiences. These themes remain salient today. Because of these themes, it continues to be necessary to rationalize the presence and service of international students at the community college.

From Oppression to Global Social Justice 175

In "Others" we argued that, because decision makers at community colleges have strategically enrolled international students, these students are now members of the campus community. The community college, therefore, has an obligation to serve international students as they would other students, which includes considering issues of access and equity. We grounded this argument within the two principles of Rawls' (1999) Theory of Justice. The liberty principle states that individuals have the right to freedoms and protection from undue harm (Rawls, 1999). The second principle can be split into two subprinciples. First, the fair and equal opportunity subprinciple (FEOP) that states that given equal talent, opportunity, motivation, and ability, anyone—regardless of their background, culture, or class in society—can obtain any career. To ensure FEOP, it is necessary to have equal access to education (Nussbaum, 2006). Second, the difference subprinciple postulates that in a society there can be unequal groups—due to economic disparity—as long as economically disadvantaged groups are not further disadvantaged (Rawls, 1999). Because globalization theory conceptualizes the world as "a single place" (Robertson, 1992), we extended these principles to geographic origin and argued that access to higher education institutions in the United States needs to be approachable for all potential international students in order to be considered just. Subsequent research further elaborated on the responsibility of US community colleges to serve diverse international populations because of the global history of colonialism (Viggiano, 2020) and a responsibility to an extended campus community (Viggiano, 2019).

In this chapter, we further reconceptualize international students in the United States as humans living in oppressive conditions that cultivate an ontological sense of powerlessness (Hernández-Plaza et al., 2010). Powerlessness is linked to psychological dynamics of exclusion and subordination that lead to the internalization of a disadvantaged position in hierarchical and asymmetrical power relations, fear, violence, tolerance, and obedience to authority (Hernández-Plaza et al., 2010). From this perspective, we assert that, when international students are rendered powerless by oppressive conditions, they become dependent on decision makers to have a fair, just, and dignified experience in the United States. This dependency is particularly problematic when decision makers reproduce inequity through their own flawed and implicit assumptions of fairness, without any accountability to ensure that these students are well treated. Decision makers at community colleges largely don't conceptualize international students as worthy of equal treatment: decision makers are largely blind to their continued participation in the reproduction of oppressive conditions for international students in the United States (Viggiano et al., 2018). This lack of self-critique, from community college decision makers, impedes accountability and necessary action required to mediate and

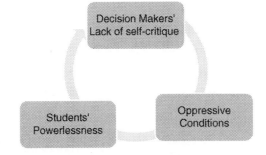

Figure 11.1 Reproduction of Hegemony and Oppressive Conditions

diminish the oppressive conditions experienced by international students. Oppressive conditions can lead to students feeling powerless have their experiences voiced or understood, which contributes to decision makers' inability to self-critique. Figure 11.1 reflects this cycle.

Rather than putting this responsibility to educate decision makers on students, critical internationalization scholarship can disrupt this cycle by helping decision makers to identify inequities and implicit biases necessary for self-critique (Viggiano, 2019, 2020). When decision makers are capable of self-critique, they can begin to collectively address the oppressive conditions that facilitate powerlessness amongst international students (Viggiano, 2019, 2020).

Critical Internationalization

In 2017, scholars coined the term Critical Internationalization Studies to describe a scholarly perspective that acknowledges the potential risk that global massification of higher education poses to reproduce global inequity and social injustice (Stein, 2017). What was previously a loose coupling of multidisciplinary and seemingly incongruent perspectives, now has overt theoretical grounding (see Stein, 2017).

Critical scholarship has the potential to serve as a tool to identifying injustice while encouraging service to those disassociated from wealth and power (Martínez-Alemán et al., 2015), but methodological nationalism impedes this work (Shahjahan & Kezar, 2013). Critical scholars recognize that there is not just one form of critical thought (Kincheloe et al., 2011). Higher education scholars tend to think critically without thinking outside the national container (George Mwangi & Yao, 2021; Shahjahan & Kezar, 2013). Shahjahan and Kezar (2013) identify the absence of critical internationalization literature on higher education as methodological nationalism: the unexamined assumption that the State is the ideal unit of analysis. Methodologically nationalist

From Oppression to Global Social Justice   177

assumptions manifest as real-world inequity (George Mwangi & Yao, 2021; Shahjahan & Kezar, 2013).

Stein (2017) describes three categories of nonmethodologically nationalist critical thought: soft critique, an approach that identifies significant shortcomings in the internationalization of higher education, but that remains supportive of and focuses on its benefits; radical critique, oriented by the idea that higher education institutions reproduce global inequality of labor and resources; and liminal critique, which suggests that universities in the global north take advantage of ongoing processes of subjugation in southern countries to maintain its supremacy under the flag of modernity. Of the critical internationalization literature, the majority falls into the category of soft critique (Stein, 2017). "Others" was no exception (Stein et al., 2019). While we were critical of the system of higher education, we failed to overtly question the superiority of Western higher education and the benevolence of internationalization (Stein et al., 2019).

We originally assumed that increased access would lead to global social justice, but this is not inherently the case (George Mwangi & Yao, 2021). The issue of epistemic dominance—the assumed superiority of Western knowledge as the Truth—creates a power dynamic critical scholars should explore. One reason many international students come to the United States is because of global pressure to attend "the best" institutions (Shahjahan et al., 2017). Because of the colonizing history of US higher education, a US degree is more valuable in their home country's job market (Shahjahan et al., 2017). Despite having quality institutions of higher education within their home countries, the illusion of superiority—reproduced by annual rankings that promote transactional outcomes—creates economic pressures that push students to go abroad for their degree (Shahjahan et al., 2017). For some, it is an economic imperative rather than a choice (Anayah & Kuk, 2015). Non-ranked US institutions of higher education, like community colleges, benefit from the quality halo-effect that surrounds US higher education in general (Anayah & Kuk, 2015). As such, plausibly, simply extending access to the community college alone—making it more affordable to attain a US degree—could further exacerbate the issue of epistemic dominance.

Moreover, while global access could be beneficial to the individual student, it is not necessarily beneficial to the country from which that student hailed or the world (Brennan & Naidoo, 2008). If the student does return home, it could amplify the issue of epistemic dominance of the Global North: those with the valued US degrees are slated for positions of power (Stein, 2017). In this way, the community college, like other institutions of higher education that Stein (2017) highlights, are utilized as a colonizing tool. In 2018, we failed to consider the deep historical and cultural roots of the biases we observed. A global

178 *Tiffany Viggiano et al.*

history of colonialism further informs conversations about international student access and equity at the community college (George Mwangi & Yao, 2021).

Importantly, in 2018 we overlooked the ways in which decision makers' rhetoric could cause larger harm by contributing to a hostile campus climate and global social injustice. Although scholars such as García et al. (2019) draw attention to campus climate by developing structures that could be employed within community colleges to support international students, they neglected the larger global context in which these students simultaneously exist. Oppressive contexts limit the freedom, autonomy, and value of individuals; and negatively influence how they experience the "acculturation processes" (Hernández-Plaza et al., 2010). Immigrants in oppressive contexts may internalize dominant negative narratives and experience feelings of "lack of control, low self-esteem, and mental health problems" (Hernández-Plaza et al., 2010, p. 250). The literature largely associates these feelings with "acculturative stress" (Hansen et al., 2018), normalizing, putting the onus on the student, shielding the xenophobic structure from responsibility. International students—a constructed minority group, discussed more as a commodity than as valued members of the institutions—may experience powerlessness due to oppressive conditions cultivated by decision makers. In the following sections, we detail how a lack of self-critique surrounding transactional arguments—similar to what we observed in "Others"—is evident in rationales related to the Travel Bans and COVID-19, cultivating oppressive conditions for international students in the United States.

2017 Travel Bans and Transactional Arguments

The US Travel Bans of 2017 [Collectively, Executive Order 13769 (2017); Executive Order 13780 (2017); Presidential Proclamation 9645 (2017)] restrict the issuance of immigrant visas, limits the entry into the United States and increase the screening processes for certain categories of people. Through a collective amicus brief, preexisting assumptions of inequity identified in "Others" were brought to the national stage.

The ACE and 32 additional associations (which included the American Association of Community Colleges) submitted a brief of amicus curiae (2018) to inform the decision of the Supreme Court case to overturn the bans: Trump v. Hawaii. These associations included among them the American Association of Community Colleges. The national rationale to overturn the bans was initially related to their seeming to target Muslim majority countries: Chad, Iran, Libya, North Korea, Somalia, Syria, Venezuela, and Yemen. Racism and xenophobia were openly critiqued. However, these 32 associations did not argue

From Oppression to Global Social Justice 179

to dispel the ban on the grounds of discrimination, but rather on the basis of transactional interest convergence (Yao & Viggiano, 2019). Where institutional decision makers in "Others" interpreted "open access" as accepting economically affluent international students to their campuses to serve as resources to generate revenue and enrich the learning environment at their institutions, "open boarders" was interpreted the same way. Yao and Viggiano (2019) identified transactional rationalization among national associations in relation to the acceptance of international students into the country in general. Similar to the issue that we identified in "Others" (2018), the amicus curiae highlighted transactional benefits did not leave space to discuss social justice.

The community college decision makers in our original study were already employing transactional arguments at the institutional level prior to the institution of the US Travel Bans of 2017. Though exacerbated by the post-2016 federal regime, this exploitative ideology did not stem from there. The rationales for the presence and treatment of international students flow between campus decision makers and the federal government. The focus on the transactional relationship reproduced a narrative that ultimately prioritized economic benefit over student welfare and further underscored the assertion that international students were not deserving of equal treatment (Yao & Viggiano, 2019). Given this normalization from national professional organizations, it is likely that community college decision makers will now more adamantly rationalize their transactional relationships with international students. As such, we observe that the transactional argument employed in response to the travel bans exacerbate the already oppressive conditions in which international students existed.

The International Access Paradox and Transaction in the COVID-19 Pandemic

COVID-19 pandemic has fundamentally changed our perceptions of international higher education, placing responsibility on humans around the world to reduce viral spread through social distancing. This resulted in the majority of colleges and universities turning to online instruction for the duration of the global pandemic. Initially, the Student Exchange Visitor Program (SVEP) modified visa restrictions so as to meet the demands of the global health crisis. International students, like all students, were permitted to take their courses online. Nonetheless, international students have unique concerns that their domestic counterparts do not, such as xenophobia and fear of deportation.

Chirikov & Soria (2020) analyzed data on international student experiences at the onset of the COVID-19 pandemic. Likely related to the political presentation of COVID-19 as a threat from abroad,

180   *Tiffany Viggiano et al.*

17 percent of international undergraduate students and 12 percent of international graduate students reported experiencing hostility, intimidation, and microaggressions based on their national origin (with higher rates for Asian students, including students from Japan, China, Vietnam, and South Korea). Chirikov and Soria (2020)reported that 52 percent of international undergraduate and 67 percent of graduate students are worried about how they can maintain good health during the pandemic. In addition, 25 percent of international students were distressed about discrimination, harassment, or xenophobia. It is in this contextual backdrop that the SVEP announced modifications to their visa requirements.

On July 6, 2020, SVEP announced that all students with F1 or M1 visas, and their families, would lose their visas if their institution made the decision to offer only online courses in the fall semester of 2020. If institutions offered a hybrid model, these students would be required to take some in-person courses in order to keep their visas. M-1 visa holders (those enrolled in nontraditional universities and who study short-term career-oriented courses) were given the most stringent regulations: they were not permitted to take even a single online course. Given the vocational focus of the majority of community colleges, the M-1 visa regulation was particularly problematic. It could be conceptualized as an attack on the internationalization of the community college. Due to the reduced distribution of H1 and J visas—those necessary to work in the United States after graduation—one month prior, on the grounds that they would "take American jobs" [Presidential Proclamations No. 10014 (2020); Presidential Proclamations No. 10052, (2020)], many speculate that all visa regulations were a purposeful political decision to "protect American jobs". Given the relationship between M-1 visas and employment, the stringent M-1 requirements lends credence to this argument.

Although this was a novel situation, the logic employed by SVEP was not novel. Similar to that of the International Access Paradox that we identified in "Others", decision makers—in this case, those at the federal level—deployed arguments of individual autonomy to exclude students from access. Efforts were made to project the appearance of access, but those that were conceptualized as less economically desirable were actually, by definition, incapable of meeting the access standards. Although SVEP was not explicitly banning international students from attending US institutions, they were functionally excluding access to M-1 holders that were required to take entirely in-person instruction that was functionally not available. In both cases, leaders present potential international students with the illusion of access and the illusion of choice.

The loss of international students due to increased COVID regulations would have been a substantial loss of revenue for the institutions

From Oppression to Global Social Justice   181

of higher education (Martel, 2020; Raby, 2020). After 200 universities filed or backed at least eight law suits, on these grounds, the decision was overturned on July 14 (Castiello-Gutiérrez & Li, 2020). The transactional arguments further reproduced the narrative of assumed inequity.

In addition, the larger symbolic messages from the Government to students could not be overturned nor forgotten. Castiello-Gutiérrez and Li (2020) publicly state the thoughts representative of many international students at this time:

> Did the policy makers thought about whether it is possible, safe, and affordable for us to travel back home amidst the pandemic? Did they think about the apartment leases we have already signed? And more importantly, did they consider that some of us may not even have a place "back home" to return to? We questioned whether the country in which we have spent years studying, growing, playing, making friends, and raising children actually values our lives and sees us as human beings no different than those who hold a U.S. passport. (p. i)

Castiello-Gutiérrez and Li (2020) draw attention to of issues of justice, dignity, and inclusion associated with oppressive conditions. International students were at the mercy of political changes and advocation of "allies" that have, historically, allied themselves primarily with their own interests. In light of oppressive conditions, the misconception that international students are a monolithic privileged group identified in "Others", does not leave space to critically discuss their safety and developmental needs.

Conclusion and Discussion

We have provided evidence that international students were not well-served when attending the US community college. In this chapter, we have focused on two political events of the 2016–2020 political regime—the 2017 Travel Bans and the SVEP response to the 2020 COVID-19 pandemic—to draw attention to what isn't new about these global challenges. We utilized an international critical frame and attention to oppressive conditions to point out the structural, tacit, and ever-present injustice perpetrated against international students. In referencing "Others", it becomes perceivable that decision maker rationales reproduced and strengthened oppressive conditions prior to these recent federal actions. The same transactional logic that we identified in "Others" permeated into the national stage. In bringing these points to bear, we demonstrate that US institutional culture is and has been incompatible with international student support since before these events.

182 *Tiffany Viggiano et al.*

We demonstrate that the illusion of choice, which we had initially observed at the institutional level, is also employed at the national level. In 2018, it was clear that a false argument of individual autonomy and choice was being employed by community college decision makers to justify the exclusion of nonaffluent potential international students. In this chapter, we have demonstrated how we can observe that same logic at the federal level to justify the exclusion of all international students, particularly those with identities that are targeted by a federal agenda. In doing so, the community college fails to favor equal access and the advantage of the disadvantaged, and thus, it does not promote justice Rawl (1999) in a globalized world (Robertson, 1992).

We demonstrate that, in times of crisis when international students relied on institutional support and guidance, decision makers were neither philosophically nor ethically prepared to help international students. In "Others", we observed that community college decision makers viewed international students as a resource and engaged in a transactional relationship. It was this transactional relationship that blinded decision makers to the responsibility to include international students in their open-access mission. In this chapter, we have pointed out how this same blindness is detrimental to advocating for just national policy as it relates to international students. Decision makers reinforced this power imbalance by normalizing and reproducing transactional relationships. US decision makers have not developed an institutionalized or formal way of advocating for the rights, safety, and justice of international students on the grounds that they had a responsibility to care for the students in their charge (Viggiano, 2019) or a responsibility to the world (Viggiano, 2019, 2020).

As such, rather than assuming that the global responses to the Pandemic or US Travel Bans were the root causes of international student stress, we are confronted with the notion that US institutional culture is and has been incompatible with international student support since before these events. Rather than dismissing these events as rare, short-term, crisis—symptomatic of a particular political regime—practitioners should consider the ways in which deeply ingrained institutional and US culture are to blame. If we focus on these occurrences as rare symptoms of a particular political regime, we continue to ignore the substantive problems that are deeply ingrained in institutional and US culture. The first step to mediating the oppressive conditions imposed on international students in the United States is to recognize this self-critique. This can help practitioners to be ideologically prepared to serve as advocates that are not simultaneously reinforcing oppressive conditions the next time similar crises arise.

Raby (2020) suggests some tangible solutions to move forward. Firstly, recognize that "local is not the opposite of global". As we have demonstrated, local and global climate are very much intertwined. Secondly,

From Oppression to Global Social Justice 183

avoid structuring programs without thought, because this would likely lead to a reproduction of hegemonic exclusion. Thus, thirdly, as you think about program structuring, reject stereotypes about students that reproduce injustice. One such stereotype that we have identified here is that international students are a monolithic privileged group. Further research should investigate the way in which race and international student identities intersect. Scholars such as George Mwangi and Yao (2021) engage with this subject. We must make ideological and institutional space for international students from economically disadvantaged and minoritized backgrounds. Fourthly, she suggests that we use caution when recruiting students as a revenue source. As demonstrated here, decision makers that recruited international students as a revenue source blinded themselves to the ways in which these students needed their protection. Lastly, remember it is that lack of support and awareness of the real needs of international students that leads to lack of academic success, not lack of student interest. As such, when we fail to recognize that international students are humans that require more support than their domestic counterparts, particularly in times of hostile global climate, then we are failing our students globally.

To what extent should decision makers be accountable for the lack of self-critique while reproducing global social injustice? The absence of self-critique facilitates oppressive conditions. We advocate for a new conceptualization of international students in the U. S. This notion promotes the humanization of this student population by confronting decision makers' long-standing assumptions that transactional relationships are just. We encourage decision makers to reimagine the role of international students in the country: individuals with similar psychosocial needs as domestic students, but also with specific challenges that will require special policies, fair treatment, and just support initiatives.

Acknowledgment

This article is expanded based on a previously published article by the same author. You can read the original article here https://journals.sagepub.com/doi/abs/10.1177/1028315317725883?journalCode=jsia.

References

American Council on Education (ACE). (2016). *Survey responses by institution type*. Washington, DC: Center for International and Global Engagement. Retrieved from http://www.acenet.edu/news-room/

Anayah, B., & Kuk, L. (2015). The growth of international student enrollment at community colleges and implications. *Community College Journal of Research and Practice*, 39(12), 1099–1110.

184 *Tiffany Viggiano et al.*

Blanco, G. L. (2020, July 9). International students and hostage taking. *Critical Internationalization Studies Network*. https://criticalinternationalization.net/2020/07/09/international-students-andhostage-taking/

Brennan, J., & Naidoo, R. (2008). Higher education and the achievement (and/or prevention) of equity and social justice. *Higher Education, 56*(3), 287–302.

Brief for American Council on Education et al. (2018). As Amicus Curiae Supporting Respondents, Donald J. Trump, President of the United States, et al. v. State of Hawaii, et al. (no. 17–965).

Castiello-Gutiérrez, S., & Li, X. (2020). We are more than your paycheck: The dehumanization of international students in the United States. *Journal of International Students, 10*(3), i–iv.

Chirikov, I., & Soria, K. M. (2020). *International students during the pandemic: Academic experiences and concerns.* SERU Consortium, University of California—Berkeley and University of Minnesota. https://cshe.berkeley.edu/seru-covid-survey-reports

Executive Order No. 13769. (2017). Executive order protecting the nation from foreign terrorist entry into the United States. Retrieved from: https://www.whitehouse.gov/presidential-actions/executive-order-protectingnation-foreign-terrorist-entry-united-states/

Executive Order No. 13780. (2017). Executive order protecting the nation from foreign terrorist entry into the United States. Retrieved from: https://www.whitehouse.gov/presidential-actions/executive-order-protectingnation-foreign-terrorist-entry-united-states-2/

García, H. A., Garza, T., & Yeaton-Hromada, K. (2019). Do we belong? *Journal of International Students, 9*(2), 460–487.

George Mwangi, C. A., & Yao, C. W. (2021) US higher education internationalization through an equity-driven lens. In Perna L. W. (Ed.), *Higher education: Handbook of theory and research* (Vol. 36, pp. 1–62). Springer.

Hansen, H. R., Shneyderman, Y., McNamara, G. S., & Grace, L. (2018). Acculturative stress and native and US culture immersion of international students at a community college. *Journal of International Students, 8*(1), 215–232.

Hernández-Plaza, S., García-Ramírez, M., Camacho, C., & Paloma, V. (2010). New settlement and wellbeing in oppressive contexts: A liberation psychology approach. In S. C. Carr (Ed.), *The psychology of global mobility* (pp. 235–256). Springer Press.

Kincheloe, J. L., McLaren, P., & Steinberg, S. R. (2011). Critical pedagogy and qualitative research. *The SAGE handbook of qualitative research* (pp. 163–177). Sage.

Kouzes, J. M., & Posner, B. Z. (2007). Leadership is in the eye of the follower. In J. Gordon (Ed.), *The Pfeiffer book of successful leadership development tools* (Vol. 154, pp. 3–10). Wiley Press.

Lee, J. J. (2020, July 8). International students shouldn't be political pawns. *Inside Higher Education.* https://www.insidehighered.com/views/2020/07/08/government-regulationabout-international-students-strong-arming-colleges-resume

Levin, J. S. (2001). *Globalizing the community college: Strategies for change in the twenty-first century.* St. Martin's Press.

From Oppression to Global Social Justice 185

Martel, M. (2020). *COVID-19 Effects on U.S. higher education campuses: New realities for global student mobility in summer and fall 2020.* Institute of International Education COVID-19 Snapshot Survey Series (Report No. 3). https://www.iie.org/en/Connect/COVID-19/COVID-19-Snapshot-Survey-Series.

Martínez-Alemán, A. M., Pusser, B., & Bensimon, E. M. (Eds.). (2015). *Critical approaches to the study of higher education: A practical introduction.* JHU Press.

Nussbaum, M. C. (2006). Education and democratic citizenship: Capabilities and quality education. *Journal of human development, 7*(3), 385–395.

Presidential Proclamation No. 9645. (2017). Presidential proclamation enhancing vetting capabilities and processes for detecting attempted entry into the United States by terrorists or other public-safety threats. Retrieved from https://www.whitehouse.gov/presidential-actions/presidential-proclamation enhancing-vetting-capabilities-processes-detecting-attempted-entry-unitedstates-terrorists-public-safety-threats/

Presidential Proclamation No. 10014. (2020). Presidential proclamation suspending entry of immigrants who present risk to the U.S. labor market during the economic recovery following the COVID-19 outbreak. Retrieved from: https://www.aila.org/infonet/proclamation-suspending-entry-immigrants

Presidential Proclamation No. 10052. (2020). Presidential proclamation suspending entry of individuals who present a risk to the U.S. labor market following the coronavirus outbreak. Retrieved from: https://www.aila.org/infonet/presidential-proclamation-suspending-entry

Raby, R. L. (2020). Celebrating the last 10 years of community college internationalization. *Journal of International Students, 10*(4), x–xiv.

Rawls, J. (1999). *A theory of justice.* Harvard University Press.

Robertson, R. (1992). *Globalization: Social theory and global culture* (Vol. 16). Sage.

Shahjahan, R. A., & Kezar, A. J. (2013). Beyond the "national container" addressing methodological nationalism in higher education research. *Educational Researcher, 42*(1), 20–29.

Shahjahan, R. A., Blanco Ramirez, G., & Andreotti, V. D. O. (2017). Attempting to imagine the unimaginable: A decolonial reading of global university rankings. *Comparative Education Review, 61*(S1), S51–S73.

Stein, S. (2017). Internationalization for an uncertain future: Tensions, paradoxes, and possibilities. *The Review of Higher Education, 41*(1), 3–32.

Stein, S., Andreotti, V., & Suša, R. (2019). Pluralizing frameworks for global ethics in the internationalization of higher education in Canada. *Canadian Journal of Higher Education/Revue canadienne d'enseignement supérieur, 49*(1), 22–46.

Viggiano, T., López Damián, A. I., Morales Vázquez, E., & Levin, J. S. (2018). The others: Equitable access, international students, and the community college. *Journal of Studies in International Education, 22*(1), 71–85.

Viggiano, T. (2019). Thinking globally about social justice. In *Study abroad opportunities for Community College students and strategies for global learning* (pp. 184–199). IGI Global.

Viggiano, T. (2020). Higher education and global social injustice. *Finnish Institute for Educational Research: Research publications, 36*(1).

Weimer, L., & Barlete, A. (2020). The rise of nationalism: The influence of populist discourses on international student mobility and migration in the UK and US. In *Universities as political Institutions* (pp. 33–57). Brill Sense.

186　*Tiffany Viggiano et al.*

Yao, C. W., & Viggiano, T. (2019). Interest convergence and the commodification of international students and scholars in the United States. *JCSCORE, 5*(1), 81–109.

Author Bios

Tiffany Viggiano, PhD, is a US based practitioner and scholar of higher education. She earned her doctoral degree in education from the University of Jyväskylä. As a co-editor of the *Critical Internationalization Studies Newsletter,* she is interested in issues of access and social justice as they relate to the internationalization of higher education.

Evelyn Vázquez, PhD, is a postdoctoral scholar at the School of Medicine, University of California, Riverside. Dr. Vázquez is a first generation immigrant, a woman of color, and English as second language learner. Dr. Vázquez is a social psychologist with research experience in: healthy inequity in higher education; community-based participatory research in public health; and professional development, mental health, and emotional well-being in graduate school. Dr. Vázquez is leading a pilot project (funded by the National Institute on Minority Health and Health Disparities) that focuses on structural vulnerability and mental health disparities among underrepresented graduate students.

Ariadna I. López Damián, PhD, is a faculty member at the Instituto Tecnológico de Chilpancingo. She earned her doctoral degree in Higher Education Administration and Policy for the University of California, Riverside. Her research interest includes part-time faculty, student-faculty relationships, students' aspirations, and faculty organizational commitment. She recently co-authored the book *University Management, the Academic Profession, and Neoliberalism.*

12 International Education and the Global Pandemic in the Community College

Reflections and Best Practices

Marc Thomas

Introduction

By March 15, 2020, at the peak of college spring-break season, 165,201 cases of COVID-19 had been recorded worldwide (WHO, n.d.). By May 8, the typical end of the American college semester, infections totaled 3,782,855 globally. As the highly contagious respiratory virus swept across continents, college faculty and staff—including those leading international education programs—maneuvered policies, programs, and people to help ensure that students around the world were safe.

On college campuses across the United States and abroad, many students were sent home, armed with personal computers, tablets, and cell phones to connect with their professor and other students. The effort to move instruction to remote delivery involved numerous moving parts—reviewing local virus infection trends, training on new technology, supporting faculty with professional development in moving their instruction to remote delivery, and reviewing attendance and grading policies, to name just a few challenges to overcome to continue teaching and learning from afar. Remote instruction took different forms in support of course learning outcome mastery:

- Online—asynchronous learning delivered through an Internet-based learning management system, typically including student and faculty interaction through a written discussion forum, podcasts or recorded lectures, learning activities, assignments, readings, and quizzes.
- Video—instruction driven by a live video connection, usually through software like Zoom, Web Ex, or Skype.
- Hybrid—a blend of the elements of online and video instruction, sometimes with a face-to-face component.

The bedrock of international study, traditionally, is the in-person interaction that leads to deep cross-cultural understanding. The decisions

188 Marc Thomas

around how to move forward with international education during a pandemic that required minimal in-person contact presented a multitude of challenges. On March 19, the US State Department issued its highest travel advisory, discouraging Americans from international travel abroad and directing any Americans abroad who could to return immediately. Two days earlier, the European Union had imposed a ban on nonessential travel for non-EU citizens.

In 2018–2019, more than 1 million international students studied in the United States, while more than 380,000 American students studied abroad the previous year for credit or noncredit experience (IIE, 2019). The large number of students studying outside their home country and the unpredictable and aggressive spread of COVID-19 within and across borders made it difficult to plan for and implement measures to keep students safe and continue their global learning.

This chapter will present an overview of how American community colleges responded to the COVID-19 pandemic in early 2020, while focusing on the effect the pandemic had on international students in the United States. Furthermore, the present chapter offers examples of best practices reported by international education practitioners and reviews research-based evidence that has guided higher education international study during the 21st century. The chapter concludes by proposing a framework that may be helpful for sustaining international education at US community colleges.

Research Method

The research for this chapter employed a mixture of interviews with community college international students and international education leaders, review of relevant literature, and review of media reports. To identify college international education leaders to participate in interviews, the 20 community colleges with the largest number of international students as reported by the IIE's 2019 Open Doors report were contacted. Of those contacted, four institutions indicated an interest in participating in the study. Information from three of those institutions is cited in this chapter. To provide geographic and institutional size balance, an additional college (Elgin Community College in Illinois) was asked to participate, and agreed to take part. Shoreline Community College and Montgomery College were asked to provide names of international students who might be interested in answering questions about their experience during the pandemic. A total of seven student names were provided; four of those agreed to respond to questions. Information from all four student responses is included in this chapter. To maximize credibility and advance the idea of sharing best practices, all those interviewed agreed to have their real names and institutions identified.

Experiences and Best Practices from the Field

This analysis section will chronicle the response of American community colleges as the COVID-19 pandemic unfolded in early 2020. Its focus is on how college instructional strategies and student support responded to the need for physical distancing between people to help reduce the spread of the virus.

Background: The Pandemic Spreads

A Washington Post report on March 6 foretold the reality that would unfold at institutions across the country: "On Thursday, Everett Community College, near Seattle, closed and its president announced a student had tested positive for covid-19" (Svrluga, 2020). By this date, the World Health Organization (WHO) had reported 214 US cases and 101,254 globally. The article identified early March as the timeframe when US higher education institutions began shifting from viewing the pandemic as being a foreign problem to a domestic one:

> They have shut down study-abroad programs, closed campuses in China and worried about the effects on international students and overseas research. But as the number of confirmed infections in the United States surged past 100 this week, with 11 deaths as of Wednesday night, many schools are ramping up planning on their campuses, bracing for the possibility of a more profound and direct hit. (para. 7)

By late March, the profound reach of the pandemic was becoming clear. A headline from the publication Inside Higher Education on March 20 described this situation: "International and Study Abroad Students See Major Disruptions." By the date of this article, the number of COVID-19 cases had grown to 15,220 in the United States and 266,097 globally (WHO, n.d.).

Learning during the Pandemic: Challenges

Key themes related to the continued ability of students to learn effectively during the pandemic, as identified by community college leaders and international students, were connection to faculty, access to technology, and support services to students. This chapter section will review challenges identified in these areas, along with solutions identified to meet these challenges.

Maghara, an international student from Indonesia studying at Shoreline Community College in Washington State, described interaction with faculty as the key to his ability to succeed after instruction

190 *Marc Thomas*

was moved to remote access on March 16. His spring statistics class included an introduction activity through a Zoom video connection, regular podcasts, homework, and open-book exams, along with support from an online math activity lab, wamap.org, provided free to students at public educational institutions in Washington (M. Adipura, personal communication, August 19, 2020).

It was the potential lack of connection with faculty that concerned Maghara most about remote instruction. He reported achieving meaningful gains in the application of statistics to practical purposes, including in the use of statistical analysis software commonly used in industry. "The professor did a great job on organizing the modules and assignments. I can still grasp the materials clearly ... because of the professor's great contributions in handling the class" (M. Adipura, personal communication, August 12, 2020).

Another international student, Mia from Madagascar, was working on fulfilling her childhood dream of a career in medicine. In early 2020 she was studying at Montgomery College in Maryland. Her biology lab included assignments and activities through Blackboard, the online learning management system, as well as activities delivered through a Zoom video connection. Mia enjoyed the flexibility of remote learning, but lamented the challenge of interacting with the faculty during the pandemic. "We have been given the best resources even remotely ... being remote means that we are lacking in the teacher-student privileges, the teachers have so many things going on" (M. Andriamanantena, personal communication, July 16, 2020). Emilia, a Montgomery international student from Mexico studying international relations, echoed the student concern for continued interaction with faculty during the pandemic. She expressed gratitude for efforts to keep students safe through remote instruction. "In general, I think that it was good to have this other way to get educated" (E. Esponda, personal communication, July 20, 2020).

About half of Shoreline international students returned to their home countries there wasn't more of a challenge for ESL classes due to students returning to home country. Transitioning to online was overall a heavier lift for ESL because prior to the pandemic, these classes had never been taught online (to comply with F-1 regulations). Shoreline added a week of preparation for students that included student reflection on readiness for online learning, identification of available resources to help them succeed, basic understanding of the learning management system, and practice of video instruction technology. The College also put special emphasis on students who returned to China to help overcome access-to-technology obstacles those students faced, including blocks to email and online test-proctoring software.

Access to technology was a challenge across colleges during the pandemic. Liza Carbajo, Executive Director of Miami Dade College's Office of International Education, pinpointed the primary challenge of shifting to remote learning: "Most international students had never enrolled in virtual classes before" (L. Carbajo, personal communication, July 17, 2020).

Miami Dade College (MDC) enrolls approximately 1,300 international students. MDC migrated to remote learning in mid-March, partway through the Spring 2020 semester. The response included adding several free technology resources for students during the pandemic, including loaner laptops for each student, software, remote testing, and cloud storage to allow remote access from wherever students were.

The New York Times on February 28, 2020, foreshadowed the reality that America would soon face: that COVID-19 was beginning an exponential spread. The article by Baker et al. (2020) reported this: "Troubling new signs that the coronavirus is spreading in the United States emerged on Friday, as cases not explained by overseas travel or contact with a person known to be infected were reported in California, Oregon, and Washington State" (para. 1). The swift spread of the virus posed challenges to the ability of colleges to support the academic, emotional and social needs of international students.

The Executive Director for International Education at Shoreline Community College Samira Pardanani, reported that her college's Washington State locale caused early and pronounced concern and response to the pandemic. "Students were talking about Seattle being the "new Wuhan," [the virus's presumed origin in China]. Many reported that their parents were asking them to return home right after the winter quarter ended. They were puzzled and nervous about why no one was wearing masks in the U.S." (S. Pardanani, personal communication, July 17, 2020). Shoreline held focus groups with international students, who reported the following concerns:

- worry about not being able to maintain their grade point average with fully online courses;
- the amount of homework being assigned;
- worry about their families back home;
- feeling conflicted about whether to stay in America or return to their home countries;
- fear of contracting COVID-19;
- financial challenges; and
- lack of access to the Canvas learning management system and Google-based email (especially for students who returned to China)

Worries from international students during the pandemic received some media attention, bringing their concerns to public attention. Dickerson (2020), in the New York Times, encapsulated the student situation that extended beyond concern about where to live: "A substantial number of international students are also watching their financial lives fall apart: Visa restrictions prevent them from working off campuses, which are now closed. And while some come from families wealthy enough to pay

192   Marc Thomas

for their housing or whisk them home, many others had already been struggling to cobble together tuition fees that tend to be much higher than those paid by Americans" (para. 3).

Mia, the international student at Montgomery, reported this reality: "Unfortunately I couldn't go home. Madagascar is in quarantine and they don't allow anyone to come in the country right now. I lived by myself until the end of the month on March 31st. Then I had to move with my sister because there was no resource coming in for me anymore, I didn't work, and my parents couldn't send any money from Home ever" (M. Andriamanantena, personal communication, July 16, 2020).

Learning during the Pandemic: Solutions

Longstanding research and theory on teaching and learning is plentiful. This chapter section will highlight some of the pre-pandemic research on effective instruction and lay the groundwork for how that research might be applied to 21st-century pandemic-era educational practice. Chickering and Gamson (1987) presented the seven principles of good practice for higher education, where faculty: "(1) encourage contacts between students and faculty; (2) develop reciprocity and cooperation among students; (3) use active learning techniques; (4) give prompt feedback; (5) emphasize time on task; (6) communicate high expectations; and (7) respect diverse talents and ways of learning" (p. 1). In the 21st century, these themes persist, and have potential application to international education as practitioners grapple with the new pandemic reality.

There is ample research support for the connection between student and faculty as fundamental. In one of the first scholarly analyses of post-pandemic instructional excellence, Tran (2020), articulated that "In such a fallout, the connection between University communities and international students is more critical than ever" (p. xii). Tran's conclusions came from a body of work drawn from interviews with about 400 international students and practitioners and centered on the importance of personal connection to help international students thrive in higher education.

Laura, an international student from Columbia studying at Shoreline, offered this advice for continued academic success during adversity: "I believe that having the goal to do well and be able to get good grades kept me motivated throughout the quarter. I started to use checklists and planners to organize my time and tasks, as well as setting a timer to do my homework. I used an app called Focus Keeper in which I was able to set a timer for 30 minutes and have a 10-minute break in between each set. I also practiced and still do meditation on a daily basis, thus meditating definitely kept me on track" (L. Florez, personal communication, September 1, 2020).

Enrolling around 3,000 international students—among the largest for 2-year American colleges—Lone Star College in Texas assembled a blend of remote and face-to-face formats, along with a variety of student engagement strategies. Katharine Caruso, Associate Vice Chancellor for Honors and International Education shared the College's instructional solutions: "Learning differed in class and faculty. Some faculty chose the synchronous learning experience, while others did recorded videos. Some of our faculty got very creative and built labs in their living rooms and garages to offer instruction" (K. Caruso, personal communication, August 13, 2020).

A Chronicle of Higher Education survey garnered feedback from 712 college faculty members and 457 administrators about their reflections on teaching through the pandemic. The survey's prevailing theme was "students," mentioned 582 times by those responding. In reporting on the survey, Williams (2020) found that "many professors discovered that some of their students were grappling with issues that made focusing on their coursework difficult. Another lesson learned: Connecting with students online was challenging; faculty members used variations of the word 'engage' 71 times to describe how hard it was to do so" (para. 6). The next-often mentioned theme was "face-to-face," in the context of online learning as a less effective delivery method. However, one faculty respondent shared a hope that reflection around teaching amid the pandemic would lead to improvement: "Pedagogy that wasn't great face to face is disastrous online; I actually think that what we are learning and sharing now because of teaching remotely is going to improve teaching overall for those who wish to improve" (para. 16).

Student Support during the Pandemic: Challenges and Solutions

Effective learning is augmented by effective student support services. Numerous community college leaders and students who shared insights for this research pointed to the heightened importance of supporting students during the pandemic. The experience of those who participated in this study, along with organizations that support the practice of international education, offered best practices in supporting international students during times of crisis. Some of these best practices are included here, arranged by category.

Communication: NAFSA, the association for international educators, places communication as a top priority. This includes not only mass updates, but also personal contact. West (2020) in the International Educator, reported on an initiative by the University of Central Florida to reach its 3,000 international students by phone, an effort that spanned a week and a half. One international student offered his take on the support: "They called me to check in on me, asking how I have been

194   *Marc Thomas*

doing, whether I was in need of something special, and they provided updates regarding the pandemic," he says. "You are thousands of miles away from home and do not know what is coming up next; the situation is highly uncertain ... so you do not know when you will be able to go home. At times of such uncertainty, such a call becomes quite empowering" (para. 2).

Students and educators alike reported that communication was fundamental to an effective college response. Emilia, from Mexico, shared her gratitude: "Montgomery College, every day, was updating us by emails about COVID and what to do in the event that we got sick" (E. Esponda, personal communication, July 20, 2020). Shoreline Community College stressed the importance of overcommunicating, along with encouraging staff to "show grace. Different people react differently in crisis" (S. Pardanani, personal communication, July 17, 2020).

Finances: Students reported funding as a source of stress. The US federal government Coronavirus Aid, Relief, and Economic Security Act, passed in late March 2020, offered support nationwide of approximately $6 billion in grants to college students, but specifically exempted undocumented and international students. In response, the Institute of International Education directed part of its Student Emergency Fund to support international students with $2,500 grants, awarded through a process that began with nomination from colleges. The grants were prioritized to students with financial needs who could not return home.

Housing: The question of whether students should stay in the United States or return to their home country is elemental. The director of the office of international students and scholars at Michigan State University, which enrolls around 9,000 international students, advocated for students themselves making the choice of staying or returning home, armed with information from their institution, taking into account:

- Personal safety and comfort level of the student and their family with being in the US during the pandemic;
- Immigration issues including establishing or maintaining eligibility for CPT and OPT [Curricular Practical Training and Optional Practical Training];
- Ability to be successful taking classes online from abroad including having a good study space, access to the internet, and access to course materials;
- Their future plans;
- Their financial situation; and
- Options such as taking a semester off, engaging in our Study Away at Home Program or our China Semester both of which allow students to take in-person courses in their home country at a partner institution" (McCallum Beatty, personal communication, August 10, 2020).

Sofia Marrufo, an international student from Venezuela and president of the international student association at Morningside College in Iowa, reported that the decision-making timeline around housing is important given quickly evolving international travel bans. "We were coming off from an extended spring break when we heard the college would close due to the threat of coronavirus," she explained to the Sioux City Journal (2020). "International students literally had a day or so to decide if they were staying in America or going back home."

Mental Health: Lone Star College's senior international education officer communicated that college's philosophy about keeping students safe: "to treat international students pre, during, and post-pandemic the way we would want our children, siblings, nieces, nephews or any family member treated if they were studying abroad" (Caruso, personal communication, August 14, 2020). Lone Star began its transition to a remote commitment to student support with virtual cultural competency training for staff, tailored to the meeting the challenges of a quick shift to remote learning for international students. The training, completed through Humber College in Canada, included a course on understanding students in transition.

Elgin Community College, in Illinois, launched a virtual course for its international students that included updates and advice for pandemic survival, including guidance for remaining in compliance with visa requirements. Shoreline Community College added a live chat link on its international education home page.

Safety: the US CDC describes COVID-19 as "an illness caused by a virus that can spread from person to person," especially through close contact with others. Guidelines for reducing likelihood of transmission include keeping six feet or more from others, wearing a mask in public, cleaning and disinfecting surfaces, and washing hands frequently (Centers for Disease Control and Prevention, 2020). Concern about keeping safe from COVID-19 was at the forefront of international student worries. Some colleges—like Shoreline—instituted a campus-wide communicable disease task force to help map out a plan.

Discussion and Conclusions

To respond and chart a course forward, international education practitioners must integrate past, present, and future in their calculation. The past and present include our experience and research. The future is mapped by how well we employ the current reality's best practices, and how well we interpret data to forge a path forward. This mission is made harder with the possibility of continued or renewed health danger. This section will discuss three parts of the international education equation, given the need to plan for the possibility of continued or future pandemic accommodations: the overarching ability of the United States

196 Marc Thomas

to navigate political and public health realities, strategies for ensuring effective instruction, and approaches for student support. In all three areas, there is room for optimism.

The community college international students interviewed for this work were largely not deterred from continued study in the United States. Maghara, from Indonesia, expressed a belief that "regardless of the pandemic and some current political matters building up in the United States, I'm still comfortable continuing my academic journey there" (M. Adipura, personal communication, August 12, 2020). Mily, from Mexico, communicated her continued comfort in American study: "I haven't hesitated in my goals, because I invest in the best thing that I can do for my life and that is my education" (M. Esponda, personal communication, July 20, 2020).

Learning during the Pandemic

Students have reported a desire for active connection between them and faculty during remote learning. Research backs up this student interest in connection as predictive of student success. The research undertaken for this chapter included review and reflection on Chickering's education research to lay a foundation for best practices in 21st-century remote learning. More recent research from Tran (2020) builds on Chickering's work, adding perspective on teaching and learning for international students. Table 12.1 presents the alignment between the Chickering's (1987) Principles of Good Practices in Undergraduate Education and the Tran Framework for Teaching and Learning for International Students. The connections between four of the principles Chickering and the framework Tran put forward, along with examples of strategies that flow from their related categories, offer a potential foundation for continued reflection and action in moving international education forward.

As international educators contemplate a future involving increased remote instruction, reflection on the foundations of higher education excellence—like Chickering's work—and contemporary scholarship—like Tran's—can offer a path forward. An important question is how these strategies might be applied to remote instruction, either asynchronous through a learning management system or synchronous through a video connection—or a mixture of both. A growing body of research on online learning can help us apply the core principles of engaging students for success to a future driven by remote learning. One recent example of this research is from Yu (2020), whose inquiry focused on students classified as members of Generation Z, born from the mid-1990s to around 2010. This research yielded interesting results, including the desire of Generation Z learners to have a choice in instructional delivery format, have control over their own learning within weekly

International Education and Global Pandemic 197

Table 12.1 Crosswalk between Chickering's Principles and Tran's International Student Framework

Chickering's Principles	Tran's Framework	Potential Strategies for Post-COVID-19 global education
Encourages contact between students and faculty	Connecting: engaging students intellectually, culturally, and socially through people-to-people connections	Virtual office hours, language instruction, and feedback through video connection
Develops reciprocity and cooperation among students	Reciprocating: positioning international students as co-constructors of knowledge and educators as reciprocal co-learners	Virtual cultural exchange and discussion between international and domestic students through an online platform
Uses active learning techniques	Integrating: weaving international examples, case studies, materials, and perspectives into the curriculum	Online cross-cultural service learning (for example, advocating for policy change via social media)
Respects diverse talents and ways of learning	Accommodating: understanding cultural and educational backgrounds, characteristics, identities, and aspirations	Online or virtual orientation programs and support for international students Online or virtual survey of students through video and learning management system platforms

online modules, and a desire to take part in online discussion forums as an acceptable alternative to in-person activities. "Online collaborations with their peers were challenging but helped them not feel isolated. An online course should accommodate their demand for more real-time interactions with teachers and peers, multimedia resources, and apps," according to the research (p. 8).

There is a pre-pandemic precedent for virtual connection. O'Dowd (2017) pointed to enhanced interest in virtual exchange, where "a growing number of higher education institutions are engaging their students in Virtual Exchange or telecollaboration—a rich and multifaceted activity which refers to online intercultural interaction and collaboration projects with partner classes from other cultural contexts under the guidance of educators and/or expert facilitators" (p. 1). Another virtual exchange project, reported by Trapè (2019), facilitated collaboration between US and Italian students through Skype including topics "chosen to foster students' reflections on culture-specific issues including stereotyping, intercultural competence, empathy and emotions" (p. 176–177).

198 *Marc Thomas*

The collaboration culminated in service projects developed virtually across cultures but carried out locally.

An additional virtual exchange, as reported in Ruther (2020), took place in spring of 2020 and involved 14 American and 19 French college students, collaborating on an international banking project using Zoom, WhatsApp, Google Classroom, Google Suite, and Survey Monkey. Learning outcomes for this project-based course included gaining proficiency at working in cross-national, cross-cultural teams and communicating complex ideas to an international audience. This pandemic-era experience grew from a partnership between a community college in the Connecticut State Colleges & Universities system and the nonprofit organization Gazelle International, which had worked together on developing virtual exchanges for community college students since 2017 (N. Ruther, personal communication, September 20, 2020).

Student Support during the Pandemic

For this research, students and educators identified several support services that were desirable in helping students persist during the pandemic. Reported challenges to overcome included ensuring that students received adequate communication from colleges and got support in their basic needs including money, food, and housing during the pandemic-inspired upheaval. The question of how to best support international students at American colleges is ubiquitous. That question—and the potential answers—is heightened as higher education leaders address it during a pandemic. There is ample research to support the benefits of engaging with students in the delivery of student services. The Center for Community College Student Engagement (2013) points to a commitment in services like advising to "making personal connections and building relationships with students to help them succeed" (p. 9). Bista (2015), in analyzing data from a survey of 705 international students from Asia, reported that "Asian students who had relatively better relationships with staff were very likely to have higher levels of gain in learning" (p. 46).

The best practices around student support presented earlier in this chapter—including regular mass communication, personal connection whenever possible, the establishment of emergency funds for students in crisis—are important. One study conducting during the 2020 pandemic, by Driessen et al. (2020) of 330 biology students whose learning shifted from in-person to remote during the pandemic reported this: "One recurring theme from students was the negative impact of emotional factors on their study habits, such as anxiety, a sense of confusion, and lack of motivation" (p. 3). Arguably, the focus of student support going forward, given the likely reality that college life will never again return to fully in-person, should be on re-building our student support services to maintain the connection that students, and the literature, say is needed. This structure could include remote or online recruitment and outreach, welcome orientations, advising, crisis counseling, and tutoring.

Implementation

The previous sections of this chapter reviewed long-standing higher-education theory, coupling it with more recent research on the value of personal connections as central to the success of international students. These models formed the basis for offering examples of specific strategies in Table 12.1 above to support global education in an increasingly unpredictable landscape. This section will offer introductory thoughts on how to best implement these or similar new instructional and support strategies. In short, implementation of these strategies in an environment of fast-changing public health and political realities should be mindful of the following:

- First and foremost, consider the student voice. Regularly reach out to students with guidance, along with inquiry. From informal chats to formal en masse survey research, this information will inform better decision-making;
- Think and act holistically. Whether advising an international student or building a new international program, reach out. Having internal alliances—from student service to the dean's office—along with external organizations including nonprofit organizations, community foundations, business organizations, employers, and libraries will help you support your students day-to-day and when in crisis;
- Think about how technology can connect you. Technology can help keep faculty, students, and staff organized (for example, keeping grades updated on the learning management system helps support student success). It can help capture student interest (like doing an online poll or group project). But do not underestimate the power of a simple message. An announcement or note to students checking in on their well-being will do more to keep them engaged than you might think.

Keep in mind, the ideas and best practices presented in this chapter are based on feedback from a small number of students and practitioners. And the practices were implemented in less than optimal circumstances. They show promise for broader application, but are beholden to the wide variety of circumstances, demographics, and political landscapes of our individual institutions. And application of these suggestions surely could benefit from additional research, in particular research that tests the

200 Marc Thomas

instructional and student support strategies presented through randomized control groups.

Concluding Thoughts

In striving to record what steps community colleges took in response to the COVID-19 pandemic and recalibrate international education amid a new culture of remote learning, this chapter is written as the international education community finds itself at a crossroads. The challenges and opportunities of the 2-year college in charting an uncertain future are on the minds of many community college leaders. Lauren Nehlsen, Director of the Center for International Education and Programs at Elgin Community College in Illinois, acknowledges the heightened resources that 4-year institutions have, but points to mission as a selling point: "community colleges are engaged and involved in their local communities and with students, who become part of that community. Community colleges are able to adjust quickly to changing external influences and are committed to student success and development. This combination makes them prepared to deal with multiple challenges" (L. Nehlsen, personal communication, July 30, 2020). Two colleges involved in this study reported modest gains in international student applications in late 2020. Some Shoreline international students opted to stay in the United States for summer classes, and Lone Star reported an initial increase in fall international applications. Shoreline Executive Director of International Education Samira Pardanani suggested a pandemic-era advantage for community colleges "at a time when some students and families are expressing reluctance about paying university tuition for an online program" (S. Pardanani, personal communication, July 17, 2020).

Community colleges are built on a 20th-century foundation of educational access for students who might not otherwise have it. In the 21st-century, these institutions are making high-impact teaching and learning strategies, along with robust support services, priorities in the drive to improve student degree completion and global competence. The challenge for continued effectiveness and relevance in international education likely lies in our willingness to research, reflect, and implement change proactively, rather than only reactively.

References

Baker, M., Fink, S., Fuller, T., & Bogel-Burroughs, N. (2020, February 28). Unexplained Coronavirus cases in three states raise specter of spread. *The New York Times*. https://www.nytimes.com/2020/02/28/us/coronavirus-solano-county.html

Bista, K. (2015). Asian international students' college experience: Relationship between quality of personal contact and gains in learning. *Journal of International & Global Studies, 6*(2), 38–54.

Center for Community College Student Engagement. (2013). *A matter of degrees: Engaging practices, engaging students (high-impact practices for community college student engagement).* Austin, TX: The University of Texas at Austin, Community College Leadership Program.

Centers for Disease Control and Prevention. (2020, June 1). *What you should know about COVID-19 to protect yourself and others.* https://www.cdc.gov/coronavirus/2019-ncov/downloads/2019-ncov-factsheet.pdf

Chickering, A. W., & Gamson, Z. F. (1987, March). American association for higher education. Seven principles for good practice in undergraduate education. *AAHE Bulletin, 39*(7), 3–7.

Dickerson, C. (2020, April 25). 'My world is shattering': Foreign students stranded by Coronavirus. *The New York Times.* https://www.nytimes.com/2020/04/25/us/coronavirus-international-foreign-students-universities.html

Driessen, E., Beatty, A., Stokes, A., Wood, S., & Ballen, C. (2020). Learning principles of evolution during a crisis: An exploratory analysis of student barriers one week and one month into the COVID-19 pandemic. *Ecology and Evolution, 10*(22), 12431–12436. https://doi.org/10.1002/ece3.6741

IIE (2019). Fast Facts. Institute for International Education. https://www.iie.org/en/Research-and-Insights/Open-Doors/Fact-Sheets-and-Infographics/Fast-Facts

O'Dowd, R. (2017). Virtual exchange and internationalising the classroom. *Training, Language and Culture, 1*(4), 8–24. https://doi-org.ezproxy.aclin.org:2443/10.29366/2017tlc.1.4.1

Ruther, N. (2020). Briefings: Gazelle International. *Gazelle International.* https://www.gazelleinternational.org/briefings

Sioux City Journal. (2020, March 29). *International students experience challenges while dealing with COVID-19 concerns.* https://siouxcityjournal.com/news/local/international-students-experience-challenges-while-dealing-with-covid-19-concerns/article_9092a037-3517-5e6a-9c09-049f22517014.html

Svrluga, S. (2020, March 6). *Two colleges close, another cancels classes and others brace for Coronavirus impact on campus.* The Washington Post. https://www.washingtonpost.com/education/2020/03/05/college-closes-others-brace-coronavirus-impact-campus/

Tran, L. (2020). Teaching and engaging international students: People-to-people connections and people-to-people empathy. *Journal of International Students, 10*(3), xii–xvii. https://doi.org/10.32674/jis.v10i3.2005

Trapè, R. (2019). Building empathy and intercultural citizenship through a virtual exchange project. *Le Simplegadi,* XVII(19), 167–180. https://doi-org.ezproxy.aclin.org:2443/10.17456/SIMPLE-136

West, C. (2020, May 6). Supporting international students during COVID-19. *International Educator.* https://www.nafsa.org/ie-magazine/2020/5/6/supporting-international-students-during-covid-19

Williams, A. (2020, June 15). In their own words: Here's what professors, chairs, and deans learned from remote courses this spring. *The Chronicle of Higher Education.* https://www.chronicle.com/article/in-their-own-words-here-s/248989?fbclid=IwAR03-kZS_NH8R8KQocMvf6b5GU9P5yZV032VAY8

fcpRrXWSkMlwwlVB4TtM&key=wYmokCnDzR4h9eFNudrs4p
TiEZ600aCSnzzv6JPbstvoexSQqbRY9z2f5W89_jz2MEcwd2huSUx5V
VZfeWJ6eGwyaTZZZHh2cVZSYVZzTUhwOFpOc2l0Wndubw

WHO. (n.d.). *WHO Coronavirus (COVID-19) Dashboard*. World Health Organization. https://covid19.who.int/

Yu, E. (2020). Student-inspired optimal design of online learning for generation z. *Journal of Educators Online*, *17*(1). https://www.thejeo.com/archive/2020_17_1/yu

Author Bio

Marc Thomas, EdD, is Dean of Teaching Excellence at Oakland Community College in Michigan. Previously, he served as academic dean in Colorado and as social science professor and global programs coordinator at Lansing Community College (LCC) in Michigan. His first experience in international education was as faculty adviser for the LCC Japan Adventure Program in the Shiga Prefecture in 2005.

13 Trends in International Student Enrollments in Canadian Community Colleges

Elizabeth Buckner, Sarah Morales, Taiya Brown, and Scott Clerk

Introduction

The number of international students in Canadian community colleges and universities has been growing markedly since 2010. In 2019, international students accounted for 21 percent of all enrollments in Canadian higher education and added 22 billion (CAD) to the Canadian economy (El-Assal, 2020; GAC, 2019). However, the literature on international students in Canada focuses primarily on universities, while the college sector has received much less attention (Bégin-Caouette et al., 2015; Cudmore, 2005; Galway, 2000). This is despite the fact that the number of international students in the college sector has been increasing at a faster rate than in the university sector. In the Canadian college sector, which enrolls 37 percent of all postsecondary students and is comprised of over 130 institutions across Canada (Statistics Canada, 2020; Colleges and Institutes Canada, 2020), the growth of international students is changing the demographics of many colleges and raising important questions for colleges concerning their educational programs, student services, and broader mandates; as such, the topic warrants greater scholarly attention.

This chapter provides an overview of the enrollment trends of international students in Canadian colleges over the past decade. Drawing on data from Statistics Canada, the chapter points to growing numbers of international students in the college sector, particularly from India. We argue that the increasing numbers of international students in Canadian colleges raise important questions for the sector, which has historically been oriented towards serving students from local communities to participate in the labor markets, and conclude with avenues for future research.

Higher Education in Canada

In Canada, higher education is highly decentralized, and responsibility for all levels of education is delegated to the provinces and territories

204 *Elizabeth Buckner et al.*

under Canada's constitutional federation (Jones, 2014). In the postwar era, demographic growth and changing labor markets, which called for new forms of advanced training in applied fields, resulted in significant pressure to expand access to higher education. At the time university leaders worried that expansion would undermine their traditional mission of liberal education and research. As a result, throughout the 1960s and 1970s, many provinces looked to a new model of postsecondary education—the public college—to expand enrollments and provide advanced training (Gallagher & Dennison, 1995; Jones, 1997; Kirby, 2009). These public colleges are often referred to informally as "community colleges," as a generic descriptor for postsecondary institutions that do not have university status in Canada, despite many of these institutions not identifying with that title (Skolnik, 2010). This parallel sector saw rapid expansion throughout the 1960s and 1980s, aimed at offering students short-cycle credentials, including one-year certificates, and diplomas ranging from two to three years in length (Gallagher & Dennison, 1995; Jones, 2009). The college sector varies significantly by province, as each made very different decisions about how to structure their expanding higher education systems. For example, the Western provinces of British Columbia and Alberta created a college model that most closely resembled the American community college model, with the option to transfer to university after a two-year diploma, whereas most of the remaining provinces focused on career-oriented diploma programs with no university transfer function (Jones, 2009). Historically, a characteristic that separated colleges and universities in Canada was the authority of the latter to grant degrees. However, this boundary has become blurred in several provinces where degree granting has fallen under the jurisdiction of several colleges as well (Jones, 2009; Skolnik et al., 2018).

Despite blurring in the sectoral divide and the variations by province, Canadian colleges share particular institutional characteristics that distinguish them from universities, including: a vocational focus, curricular flexibility, an emphasis on accessibility, teaching and learning, a community orientation, and high levels of responsiveness to provincial governments. Moreover, the primary mandate of Canadian colleges is to prepare adults for the workforce (Dennison & Gallagher, 1986; Gallagher & Dennison, 1995; Shanahan & Jones, 2007). Their public mission is exemplified by the fact that almost all colleges remain under the control of provincial governments. In this way, they differ significantly from Canadian universities, which are legally autonomous from government and are oriented towards both teaching and research (Dennison & Gallagher, 1986; Kirby, 2007; Shanahan & Jones, 2007). The student population in college tends to be more heterogeneous than their university counterparts due to their variety of programming and open admission policies. As a result, an emphasis on student support services has always been an important characteristic of these institutions. However, over the past two decades, globalization has brought significant changes to the Canadian college sector, including a growing orientation towards new and increasingly international stakeholders (Levin, 1999) and an increased emphasis on international student recruitment, as discussed below.

International Student Recruitment as Policy Goal

In Canada, despite the fact that higher education policy is a provincial domain, international student recruitment is an explicit policy goal of the federal government. The federal government closely links international student recruitment to both economic growth and to a broader policy goal of attracting highly skilled immigrants (Sá & Sabzalieva 2018; Scott et al., 2015). In 2014, Canada launched its first International Education Strategy, which was produced by the federal government's Department of Foreign Affairs, Trade, and Development. The strategy discusses international students primarily in terms of the economic benefits they bring to Canada. Specifically, it states that international students create jobs and generate tax revenues through their spending, and in the long-term, can also play a role in addressing shortages of skilled labor or counteracting demographic declines in parts of the country. The 2014 strategy set the goal of doubling the number of international students studying in Canada between 2011 and 2022 and specifically, attracting 450,000 international students by 2022, a goal that was surpassed five years early, with 494,525 international students in 2017 (CBIE, 2018).

In 2019, under the rebranded foreign affairs Ministry, Global Affairs Canada, a new strategy was launched titled Building on our Success. The new strategy celebrates the significant increases in international students in Canada, and continues to emphasize many of the same themes, explicitly identifying international students as "excellent candidates for permanent residency" who can "help address [Canada's] current and pending labor market needs" (p. 5). In addition to maintaining high numbers of international students, one of the strategy's three targets is to diversify the global pool of students who are from different countries of origin. This is because in 2018, over 50 percent of international students in Canada came from only two countries—India and China (GAC, 2019).

In response to the 2020 COVID-19 pandemic, the Canadian government also made a number of policy adjustments related to international students and their eligibility for future immigration. Several temporary policy changes were specifically aimed at protecting international students' eligibility for postgraduation work permits, which allow international students to live and work in Canada after graduating. Specifically,

206 *Elizabeth Buckner et al.*

they allowed international students to begin their studies online from their home countries without disqualifying them for a postgraduation work permit (IRCC, 2020). As of August 2020, students enrolled in an educational program that started in the summer or fall terms (from May to September) of 2020 that lasted between 8 and 12 months would be able to complete the full-length of their program online and still be able to apply for a postgraduation work permit, even if they were outside of Canada for their entire program (IRCC, 2020). These temporary policy changes represent a significant departure from the pre-COVID policy that required in-person attendance. In doing so, they seem designed to encourage international students to continue to enroll in Canadian institutions by promising the possibility of future immigration. In fact, they are arguably targeted specifically to the college sector, as international students in colleges are more likely to seek permanent residency after graduation than those in university (Esses et al., 2018) and whose short-cycle programs are more directly impacted by these policies.

Many provincial governments have also encouraged international student recruitment. Examining the case of Ontario, Arvast (2008) argues that globalization has brought a shift in focus from the local community to the global market, evidenced through the removal of the formal catchment areas in the new Ontario college charter and references to a "global marketplace." Moreover, in a throne speech in 2010, former Ontario Premier Dalton McGuinty advocated that the province "get serious about competing for international students" (Benzie, 2010), in the same way Australia has, in order to generate funds for the province's postsecondary institutions and to promote job creation.

Canadian institutions have increasingly sought to enroll international students as well. Growing international student enrollments have been an explicit strategy of both colleges and universities that view international student tuition as a way to offset stagnant public revenues, and see international students' presence on campus as helping expose domestic students to others from diverse backgrounds (Buckner et al., 2020). These practices have generated significant funding for Canadian higher education. Usher (2020a) reports that nationwide, between 2007–2008 to 2018–2019, "international student fees grew from $1.5 billion to $6.9 billion (both figures in 2019 dollars), and from 4 percent to 13 percent of total system income (colleges and universities combined)" (p. 9). As a result, the Canadian higher education system is increasingly financially reliant on international students.

However, most reports on international students tend to combine data from colleges and universities, which obscures trends specific to the college sector. In the section below, we draw on data from Statistics Canada to document the changing enrollment trends in the Canadian college sector. We then discuss what these changing demographics

International Students in Canadian Community Colleges

Over the past decade, Canadian colleges have experienced a major shift in international student enrollments. Traditionally, international students have been more likely to enroll in universities, seeming to prefer the degrees they provide over colleges' short-cycle diplomas (Statistics Canada, 2020). Although total international student enrollments are still higher in the university sector, the numbers of international students in community colleges, both in terms of raw numbers, and as a percentage of total enrollments, has grown rapidly.

Table 13.1 shows international students as a percentage of total enrollments over the past decade, disaggregated by institution type. The table shows that in the 2008–2009 academic year, international students made up roughly 8 percent of all university students and 5 percent of all students in the college sector. By 2017–2018, the proportion of international students had increased significantly in both sectors, to 15 percent in the university sector and 13 percent in the college sector. Within the Canadian college sector, the top five countries of origin for international students are India, China, South Korea, Brazil, and Vietnam, meanwhile for Canadian universities, the top five are China, India, France, United States, and Nigeria (CBIE, 2019).

This period of growth also aligns with a second clear trend: the rise of India as Canada's top country of origin for international students. China has been the primary source of international students in Canada

Table 13.1 International Students as a Percentage of Total Enrollments, by Year and Sector

Year	International University Students	% Total University	International Community College Students	% Total College
2008/2009	88,014	8%	35,292	5%
2009/2010	98,874	8%	36,693	5%
2010/2011	107,514	9%	34,653	5%
2011/2012	119,889	10%	38,220	5%
2012/2013	131,739	10%	42,510	6%
2013/2014	144,351	11%	54,723	7%
2014/2015	159,405	12%	58,089	8%
2015/2016	168,591	13%	60,285	8%
2016/2017	179,796	14%	76,662	10%
2017/2018	196,563	15%	99,909	13%

Source: Statistics Canada.

208   *Elizabeth Buckner et al.*

Table 13.2 Enrollments of International Students from India, by Year and Sector

Year	University	College	% in College Sector
2008/2009	3366	1641	33%
2009/2010	3984	2325	37%
2010/2011	4854	5073	51%
2011/2012	5658	7221	56%
2012/2013	6543	8088	55%
2013/2014	7710	8907	54%
2014/2015	9027	10107	53%
2015/2016	10575	15768	60%
2016/2017	12924	22479	63%

Source: Postsecondary Student Information System (5017). https://www150.statcan.gc.ca/n1/daily-quotidien/181128/cg-c001-eng.html.

since the early 2000s (Lu & Hou, 2015), but was overtaken by India in 2018. The increase in Indian students studying in Canada has been concentrated in colleges, while Chinese students continue to prefer universities (and remain by far the top source country for Canadian universities). In just two years, from 2015 to 2017, Indian student enrollments in Canadian colleges more than doubled, with 122 percent growth (Statistics Canada, 2020). Table 13.2 shows the total number and proportion of all international students from India, disaggregated by year and institution type.

The table clearly demonstrates the growth of Indian student enrollment, particularly in Canadian colleges. In 2008–2009, there were 1,641 students from India in the college sector, compared to 3,366 in the university sector. By 2017–2018, the number of Indian international students in the college sector had increased to 22,479, a more than tenfold increase. Over the same time period, the total number of Indian international students in Canadian universities also increased, from 3,366 to 12,924. While substantial, this growth represents an increase of 383 percent, compared to an increase of 1,369 percent in the college sector over the same time period. Table 13.2 also shows that in 2008–2009 the college sector enrolled only about a third of all Indian international students; however, by 2018, the proportions had reversed. The college sector is now enrolling roughly two-thirds of all Indian international students. These rapidly changing demographic trends mean that many Canadian colleges have only very recently begun enrolling high proportions of Indian students. This new trend poses new challenges for institutions, as faculty and staff may have little knowledge or understanding of their students' backgrounds or needs.

A third clear trend is that international student enrollments vary significantly across provinces, and are heavily concentrated in only two

Table 13.3 International Students in the College Sector, by Province (2018)

Province	International	Total	% International
Canada	99,909	774,654	13%
Ontario	68,037	331,485	21%
British Columbia	17,409	99,732	17%
Manitoba	2,148	16,233	13%
Prince Edward Island	180	2,073	9%
Alberta	5,067	60,978	8%
New Brunswick	600	8,079	7%
Saskatchewan	723	19,563	4%
Quebec	5,682	214,383	3%
Nova Scotia	60	7,908	1%
Newfoundland and Labrador	3	10,686	0%

Source: Statistics Canada.

provinces: Ontario and British Columbia (BC). Table 13.3 shows the total number of international students and their percentage of total enrollments in the college sector in 2017–2018, disaggregated by province. The table points to significant differences across provinces. Of the nearly 100,000 international students in Canadian colleges in 2017–2018, more than 68,000 of them studied in Ontario, while only three were enrolled in Newfoundland and Labrador. The table shows that international students make up 21 percent of all students in the college sector in Ontario, and 17 percent of all students in BC. Meanwhile, international students make up less than 10 percent of all students in most other provinces, and only 1 percent of college students in Nova Scotia and 0 percent in Newfoundland and Labrador. Combined, Ontario and BC enroll more than 85 percent of all international students in the college sector. While the concentration of enrollments in Ontario and BC is partially due to the regions being the two largest English-speaking provinces, there are likely other factors at play as well, including the appeal of large metropolitan areas such as Toronto, Ontario and Vancouver, BC, the large South Asian and Chinese immigrant populations in these provinces, and the international education policy and coordination infrastructure in these provinces, such as the BC Council on International Education.

However, this provincial imbalance creates policy challenges: the economic benefits of international students on local communities are highly uneven, with the more populous provinces benefitting more. Canada's most recent internationalization strategy makes reference to this imbalance, stating that it seeks to diversify the regions and institutions where international students study, and that doing so would "distribute the benefits more equitably across the country" (p. 4). For

210 *Elizabeth Buckner et al.*

example, relatively populous and urban provinces, such as Alberta and Quebec, could follow Ontario and BC's strategies of more explicit recruitment and marketing strategies.

Discussion and Conclusion

In this chapter, we examine the changing context and demographics of international student recruitment. We identify three major trends: (1) a rapid, recent, and unprecedented increase in international student enrollments in the college sector; (2) significant growth in the number and proportion of international students from India; and, (3) a concentration of enrollments in only two provinces: Ontario and BC. Notably, we also point out that the federal government, despite having no official mandate over higher education policy, has supported and facilitated these increases in international student enrollments due to their presumed short- and long-term economic benefits.

That being said, increasing international students raises concern about the growing financial dependence on international tuition fees in the college sector, specifically on tuition fees from Indian international students. The sector's reliance on high numbers of Chinese and Indian students could also result in severe financial consequences for the college sector should students from these countries seek educational opportunities elsewhere, including in their own countries. For example, Canadian institutions were financially impacted when the Saudi Arabian government pulled thousands of its scholarship students from Canadian institutions during a diplomatic conflict in 2018 (Usher, 2018). The ongoing COVID-19 pandemic has now pushed this concern to the forefront for college administrators and government, resulting in the swift immigration policy changes referenced above to help mitigate the impact on the sector. Even with these changes, there are concerns that Canadian colleges will face budgetary shortfalls due to the decreased enrollments associated with the pandemic (Usher, 2020b).

The increasing numbers of international students in Canadian colleges also raises important questions for the provision of student services. Colleges have long been associated with serving a more heterogeneous student population than universities, including higher proportions of Indigenous students, persons with disabilities, single-parent families, and students from lower income families (Skolnik et al., 2018). However, they have not traditionally served many international students. As they enroll increasing numbers of international students, colleges will likely need to add new services and staff to provide targeted academic and nonacademic supports to these students.

The findings also point to many avenues for future research. First, there is a need for more research on the backgrounds of international college students and their experiences on college campuses. Specifically, research should examine whether college students' experiences differ from those of their university-bound peers. Understanding differences between the demographics, prior academic experiences, and socio-economic status of international students in colleges could inform the development of more specialized college support services.

More research is also needed on international college students' post-college outcomes. One survey, conducted by the Education (CBIE) in 2016–2017, found that 50 percent of international students in Canada intended to apply for permanent residency, and 61 percent intended to work in Canada. Moreover, they also found that international students attending a college were 1.44 times more likely to seek permanent residency than international students enrolled at universities (Esses et al., 2018). However, in their study of international students' transition to permanent residency, Lu and Huo (2015) found that among international students enrolled in Canadian institutions in the early 2000s, 32 percent of university students transitioned to permanent residency within ten years, compared to only 26 percent of college students. More research is needed to determine what proportion of international college graduates actually obtain postgraduate work permits and remain in Canada after graduation, what kinds of jobs they secure, and where they work.

Relatedly, given the growing enrollments from India, studies should examine why a growing proportion of international students from India are attracted to Canadian colleges as compared to universities. On one hand, we might posit that some Indian international students are attracted to the college sector in the hopes of obtaining permanent residency, as short-cycle diploma and certificate programs may offer a quicker route to a postgraduate work permit. However, there has been little research on the proportion of Indian college graduates who do remain in Canada, their backgrounds, and their employment outcomes. According to Lu and Hou (2015), among Indian international students enrolled in Canadian institutions in the early 2000s, roughly half (55 percent) had transitioned to permanent residency in the next ten years. More research is needed to see whether this proportion has changed in recent years, as Indian students increasingly enroll in the college sector.

Similarly, more research is also needed to determine whether international students are enrolling in colleges as a pathway to university, and if so, whether they are able to do so. Provincial comparisons will be particularly important in these studies, as transfer pathways vary significantly between provinces, and are much less common in Ontario than other provinces, such as Alberta and BC (Gallagher & Dennison, 1995; Jones, 2009).

Finally, researchers might ask how colleges are reframing their shifting mandates from one of serving the local community for primarily labor market preparation to educating students from all over the world. Given colleges' long history serving local students, and particularly those

212 *Elizabeth Buckner et al.*

underserved by universities, it is worth exploring what "accessibility" means in this new context of globalized enrollments. In particular, we might ask if many international students are attracted to colleges over universities due to their perceived "accessibility" in terms of their lower tuition fees and lower admission requirements. Moreover, we might ask whether notions of "accessibility" are undermined if international students are unable to secure either the employment or path to immigration they seek.

References

Arvast, A. (2008). The new CAAT: (Dis)illusions of freedom and the new college charter in Ontario. *Canadian Journal of Higher Education, 38*(1), 105–121. https://files.eric.ed.gov/fulltext/EJ802487.pdf

Bégin-Caouette, O., Khoo, Y., & Afridi, M. (2015). The processes of designing and implementing globally networked learning environments and their implications on college instructors' professional learning: The case of Québec CGÉPs. *Comparative and International Education, 43*(3), 1–22. https://ojs.lib. uwo.ca/index.php/cie-eci/article/view/9260

Benzie, R. (2010, March 8). *Ontario wants more foreign students.* The Toronto Star. https://www.thestar.com/news/ontario/2010/03/08/ontario_wants_more_foreign_students.html

Buckner, E., Clerk, S., Marroquin Rodriguez, A., & Zhang, Y. (2020). Symbolic commitments, strategic benefits: How Canadian colleges and universities frame internationalization. *Canadian Journal of Higher Education, 50*(4), 20–36.

Canadian Bureau of International Education (CBIE). (2018). *International students in Canada.* https://cbie.ca/wp-content/uploads/2018/09/International-Students-in-Canada-ENG.pdf

Canadian Bureau for International Education (CBIE). (2019). *International students in Canada.* https://cbie.ca/wp-content/uploads/2018/09/International-Students-in-Canada-ENG.pdf

Cudmore, G. (2005). Globalization, internationalization, and the recruitment of international students in higher education, and in the Ontario Colleges of Applied Arts and Technology. *Canadian Journal of Higher Education, 35*(1), 37–60. https://files.eric.ed.gov/fulltext/EJ720728.pdf

Dennison, J. D., & Gallagher, P. (1986). *Canada's community colleges: A critical analysis.* University of British Columbia Press.

El-Assal, K. (2020, February 20). *642,000 international students: Canada now ranks 3rd globally in foreign student attraction.* CIC News. https://www.cicnews. com/2020/02/642000-international-students-canada-now-ranks-3rd-globally-in-foreign-student-attraction-0213763.html

Esses, V., Sutter, A., Ortiz, A., Luo, N., Cui, J., & Deacon, L. (2018). Retaining international students in Canada post-graduation: Understanding the motivations and drivers of the decision to stay. *CBIE Research in Brief No. 8*, 1–8. https:// cbie.ca/wp-content/uploads/2018/06/Intl-students-post-graduation-RiB-8-EN-1.pdf

Gallagher, P., & Dennison, J. D. (1995). Canada's community college systems: A study of diversity. *Community College Journal of Research and Practice, 19*(5), 381–393. https://doi.org/10.1080/1066892950190502

Galway, A. (2000). *Going global: Ontario Colleges of Applied Arts and Technology, international student recruitment and the export of education.* [Unpublished Doctoral Thesis]. University of Toronto.

Global Affairs Canada (GAC). (2019). *Building on success: International education strategy (2019–2024).* Global Affairs Canada. https://www.international.gc.ca/education/assets/pdfs/ies-sei/Building-on-Success-International-Education-Strategy-2019-2024.pdf

Immigration, Refugees, and Citizenship Canada (IRCC). (2020). *Measures to support international students during the COVID-19 pandemic.* https://www.canada.ca/en/immigration-refugees-citizenship/news/2020/07/measures-to-support-international-students-during-the-covid-19-pandemic.html

Jones, G. A. (1997). A brief introduction to higher education in Canada. In G. Jones (Ed.), *Higher education in Canada: Different systems, different perspectives* (pp. 1–8). Taylor & Francis Group.

Jones, G. (2009). Sectors, institutional types and the challenges of shifting categories: A Canadian commentary. *Higher Education Quarterly, 63*(4), 371–383. https://doi.org/10.1111/j.1468-2273.2009.00439.x

Jones, G. (2014). An introduction to higher education in Canada. In K. Joshi & S. Paivandi (Eds.), *Higher education across nations* (1st ed., pp. 1–38). B.R. Publishing.

Kirby, D. (2007). Reviewing Canadian post-secondary education: Post-secondary education policy in post-industrial Canada. *Canadian Journal of Educational Administration and Policy, 65,* 1–24. https://cdm.ucalgary.ca/index.php/cjeap/article/view/42746

Kirby, D. (2009). Widening access: Making the transition from mass to universal post-secondary education in Canada. *Journal of Applied Research on Learning, 2*(3), 1–17. http://en.copian.ca/library/research/jarl/widening/widening.pdf

Levin, J. S. (1999). Missions and structures: Bringing clarity to perceptions about globalization and higher education in Canada. *Higher Education, 37*(4), 377–399. https://doi.org/10.1023/A:1003635731222

Lu, Y., & Hou, F. (2015). *International students who become permanent residents in Canada.* Statistics Canada. http://www.statcan.gc.ca/pub/75-006-x/2015001/article/14299-eng.pdf

Sá, C. M., & Sabzalieva, E. (2018). The politics of the great brain race: Public policy and international student recruitment in Australia, Canada, England and the USA. *Higher Education, 75*(2), 231–253. https://doi.org/10.1007/s10734-017-0133-1

Scott, C., Safdar, S., Desai Trilokekar, R., & El Masri, A. (2015). International students as "ideal immigrants" in Canada: A disconnect between policy makers' assumptions and the lived experiences of international students. *Comparative and International Education, 43*(3). https://doi.org/10.5206/cie-eci.v43i3.9261

Shanahan, T., & Jones, G. A. (2007). Shifting roles and approaches: Government coordination of post-secondary education in Canada, 1995–2006. *Higher Education Research & Development, 26*(1), 31–43. https://doi.org/10.1080/07294360601166794

Skolnik, M. L. (2010). A look back at the decision on the transfer function at the founding of Ontario's Colleges of Applied Arts and Technology. *Canadian Journal of Higher Education, 40*(2), 17. https://doi.org/10.47678/cjhe.v40i2.1915

Skolnik, M. L., Wheelahan, L., Moodie, G., Liu, Q., Adam, E., & Simpson, D. (2018). Exploring the potential contribution of college bachelor degree programs in Ontario to reducing social inequality. *Policy Reviews in Higher Education*, 2(2), 176–197. https://doi.org/10.1080/23322969.2018.1455532

Statistics Canada. (2020). *Postsecondary enrolments, by registration status, institution type, status of student in Canada and gender* [Table: 37-10-0018-01]. Statistics Canada. https://www150.statcan.gc.ca/t1/tbl1/en/tv.action?pid=3710001801

Usher, A. (2018, August 29). Canadian universities have become addicted to the revenues brought in by international students. But how much should they subsidize our institutions? *Policy Options*. https://policyoptions.irpp.org/magazines/august-2018/canadas-growing-reliance-on-international-students/

Usher, A. (2020a). *The state of postsecondary education in Canada, 2020*. Higher Education Strategy Associates. https://higheredstrategy.com/the-state-of-postsecondary-education-in-canada-2/

Usher, A. (2020b, November 2). So how are enrolments looking, anyway? *Higher Education Strategy Associates*. https://higheredstrategy.com/so-how-are-enrolments-looking-anyway/

Author Bios

Elizabeth Buckner, PhD, is an Assistant Professor of Higher Education at the Ontario Institute for Studies in Education of the University of Toronto. Her research examines how globalization affects higher education. Her recent publications have appeared in *Comparative Education Review, Higher Education,* and the *Sociology of Education.*

Sarah Morales, is an MEd student in Higher Education at the Ontario Institute for Studies in Education of the University of Toronto. Professionally she works as a Student Advisor at Sheridan College Institute of Technology and Advanced Learning. Her major research interests lie in the area of comparative higher education, internationalization, community colleges, and student support services.

Taiya Brown, MEd, is a recent graduate from the Higher Education program at the Ontario Institute for Studies in Education of the University of Toronto and professionally works at Humber College as a Field Placement Advisor. Her major research interests lie in the areas of internationalization, student support services, and comparative higher education.

Scott Clerk, is a PhD student in Higher Education at the Ontario Institute for Studies in Education of the University of Toronto, as well as the Director of International Education at Northern Lights College, in British Columbia, Canada. His primary research interests are in the field of international and comparative higher education.

14 Global Begins from Local

International Students and International Programs at Historically Black Community Colleges and Tribal Community Colleges

Krishna Bista

Introduction

As a special category of minority-serving institutions of higher education, Historically Black Colleges and Universities (HBCUs) primarily serve the African-American communities whereas Tribal Colleges and Universities (TCUs) provides a rich tapestry of the American Indian experiences. Unique by their mission and historical foundations, historically Black community colleges and tribal community colleges in the United States are the hidden treasures for expanding international education programs including study abroad, international student mobility, and internationalization initiatives. They are in the veil and only a handful of them have explored the possibilities and potential of expanding international programs—creating opportunities for cross-cultural competency and ensuring their graduates are globally educated and work independently in the 21st-century job market. This chapter offers an overview of international students and international education programs and initiatives at historically Black community colleges and tribal community colleges in the United States. This chapter also highlights the strengths and challenges of these community colleges and international programs.

Of 1,462 American community colleges, 941 are public, 148 private, and 32 tribal community colleges (US Department of Education, 2020). In the United States, there are 107 HBCUs—53 public, 51 private nonprofit institutions, and 3 closed located in 19 states and the US Virgin Islands. Of these HBCU institutions, 27 offer doctoral programs, 52 offer master's programs, 83 offer bachelor's degree programs, and 38 offer associate degrees. There are several HBCUs community colleges (2-year institutions) with locations in Alabama (e.g. Bishop State Community College), Mississippi (e.g. Coahoma Community College), Washington DC (e.g. University of the District of Columbia Community College), South Carolina (e.g. Denmark Technical College), Arkansas (e.g. Shorter College), Texas (e.g. Southwestern Christian College), and Alabama (e.g. Trenholm State Community College) which are popular for the HBCU experience.

216   *Krishna Bista*

Both Black community colleges and tribal community colleges are distinctive institutions of learning in American higher education because of their strong historical mission to the historically marginalized and underserved student population. Despite their strengths and potentials, as Malvaux an Raby (2019) mentioned, there is no "national benchmark to measure the magnitude and application in which international programs are part of the community colleges" (p. xix) and only 309 commity colleges out of 1462 support international programs. Similarly, nearly half of all 107 HBCUs offer no study abroad programs or do not have enough resources to host international programs and initiatives (Charles & Togunde, 2020). Tribal colleges and universities have not yet expanded their programs and resources to international students because of their limited resources as well their local mission to serve Native and Alska American populations.

Black Community Colleges: Historical Contexts and Shifting Demographics

Most HBCUs were established as religious missionary organizations after the American Civil War (1861–1865), primarily serving the African-American community. HBCUs opened their doors for African Americans for higher education as many other colleges and universities had prohibited them from attending or had used quotas to limit admissions of Blacks (Gasman, 2007; Gasman & Commodore, 2014). As Elliott et al (2019) indicated, "25 private HBCCs closed due to financial issues. A few were able to merge with nearby four-year HBCUs. The only public HBCCs or HBCUs to be closed were the 12 Black junior colleges in Florida. Eleven of the 12 were founded after the passage of Brown v. Board in full defiance of the case's call for integration. All 12 were abruptly closed and merged with local white junior colleges between 1964 and 1966" (p, 772). According to the National Center for Education Statistics (NCES, 2017), the number of students enrolled at HBCUs rose by 32 percent between 1976 and 2015, from 223,000 to 293,000. Of which, 8,327 were international students pursuing degrees in various disciplines and programs. HBCUs are global institutions and their global footprints are recognized as they allow African American students to engage internationally. Students and faculty demographics at the historically Black community colleges are constantly shifting in the last decades. For instance, Bishop State Community college in Alabama enrolled 2,860 students in 2018 out of which 36.75 percent were minority students, 59.56 percent were female, and 49.83 percent were full-time (Bishop State, 2020). There is limited awareness of existing Black community colleges and their existence. Table 14.1 list selected 2-year Black community colleges and general information related to international programs and international students.

Global Begins from Local   217

Table 14.1 Selected 2-Year Black Community Colleges and Online Information for International Students

Institutions	Information for International Students	College Information
Bishop State Community College (Mobile, Alabama)	The Office of International Students at Bishop offers services related to F-1 visa paperwork and other services They also offer information and forms to complete the admissions process. The information page includes stories, pictures, and testimonies of current and former international students https://www.bishop.edu/new-students/international-student-program	Bishop State offers certificate programs and associate degrees in over a dozen areas including welding and air conditioning & refrigeration technology
Coahoma Community College (Clarksdale, Mississippi)	Coahoma offers information for international students related to admissions and immigration issues http://www.coahomacc.edu/admissions-financial-aid/admissions/general-admissions/international-student/index	Coahomas started junior college courses in 1949. Academic programs include technical programs like Collision Repair Technology and culinary arts as well as health science programs (nursing, EMT)
Denmark Technical College (Denmark, South Carolina)	Denmark offers information and services for all international students who desire a student visa or who are transferring from another college on a student visa https://www.denmarktech.edu/wp-content/uploads/2017/04/DTC-Catalog_Section-II.pdf	Denmark Tech offers a large number of certificate, associate's degrees, and diploma programs. Associate's degree programs are also offered. Courses include gerontology, plumbing, cybersecurity, cosmetology, and criminal justice technology
University of the District of Columbia Community College (Washington, DC)	University of the District of Columbia (UDC) Community Colleges offers information for international students who are seeking an Associate's degree from UDC's Community College or a Bachelor's degree from UDC's Flagship University https://www.udc.edu/admissions/international-students/	Opened as a branch of the UDC in 2009, UDC Community Colleges offers associate's degrees and certificate programs. Academic programs include fashion merchandising, graphic design, mortuary science, and aviation maintenance technology
Hinds Community College—Utica Campus (Utica, Mississippi)	Hinds offers information and resources for international students related to admissions, immigrations, and scholars https://www.hindscc.edu/admissions/international-students/	Hinds Community College is one of the top community colleges in the nation for graduating African-Americans with associate's degrees, especially in construction, legal studies, and health science fields like nursing and dental assisting. It has been recognized as a military-friendly college

(Continued)

218 *Krishna Bista*

Table 14.1 (Continued)

Institutions	Information for International Students	College Information
Southwestern Christian College (Terrell, Texas)	The Office of Admissions offers the information to process admission applications for international students. This is one of the popular colleges for many international students https://www.swcc.edu/admissions_international.html	A small, private, Christian college, Southwestern offers Associate's degrees in Arts and Sciences and a Bachelor's degree program in Religious Studies. On-campus housing is available
St. Philip's College (San Antonio, Texas)	This college offers 150 academic programs for international students. International Student Services is in partnership with the West African Management Services (WAMS) and the Saudi Arabian Cultural Mission (SACM). This college hosts students from Africa, Asia, the Caribbean, Central America, Europe, South America, and the Middle East https://www.alamo.edu/spc/admissions/specific-populations/international-student-services/	The only college in the United States to be both an HBCU and a Hispanic Serving Institution, St. Philip's College is now one of the nation's top producers of minorities with associate's degrees in Mechanics and boasts the highest passing rate in Texas for the Licensed Vocational Nurses exam. St. Philips offers associate's degrees, professional certificates, and online classes

Source: Information related to international student admissions and programs were browsed from individual college's websites and the consortium of HBCUs (http://www.thehundred-seven.org/index.html). All current and updated information might not be available on the website.

Many historically Black community colleges offer a wide range of associate's degree and certificate programs and they are open to international students. For example, St. Philip's Community College that runs 150 academic programs has been an attractive destination for international students and this college offers a full range of services to international students including immigration, housing, transportation, and transfer to other institutions.

While some thriving Black community colleges have developed global understanding and communication as integral to their mission and expanded their partnerships and collaborations with other local and international agencies to expand their international footprints (see, Table 14.1), some small, private, and religious Black community colleges are shrinking their enrollments and are on the verge of collapse. For instance, Clinton College, affiliated with the African Methodist Episcopal (AME) Church Zion, is a historical Black college located in South Carolina that offers religious studies, liberal arts, and early childhood development. Such programs are not on the top priority or interests for international students, and Clinton College does not offer courses to international students as admission information is not available on its website. Similarly, Shorter College, located in Little Rock, Arkansas,

Global Begins from Local 219

is a private 2-year college established by the AME Church that offers limited associate's degrees in general studies, childhood development, church leadership and ministry, criminal justice, and entrepreneurial studies (with mandatory chapel services). This college also does not indicate whether they enroll international students to their academic programs. These small and religious Black community colleges encounter limited resources for their students and faculty members, and lack of support—culturally and economically, from trustees and presidents to expand study abroad opportunities or enrolling international students at their campuses. However, the Black community colleges also have great potential to serve the needs of international students, as some are. For example, Bishop State Community College and St. Philip's College have expanded their programs for both local and international students.

Why International Students and Internationalization are Important

Are Black community colleges the important destinations for international students? How do internationalization initiatives at Black community colleges support the mission and vision of these colleges? There is a greater need of developing a new mind-set toward international education that emphasizes holistic development of all students (Bista, 2019; Boggs & Irwin, 2007; Charles & Togunde, 2020). Many colleges have not seen the full potential of having international students on campus or integration of international students with domestic students, study abroad programs and exchange programs in which students get an opportunity to experience new languages and cultures (Bista, 2019). Charles and Togunde (2020) mentioned that some HBUCs have already started the mission-driven focus on internationalization, foreign language requirement, and international initiatives which might bring an institutional transformation after the COVID-19 pandemic. Because of the strong race, identity, and historical connection at historically Black community colleges, international students would gain novel experience while working and studying with their African-American counterparts. As an advocate for social justice, I am proposing such experiences that will help reduce stereotypes that are detrimental to Black students and minority students in general. In addition, the visiting students gain an important Afro-centric curriculum and perspective. As Mandishona (2018) mentioned, many international students "lack the knowledge of the history of slavery in the American South and the economic, legal, and social consequences it had on the Black community" (p. 3). Such knowledge helps them understand racism, sexism, xenophobia and social injustice globally.

Similar to their 4-year counterparts, community colleges have noticed a pressure to develop programs and initiatives that promote comprehensive internationalization which includes institutional commitment, development of curricula and learning outcomes, programs and resources for

220   *Krishna Bista*

student mobility, administrative structure and staffing, and local and international collaboration and partnerships. American Council on Education (2020) defines comprehensive internationalization as:

> a strategic, coordinated framework that integrates policies, programs, initiatives, and individuals to make colleges and universities more globally oriented and internationally connected. In order to foster sustainable and just global engagement, the comprehensive internationalization model embraces an organizational growth mindset. It frames internationalization as an ongoing process rather than a static goal. To that end, it recognizes that all constituents at a college or university—students, faculty, and staff—are learners and central to the institution's equitable, intercultural transformation. Intentional comprehensive internationalization is not an ancillary enterprise, but a means to advance an institution's distinct teaching-research-service mission. (para 1)

When these community colleges engage local values and institutional mission through internationalization, the entire campus community gets connected to the world. International student mobility or outward and inward mobility of student, faculty, staff, or exchange programs is just one component of the bigger picture of comprehensive internationalization. As ACE (2020) highlighted, comprehensive internationalization target areas include institutional commitment by its leaders for global engagement, support leadership and reporting structures, curriculum, and co-curriculum with critical element of internationalization, faculty and staff support for teaching and knowledge production, outward and inward physical mobility of students and faculty, and both internal and external partnerships and networks locally and globally.

The bigger goal behind this idea is to help students understand the interconnectedness of humankind and re-imagine togetherness to fight against challenging situations such as climate change, pandemic or social injustice globally. Deardorff (2020) asked us to think this way: What if we viewed ourselves through the lens of "we" given our interconnectedness? What if we viewed others through the lens of neighbor, both our local and global neighbors? This could shift our way of thinking about global citizenship and make it more real.... How do we behave toward our neighbors-locally and globally? What does it mean to be a "good neighbor?" Even more than that, how might the world be different if humans actually practiced loving their neighbors (and enemies) and putting others' needs as equal to their own? This "loving one's neighbor" goes far beyond greeting card sentiment. It is hard and sometimes even dangerous work, when such love means standing up for what's right, sacrificing for others' good, and even risking one's life, as in the case of healthcare workers today. (p. xvi)

Tribal Community Colleges: Historical Context, Mission, and Shifting Demographics

Currently, there are 32 fully accredited TCUs in the United States (US Department of Education, 2020). These colleges and universities offer 358 total programs that reflect Indigenous values and beliefs, mainly within the curriculum, including apprenticeships, diplomas, certificates, and degrees. Out of approximately 30,000 full-time and part-time students, 8.7 percent of American Indian and Alaska Native (AI/AN) college students attended these institutions in 2018/19. Diné College, originally named Navajo Community College, is the first tribally controlled college in the United States. The mission of tribal colleges is to preserve and honor tribal culture and to improve the educational, social, and economic development of their communities.

Tribal colleges are diverse in terms of student demographics as their nonnative enrollment consists of 29 percent and higher from other ethnic groups including international students. For instance, Bay Mills Community College, College of Menominee Nation, and Ilisagvik Colleges enrolled more than 50 percent nonnative enrollment. According to the Community College Survey of Student Engagement (CCSSE, 2019) indicated that 73 percent ($N=1,033$ students) from 25 tribal colleges reported that their college's focus on native language and culture improves their self image and confidence a lot or a moderate amount. On relationships with other students, 48 percent ($N=2,367$) of tribal college students reported that their college stresses their having support to thrive socially "quite a bit" or "very much."

List of Tribal Community Colleges and Universities

1 Iḷisaġvik College, Barrow, Alaska
2 Diné College, Tsaile, Arizona
3 Tohono O'odham Community College, Sells, Arizona
4 Haskell Indian Nations University, Lawrence, Kansas
5 Bay Mills Community College, Brimley, Michigan
6 Keweenaw Bay Ojibwa Community College, Baraga, Michigan
7 Saginaw Chippewa Tribal College, Mount Pleasant, Michigan
8 Fond du Lac Tribal and Community College, Cloquet, Minnesota
9 Leech Lake Tribal College, Cass Lake, Minnesota
10 Red Lake Nation College, Red Lake, Minnesota
11 White Earth Tribal and Community College, Mahnomen, Minnesota
12 Aaniiih Nakoda College, Harlem, Montana
13 Blackfeet Community College, Browning, Montana
14 Chief Dull Knife College, Lame Deer, Montana
15 Fort Peck Community College, Poplar, Montana
16 Little Big Horn College, Crow Agency, Montana
17 Salish Kootenai College, Pablo, Montana
18 Stone Child College, Box Elder, Montana

222 *Krishna Bista*

19 Little Priest Tribal College, Winnebago, Nebraska
20 Nebraska Indian Community College, Macy, Nebraska
21 Institute of American Indian Arts, Santa Fe, New Mexico
22 Navajo Technical University, Crownpoint, New Mexico
23 Southwestern Indian Polytechnic Institute, New Mexico
24 Cankdeska Cikana Community College, Fort Totten, North Dakota
25 Nueta Hidatsa Sahnish College, New Town, North Dakota
26 Sitting Bull College, Fort Yates, North Dakota
27 Turtle Mountain Community College, Belcourt, North Dakota
28 United Tribes Technical College, Bismarck, North Dakota
29 University of North Carolina at Pembroke, North Carolina
30 College of the Muscogee Nation, Okmulgee, Oklahoma
31 Pawnee Nation College, Pawnee, Oklahoma
32 Oglala Lakota College, Kyle, South Dakota
33 Sinte Gleska University, Mission, South Dakota
34 Sisseton Wahpeton College, Sisseton, South Dakota
35 Northwest Indian College, Bellingham, Washington
36 College of Menominee Nation, Keshena, Wisconsin
37 Lac Courte Oreilles Ojibwa Community College, Wisconsin
38 Wind River Tribal College, Ethete, Wyoming

Tribal community community colleges are often small with limited resources and do not take international students. For example, Fond du Lac Tribal and Community College no longer has the ability to issue student visas to any international student (Fond du Lac, 2020). Saginaw Chippewa Tribal College does not have any international students on its campus. Tribal colleges are limited with local, state, and federal funding and many of these colleges are shrinking their enrollment. As Nelson and Frye (2016) mentioned, "TCUs are perpetually underfunded through the federal Tribally Controlled Colleges and Universities Assistance Act of 1978; TCUs receive zero federal funding for nonnative students; TCUs are limited in their ability to increase tuition to fill revenue gaps because the majority of their students live in poverty and cannot afford to pay higher tuition costs and are less likely to take out student loans" (p. 2). Some Tribal colleges have expanded their programs to nonnative populations and international students to make the financial status stronger. For example, Ilisagvik College (46.64 percent), Bay Mills Community College (44.05 percent), College of Menominee Nation (41.01 percent), and Keweenaw Bay Ojibwa Community Colleges (32.36 percent) are the tribal colleges with highest nonnative enrollment. The COVID-19 pandemic has made the situation worse. Amour (2020) writes for the *Insider Higher Ed*:

> Tribal college students tend to be less traditional. They're often older (the average age is about 31), or parents, or low income. Funding from the CARES Act has helped some colleges support students, for now. The college has been providing fuel vouchers for those who

Global Begins from Local 223

have to come to the college, as well as food vouchers for groceries. It's also cutting checks to vendors for rent and utilities if students need it. (para 14)

These tribal community colleges are small in terms of program and enrollment and serve the isolated Indigenous communities with a mission to serve the local needs. Students and faculty members of these colleges are disconnected with institutional international programs in international education or exchange study opportunities to see the outside world (see, Table 14.2). In recent decades, student enrollment in these colleges has declined sharply whereas some colleges have merged their programs with other colleges. For instance, Lac Courte Oreilles Ojibwa Community

Table 14.2 Selected 2-Year Tribal Community Colleges and Online Information for International Students

Institutions	Information for International Students	College Information
Tohono O'odham Community College (TOCC), Sells, Arizona	This community college does not admit international students or offer study abroad programs or any international education-related activities although there are sponsored projects listed with the University of Arizona	This is a public tribal land-grant community college with 216 students (61 percent female; 39 percent male), 88 percent American Indian/Alaskan Native. TOCC offers associate degrees in liberal arts, business administration, science, and numerous certificates
Bay Mills Community College, Brimley, Michigan	BMCC does not admit international students or offer study abroad programs for its students. In collaboration with the Michigan Association of Collegiate Registrars and Admission Officers, BMCC students transfer education credits between public and private community colleges and universities in Michigan	This is a public tribal land-grant community college with approximately 500 students and 60 percent of them are Native American. BMCC offers associate of applied science (computer information, construction technology, administration, paramedic), associate of arts (education, social science), and associate of science degrees
Nebraska Indian Community College (NICC), Macy, Nebraska	No international program. Offer courses in carpentry, business, early childhood, human services, and Native American Studies with a focus on preserving and revitalizing the cultures of the Omaha and Santee people	Established in 1973, NICC is a public tribal land-grant community college with three locations in Nebraska: Macy, Santee, and South Sioux City. Currently, there are 95 students enrolled at NICC
College of the Muscogee Nation (CMN), Okmulgee, Oklahoma	No programs related to international education or international students or exchange programs for CMN students	Established in 2004, CMN is a public tribal college with 318 students; offers general education and Tribal-specific courses—associate degrees or certificates in programs that focus on needs or interests of the Muscogee Nation

(Continued)

224 *Krishna Bista*

Table 14.2 (Continued)

Institutions	Information for International Students	College Information
Northwest Indian College, Bellingham, Washington	No international education programs or resources exist for both students and faculty members. Offers both associate programs and four bachelor's degrees. College's primary focus is on recruiting Native American and First Nations (Canadian) students	This is a public tribal land-grant community college with 2,320 students. It was established by the Lummi Nation. Became a 4-year institution in 2008 offering programs in six sites
Cankdeska Cikana Community College, Fort Trotten, North Dakota	No international education programs or opportunities for students and faculty members	Started in 1970, this is a public tribal land-grant community college with 251 students
Lac Courte Oreilles Ojibwa Community College, Hayward, Wisconsin	No international programs or opportunities for its faculty and students. Offers 13 associate degree programs, technical diploma programs, certifications, and adult continuing education programs	Established in 1982, this is a public tribal land-grant community college with 201 students (148 Native, 53 nonnative) in its four locations

Source: Information and facts were collected from the website of these colleges. All information might not be available or updated as the time of web search.

College in Wisconsin student enrollment dropped from 575 students in 2007 to 313 in 2020 (Fall enrollment, 2020). The questions are: can the tribal college survive limiting itself to a local mission? Can international education promote local Indigenous knowledge and misrepresentations of minority and underrepresented populations? Why not expand the Indigenous knowledge curriculum and provide extracurricular activities for minority students who are working in today's complex workplace?

Local is the Beginning of the Global: International Students and Programs

Both historically Black community colleges and tribal colleges share distinctive characters in terms of their history, identity, and mission to serve an underrepresented minority population. This local authenticity and uniqueness is potential to translate into international collaborations and comprehensive internationalization initiatives for these community colleges. This unique characteristic is one of the main reasons why international students and scholars would choose these community colleges for further studies and professional growth. Many of today's historical Black colleges (and universities) are centers of attraction for international students and scholars because they can relate to their cultural identities or learn about minority cultures and traditions. Internationalization initiatives begin from the highlights of local attractions for the people and countries who never had such experiences before. Therein academic

Global Begins from Local 225

mobility of students and faculty brings a meaningful discourse on examining their assumptions and values, and reassessing skills to work globally. Indigenous worldviews and frames of references are equally important to explore global issues such as war, hunger, climate change (Makomenaw, 2012). Ideologically, both tribal community colleges and historically Black colleges are in such good positions to expand their programs and are unique to the entire world despite their limited resources at present. Although some of them have already advanced this potential, many of these community colleges—both tribal and Black, are still in their blind spots and not able to see the full potential on the horizon.

Institutional leaders of these community colleges must develop a new mind-set toward international programs and initiatives that support the entire campus community and globally engage their students and faculty members. Unlike four-year institutions, these community colleges are in a better position to expand international education and offer reach cross-cultural experience to their students because of low to free tuition, open access admission, career and workforce education, and minimum qualification for faculty hiring (Malveaux & Raby, 2019). To expand upon the local culture, indigenous values, and traditions of minorities globally, international education should be embedded with the college's mission, vision, and values statements. Boggs and Irwin (2007) write, "creating such an environment, however, is tempered and challenged by the reality of constricted attitudes, isolationist views, and lack of understanding that diversity and multiplicity are essential to surviving in the twenty-first century" (p. 25).

Moving Forward

The COVID-19 pandemic has given a greater lesson to the institutions of higher education when they moved their classes completely online, yet connecting with students and faculty globally. For smaller institutions with limited resources, it was a desperate harsh experience to go through the pandemic, considering the limited resources and technology. Meanwhile, modern technology has connected these institutional leaders and their students with other institutions and explored the best of the best resources to keep updated every day. With becoming borderless and out of choices, these colleges recognize a need to address the bigger challenges (e.g. health and safety crisis, global warming, food insecurity, war and refugees, and now pandemic) and how to work and engage with others in highly competitive environments.

The call for internationalization at community colleges began a long time ago (Raby & Valeau, 2007), although Black and Tribal community colleges have not fully developed the value of expanding resources and international initiatives for the greater good of the students. The presidents of these institutions and their worldviews are at the center of understanding and expanding international education, to make it an achievement instead of a matter of lip-service. At community colleges, Bissonette (2017) writes,

226 *Krishna Bista*

"preparing presidents to lead internationalization is the first step" (p. 60). In addition, the resources and expertise in specific knowledge areas, experiences, and skill-sets are equally important for the persons-in-charge of internationalization and international initiatives (Kumari, 2017). Given the resources and institutional priorities, both tribal community colleges and historically Black community colleges are in unique positions to leverage their existing localness (legacy, identity, and culture) to promote and expand global programs for both students and faculty members.

Acknowledgment:

The author would like to thank two experts: *Dr. Rosemary Gillett-Karam*, Associate Professor of Community College Leadership at Morgan State University, Maryland and former President of Louisburg College; *Dr. Rosalind Latiner Raby*, senior lecturer at California State University, Northridge and Director of California Colleges for International Education for their valuable suggestions and constructive feedback to the earlier draft of this chapter.

References

Amour, M. (2020, Oct 6). Innovating and adapting: Tribal colleges in the pandemic. https://www.insidehighered.com/news/2020/10/06/tribal-colleges-are-innovating-fall-will-still-need-long-term-support

Bishop State. (2020). Bishop State a glance. https://www.bishop.edu/about-us/bscc-at-a-glance

Bista, K. (2019). Touching the elephant: A holistic approach to understanding international student experiences. *Journal of International Students, 9*(4), i-v. https://doi.org/10.32674/jis.v9i4.1636

Bissonette, B. S. (2017). *What's happening with internationalization at community colleges?: Community college presidents' perceptions of internationalization actions, the desirability and feasibility of internationalization actions, and the importance of internationalization* (Order No. 10286396). Available from ProQuest Dissertations & Theses Global. (1935580063).

Boggs, G., & Irwin, J. (2007) What every community college leader needs to know: Building leadership for international education. *New Directions for Community Colleges, 138*, 25–30. DOI: 10.1002/cc.278

Bull, C. C., & Guillory, J. (2018). Revolution in higher education: Identity and cultural beliefs inspire tribal colleges & universities. *Daedalus, 147*(2), 95–105. DOI: 10.1162/DAED_a_00493

Carter, L. S. (2018). *Institutional advancement at historically Black community colleges: A multi-case study* (Order No. 10785768). Available from ProQuest Dissertations & Theses Global. (2033480223).

Charles, H., & Togunde, D. (2020). Historically black colleges and universities: A 2020 perspective. *International Educator.* https://www.nafsa.org/ie-magazine/2020/12/8/historically-black-colleges-and-universities-2020-perspective

Community College Survey of Student Engagement (2019). Preserving culture and planning for the future: An exploration of student experiences at tribal colleges https://cccse.org/sites/default/files/Tribal_Colleges.pdf

Global Begins from Local 227

Deardorff, D. K. (2020). (Re)learning to live together in 2020. *Journal of International Students*, 10(4), xv-xiii. https://doi.org/10.32674/jis.v10i4.3169

Elliott, K. C., Warshaw, J. B., deGregory, C. A. (2019). Historically Black community colleges: A descriptive profile and call for context-based future research. *Community College Journal of Research and Practice, 43*(10), 770-784. https://doi.org/10.1080/10668926.2019.1600612

Fond du Lac (2020). International students. https://fdltcc.edu/admissions/apply-here/international-students/

Fall enrollment history (2020). Lac Courte Oreilles Ojibwa community college. https://43e25334-378a-4f98-bcac-23aae7f80efb.filesusr.com/ugd/b47198_8ed5d705628c44ea98d7cdce34318a77.pdf

Gasman, G. (2007). *Envisioning Black colleges: A history of the United Negro College Fund.* Johns Hopkins University Press.

Gasman, G., & Commodore, F. (2014). *Opportunities and challenges at historically black colleges and universities.* Palgrave Press.

Kumari, S. (2017). *Leadership in higher education: Role of persons-in-charge of internationalization efforts in community colleges* (Order No. 10262732). Available from ProQuest Dissertations & Theses Global. (1891348920).

Mandishona, T. C. (2018). *Consciously becoming Black: A phenomenological exploration of black sub-Saharan African international students' racial identity development at historically Black colleges and universities in the American South* (Order No. 10786771). Available from ProQuest Central; ProQuest Dissertations & Theses Global. (2038866080).

Makomenaw, M. V. A. (2012) Welcome to a new world: Experiences of American Indian tribal college and university transfer students at predominantly white institutions. *International Journal of Qualitative Studies in Education, 25*(7), 855–866. https://doi.org/10.1080/09518398.2012.720732

Malveaux, G. F., & Raby, R. L. (2019). *Study abroad opportunities for community college students and strategies for global learning.* IGI Global.

Nelson, C. A., & Frye, J. R. (2016). Tribal college and university funding. https://www.acenet.edu/Documents/Tribal-College-and-University-Funding.pdf

Raby, R., & Valeau, E. (2007) Community college international education: Looking back to forecast the future. *New Directions for Community Colleges, 138,* 5–14. DOI: 10.1002/cc.276

U.S. Department of Education. (2020). Tribal colleges and universities https://sites.ed.gov/whiaiane/tribes-tcus/tribal-colleges-and-universities/

Author Bios

Krishna Bista, EdD, is a Professor of Higher Education in the Department of Advanced Studies, Leadership and Policy at Morgan State University, Maryland. Dr. Bista is founding editor of the *Journal of International Students*, a quarterly publication in international education. He is also founding chair of the Study Abroad and International Students SIG at the Comparative and International Education Society. His latest books are *Inequalities in Study Abroad and Student Mobility*, w/Kommers, (Routledge, 2021), *Higher Education in Nepal*, w/Sharma and Raby (Routledge, 2020), and *Global Perspectives on International Experiences in Higher Education* (Routledge, 2019).

15 Epilogue

Voices and Perspectives on International Student Mobility: Where Are Community Colleges?

Krishna Bista and Gregory F. Malveaux

Introduction

The book also highlights issues related to international programs and student-faculty expertise and experiences in teaching, as well as study abroad research opportunities at community colleges. Our contributors, comprised of international student advisers, Principal Designated School Officials (PDSOs), International Education Directors, Study Abroad Coordinators, advising administrators and faculty, businesspeople, and graduate students in the field, examine a wide range of challenges, patterns of mobility, and successes of international students at US community colleges so that one can better understand how to serve these students; and to advise faculty, staff, administrators, and the community.

While finishing up this book, there have been some major changes in the United States and globally which might alter the landscape of international higher education, particularly for community colleges:

a Around 2,103,664 lives were lost worldwide from the coronavirus COVID-19 outbreak as of January 22, 2021. In the United States, an American died every 19 seconds on Jan. 12—the only time the rate fell below 20 seconds; and 400,000 lives were lost in the United States alone (Maxouris & Hanna, 2021).

b It has been more than a year since COVID-19 started in December of 2019. With the pandemic came mandated nationwide closures in which 1,500 million students did not attend school, face to face; this represents almost 90 percent of the world student population (UNESCO, 2020). There are limited travels and flights available; many cities and countries have used restrictive measures to slow the spread of the virus. Like their counterparts, international students at home and abroad, both at community colleges and four-year universities, are taking classes online or remotely. Study abroad and exchange programs are postponed or highly discouraged by the leaders of institutions and the governments. Like their four-year

Epilogue 229

counterparts, community colleges extended remote learning and services through summer 2021, citing high COVID-19 infection rates in the United States (*Inside Higher Ed*, 2021).

c American democratic values, safety and securities of citizens, and prestige in higher education were questioned during Donald Trump's presidency. Protests on January 6, 2021, on the US Capitol Hill, gave amazement and alarm to the world, including American allies, international students, and everyone in the country (Marcus, 2021). Several presidents of community colleges and universities put out statements criticizing the January 6 violence at the US Capitol (Burke, 2021).

d Joseph R. Biden became the 46th president of the United States on January 20, 2021. Fisher (2021) writes, "he is setting a clear tone from Day One, of openness and global engagement, still, attitude and action are different things, and there is no guarantee about what comes next."

e The Biden Administration Immigration Portal has issued new policies related to international students and immigration. New international students who arrive from abroad and begin F-1 or J-1 status are required to have one in-person class to meet their immigration status and many other updates that apply to international students both at community colleges and four-year institutions (NAFSA, 2021). This requires institutions to make hybrids or remote instructions for their students during the pandemic.

f New international enrollments decreased by 43 percent in the United States because of COVID-19; and particularly at community colleges, there is a sharp decline (Redden, 2020a). One in five international students was studying online from outside the United States. There was also a sharp decline in the visa rate for international students at all educational levels, including international students attending K-12 schools (Redden, 2020b).

g In the United Kingdom, the Brexit deal made students eligible for the Erasmus program, the continent's flagship student exchange program that offered grants to more than four million students on international education (Redden, 2021).

h The Biden-Harris Plan is to increase access to community colleges, making them free (Dickler, 2021; Weissman, 2020), which will attract more international students.

Are these local and international socio-political events changing student mobility patterns in community colleges? Does it create a different level of attractiveness and appeal for students who are considering American community colleges from overseas? Will the leaders of community colleges act differently to increase the presence of international students or exchange programs for domestic students? Considering the

230 *Krishna Bista and Gregory F. Malveaux*

unprecedented impact of COVID-19, are community colleges putting "international initiatives" on their institutional strategic priorities? Will the multi-billion dollar industry of international education die out after the pandemic? Are these institutions prepared to host new international students? How do colleges help support international student health and wellbeing in 2021 and beyond? There are certainly many questions and assumptions among educators and researchers. The pandemic and world politics has certainly changed the perceptions of people, particularly educators in the institutions of higher education. There might be drastic changes, yet one sure thing is that there will be a boom in international education after the pandemic, and colleges and universities are likely to restructure their institutions' needs and international engagements. Community colleges with a larger enrollment, and with some existing programs and resources for international students and study abroad students, will once again be on the rise as they continue expanding their programs and needs. Small institutions with limited resources and already low enrollment are on the verge of collapse and may merge with another institution.

There are also emerging issues and challenges seen in American community colleges related to immigration, admissions, and programs for international students. For example, Western Iowa Tech Community College made this headline in the newspapers:

> International students at Western Iowa Tech Community College sued the institution, alleging they came to the U.S. with promises of scholarships and professional internships only to be coerced into menial jobs with long hours and low pay. A group of students from Brazil and Chile sued Western Iowa Tech Community College in federal district court this week alleging that the college coerced them to work in food processing and packaging jobs under threat of deportation. The 11 students all participated in an exchange program under the J-1 student visa program. The lawsuit, filed in U.S. District Court for the Northern District of Iowa, relates that the students were led to believe they'd be enrolling in a two-year program in which they would study at Western Iowa Tech and participate in internships relating to their field of study, working no more than 32 hours a week.
>
> (*Inside Higher Ed*, January 13, 2021)

Bright Aspect of Community Colleges for International Student Mobility

Despite the pandemic, geopolitical, tensions and global debates, there is always "light at the end of the tunnel." American community colleges have the potential for expanding their current and future

Epilogue 231

international programs for domestic and international students. Of 1,462 community colleges, there are several institutions with the largest international student enrollment including Houston Community College System (4,923); Lone Star College System (3,097); Santa Monica College (2,714); and De Anza College (2,352). The following community colleges include between 1,000 and 1,500 international students: Montgomery College, Valencia College, Northern Virginia Community College, Orange Coast College, Green River College, Miami-Dade College, Edmonds Community College, Seattle Central College, Foothill College, Bellevue College, and San Mateo County Community College.

According to the Institute of International Education (IIE), around 94,562 international students studied at American community colleges during the 2017–2018 academic year, which decreased to 79,187 in 2019/2020 (Open Doors, 2020). In 2019/2020, 127 international students were studying at two-year historically Black community colleges in the United States. The top three two-year historically Black community colleges hosting international students in 2019/2020 were Gadsden State Community College, Bishop State Community College, and Shelton State Community College. There were nine international students who studied at Tribal College and Universities in 2019/2020. The top four states hosting international students at community colleges were California (22,825), Texas (13,291), Washington (8,849), and Florida (6,082). The most popular fields of study for international students were science, technology, engineering, mathematics (STEM) majors; Liberal Arts or General Studies; and Business and Management.

Many American community colleges have expanded their agreements and exchange programs such as the 2+2 pathway for international students to pursue further education in the United States. Community college leaders, along with their membership consortiums, are looking to overseas four-year institutions to increase international student transfer, among other things. For example, the Maryland Community College International Education Consortium (MCCIEC), which houses 16 of the state's community colleges, created a 2+2 program with Swansea University in South Wales, as an opportunity to expand its students' global education, increase international outreach, and improve international student exchange (Malveaux, 2019). With such partnerships, community college and overseas four-year institutions work together to ensure all of the courses they offer complement each other for an overall, comprehensive degree program; and the seamless transition process ensures students, including international students, do not waste any time or money on classes that will not be a good fit for their final goals (Chen, 2017).

In addition, according to Baer and Martel (2020), at least 44 percent of US institutions cite that they are actively recruiting international students at community colleges. Study abroad serves as a natural

232   *Krishna Bista and Gregory F. Malveaux*

recruitment tool for the community colleges that utilize it. The primary reason why community colleges are so successful is because the student population, and those who study abroad, reflect local multi-racial/ethnic or racial/ethnic homogenous communities. Diversity begets internationalization. Community colleges draw international students with their extensive populations of racial, ethnic, gender, and minoritized groups; and these institutions have a history of sending more students of color abroad than any higher education institutional sector (Raby, 2019). Through study abroad, community colleges unveil their diversity to the world and, in turn, draw international populations to their home communities. Again, when the student population represents a homogeneous profile, the study abroad population will also then represent the same profile, which then increases diversity for the education abroad field, assuming the profile includes a preponderance of or significant percentage of students of color (Raby, 2019); and in turn, those students engage people of color from around the world to their campus.

Book Themes and Findings

At the backdrop of this book, there is a deep understanding of the very natural and valuable partnership that has come to exist between international students and US community colleges. The book is logically organized into three sections—Part I: Reimagining International Student Mobility in Community Colleges; Part II: Understanding Support Systems and Challenges of International Students at Community Colleges; and Part III: Promoting Diversity and International Education at Community Colleges.

The first section, Part I: Reimagining International Student Mobility in Community Colleges, contains the following chapters—Chapter 1: Reimagining International Student Mobility in American Community Colleges, Chapter 2: Community College International Student Research: A Critical Time Series Analysis, Chapter 3: Characteristics and patterns of International Students at Community Colleges: Lessons from the Open Doors Data, Chapter 4: International Students at Canadian Community Colleges: Origins, Evolution, and Current Trends, and Chapter 5: Community College Finances and International Student Enrollment.

This first chapter of the book, Chapter 1: Reimagining International Student Mobility in American Community Colleges, written by the editors, Gregory Malveaux and Krishna Bista, presents findings that US community colleges are an immense draw for international students. Large numbers of these students have enrolled due to the low-cost, workforce-based college instruction at these institutions that prepare nontraditional students—students of color, veterans, international students, low socio-economic status students, parent-students, and more—with essential higher education and workforce development background to thrive in the US and global economy. In addition, the chapter reveals how international students have brought enormous benefits, including campus diversity, internationalization initiates, and national revenues, to American community colleges and the entire country.

With Chapter 2: Community College International Student Research: A Critical Time Series Analysis, Rosalind Latiner Raby examines publications that have helped to define the impact and reach of international students at US community colleges. The chapter uses a critical discourse and time series analysis to capture patterns in publications over time in the study of community college international students by considering 305 forms of scholarship published from 1950 to 2020. Critical discourse analysis is used to see how publications influence what and whose scholarship matters, what narratives are found in the publications and whose voices are missing, and if the publications support or counter dominant knowledge dissemination. Chapter findings show that publications on community college international students have existed for multiple decades and yet, are marginalized in the field.

In Chapter 3: Characteristics and patterns of International Students at Community Colleges: Lessons from the Open Doors Data, Julie Baer pulls from data ascertained by Open Doors®, highlighting the patterns and characteristics of international student mobility to community colleges over the past 50 years. Also, the chapter provides statistical insights on the profile of international students at community colleges compared to national trends, such as international students' gender, marital status, place of origin, enrollment status, primary funding source, and field of study. Baer concludes with how COVID-19 has impacted international student mobility in the United States based on IIE's Fall 2020 International Student Enrollment Snapshot.

International students' interest to take part in the community college educational model has been a global phenomenon. Chapter 4: International Students at Canadian Community Colleges: Origins, Evolution, and Current Trends, by Oleg Legusov and Hayfa Jafar, reveals this occurrence by examining historical and emerging trends involving international students at Canadian community colleges. Chapter findings show that the provinces' cultural differences and immigration policies significantly affect the number of international students on college campuses. In addition, the study explores new approaches used to increase the market share of international students, such as campuses exclusively for international students and partnerships with private career colleges.

With the major move of international students to community colleges, Ji Yeon Bae and Manuel S. González Canché scrutinize whether real financial benefit results from these students' enrollment in Chapter 5:

234 *Krishna Bista and Gregory F. Malveaux*

Community College Finances and International Student Enrollment. Institutional-level and county-level data on community colleges and panel regression techniques to examine the relationship between international student enrollment and institutional finances are provided. Findings show that although a subset of institutions have enrolled a high number of foreign students, the sector as a whole still retains its local nature, as evidenced in the weak relationships between the number of international students and institutional finances.

The second section of the book, Part II: Understanding Support Systems and Challenges of International Students at Community Colleges, contains the following chapters—Chapter 6: International Students' Career Development and Preparation at the American Community College, Chapter 7: Barriers and Promoting Factors in Hispanic English as a Second Language (ESL) Students' Successful Transition to English Language Learning from Home Countries to US Community Colleges, Chapter 8: Assessing Acculturative Stress of International Students at a US Community College, and Chapter 9: Frontline Advising for International Students at American Community Colleges: Understanding the Challenges and Policy Issues during the COVID-19 Crisis.

Community colleges have had strong support systems in place to aid international student workforce development and job training. In Chapter 6: International Students' Career Development and Preparation at the American Community College, Hannah Rapp, Ran Liu, Wi-jung Wu, and Xiaoli Jing study the career expectations and aspirations of international students attending US community colleges, common challenges during their career preparations, and the effectiveness of on-campus career services provided by community colleges; in addition, the chapter concludes with recommendations for how community colleges may better support international student career development needs.

Language deficiency is another major obstacle for many international students navigating through community college course curriculum with English being their second or third language. DuEwa Frazier's Chapter 7: Barriers and Promoting Factors in Hispanic ESL Students' Successful Transition to English Language Learning from Home Countries to US Community Colleges, illuminates the successful English language transition of Latinx ESL students who matriculated to college English at three community colleges in the Northeastern and Mid-Atlantic regions of the United States. Three themes emerged as influencing factors on their matriculation to college English: student engagement in active learning, students' motivation to learn English, and faculty communication that guides English language learning. Students reported on their motivation to learn English. Students also discussed the faculty communication and instructional strategies that helped them persist in completing English coursework.

Epilogue 235

The research of Hardaye R. Hansen, Yuliya Shneyderman, Gloria S. McNamara, and Lisa Grace in Chapter 8: Assessing Acculturative Stress of International Students at a US Community College shows that international college students experience high levels of acculturative stress, which can adversely impact their health and college success. This cross-sectional study examined community college international students, in particular. Immersion in a student's native culture was positively associated with acculturative stress, while immersion in the US culture was negatively associated with acculturative stress. The results of the study imply that some international students may require more support in order to succeed in their college environment.

Access and equity into the US higher education system, including community colleges, is a true hurdle for international students. In Chapter 9: Frontline Advising for International Students at American Community Colleges: Understanding the Challenges and Policy Issues during the COVID-19 Crisis, Gregory Malveaux and Marlon Vallejo examine hindrances placed on international students at community colleges, mainly fueled by US government policies and COVID-19 pandemic restrictions. Some noted restrictions are DACA stoppage, student visa filing slowdown, a technological and time zone divide, and exclusion from federal relief funds for students during the COVID-19 crisis period. These findings are aimed to assist international student counselors, including the PDSO, International Education Directors, Study Abroad Coordinators, and faculty, with remaining compliant with US government policies, and to provide proper advising for F-1 visa holders and other international student groups.

The third section of the book, Part III: Promoting Diversity and International Education at Community Colleges, includes the following chapters—Chapter 10: Community College as a Pathway to Baccalaureate Success for International Students, Chapter 11: From Oppression to Global Social Justice: Practitioners' Responsibility to International Students in the US Community College, Chapter 12: International Education and the Global Pandemic in the Community College: Reflections and Best Practices, and Chapter 13: International Students in Canadian Colleges: A Critical Analysis of Internationalization Strategy Discourses.

It is well known that four-year institutions actively pursue international students from community colleges. Top universities recruit international students from community colleges because of their proven academic performance in college-level courses, English speaking and comprehension skills, and knowledge of how American school systems work (Gobel, 2012). With Chapter 10: Community College as a Pathway to Baccalaureate Success for International Students, Elizabeth S. Park and Veronika Rozhenkova study how students from community colleges, upon enrollment in four-year institutions, become a part of

236 *Krishna Bista and Gregory F. Malveaux*

the campuses' international student population and are frequently not being recognized as a potentially different subgroup of students with their own academic characteristics, challenges, and needs. The chapter also identifies the need for additional institutional support services and transfer assistance for baccalaureate success.

In Chapter 11: From Oppression to Global Social Justice: Practitioners' Responsibility to International Students in the US Community College, Tiffany Viggiano, Evelyn Vázquez, and Ariadna I. López Damián articulate rhetorical roots of oppressive conditions experienced by community college international students in the United States. Through a revisit of a previously published work, The Others: Equitable Access, International Students, and the Community College, the authors demonstrate that the pattern of paradoxical and transactional arguments recently observed on the national stage is not new, but rooted in institutional culture. In addition, they assert that current global contexts and nascent critical international literature cast a new light on their previous conceptualization of practitioners' rationales for the enrollment of international students on their campuses.

Marc Thomas's Chapter 12: International Education and the Global Pandemic in the Community College: Reflections and Best Practices, wholly addresses the impacts of COVID-19 on community college international students, while chronicling the institutions' reactions to the pandemic in 2020. Instructional and student support lessons for future best practices are also provided.

Chapter 13: International Students in Canadian Colleges: A Critical Analysis of Internationalization Strategy Discourses, written by Elizabeth Buckner, Sarah Morales, Taiya Brown, and Scott Clerk, assesses trends in international student enrollments in the Canadian community college sector over the past decade. Three major trends are brought forth: (1) the unprecedented growth of international student enrollments in the college sector; (2) an increasing proportion of international college students from India; and, (3) a high concentration of international college students in only two provinces, namely Ontario and British Columbia. In addition, the chapter provides an overview of the Canadian community college sector and its longstanding mandate of training students for local labor markets, as well as how federal, provincial, and institutional authorities have all supported increasing international student enrollments for primarily economic rationales.

Finally, in Chapter 14: Global Begins from Local: International Students and International Programs at Historically Black Community Colleges and Tribal Community Colleges, Krishna Bista offers an overview of international students and international education programs and initiatives at historically Black community colleges and tribal community colleges in the United States. Building on their unique historical identities, heritage, and indigenous values of these institutions, he argues

Epilogue 237

that local is the beginning of global initiatives and draws some examples of exemplary community colleges that can be role models for other institutions.

Future of International Students at Community Colleges

The importance of international education at American community colleges has been increasingly acknowledged in recent years as a foundation to "ensure a civil society in a nation of rapidly changing demographics, to transform everyday Americans into competent global citizens who can successfully navigate an increasingly interconnected world, and to provide American businesses with a globally competent—as well as globally competitive—workforce that can ensure the nation's future economic prosperity" (p. 1). International students and foreign investments have the potential to leverage the economic development of the rural areas and their community colleges as the rural areas experienced the largest growth of immigrant populations (AACC, 2020). For example, there are at least 26.8 million US immigrants who are 16 years or older. In the United States, the largest percentage of international students (19 percent of them are from China alone) are enrolled at community colleges, and California is the most popular destination for all international students.

There are certainly new challenges for American community colleges to strengthen international programs and campus internationalizations, during and post-COVID, due to the greater economic impact of closed campuses that forced remote teaching and learning. Therein meanwhile, these institutions, similar to their four-year counterparts, have learned about the technological transformation and positive potential of distance and virtual learning. More than ever, community college officials are eager to explore and establish new exchange programs, international collaborations, and international student recruitment. International student enrollment is a multi-billion-dollar industry that brings a number of positive changes in socio-cultural diversity by enriching classroom practices, bilateral research, and publications. As editors of this book project, we strongly believe that American community colleges are very promising destinations for international students. These colleges are also rapidly expanding their overseas exchange programs for domestic students to study overseas. Once we are at the post-pandemic period, student mobility will be revived with an exceptional growth of two-way traffic with students leaving for study abroad and international students entering into American community colleges. Internationalization and international initiatives will remain integral to American community colleges and international students will aggressively transcend geographical boundaries to expand their professional fields. We are optimistic that community college senior leadership will

238 *Krishna Bista and Gregory F. Malveaux*

put international students and study abroad programs as their top priority; develop systematic recruiting plans in partnership with local and international four-year institutions; support services and resources for both domestic and international students; develop and globalize curriculum; and create campus internationalization strategies for inclusive campus communities.

References

American Association of Community Colleges [AACC]. (2020). The importance of global education. https://www.aacc.nche.edu/wp-content/uploads/2020/01/Importance-of-Global_Education_2020.pdf

Baer, J., & Martel, M. (2020). *Fall 2020 international student enrollment snapshot*. https://www.iie.org/en/Research-and-Insights/Publications/Fall-2020-International-Student-Enrollment-Snapshot

Burke, L. (2021, Jan 8). Pushback at community colleges. *Inside Higher Ed.* https://www.insidehighered.com/news/2021/01/18/california-community-college-leaders-face-aggressive-responses-capitol-statements

Chen, G. (2017, May 17). 2+2 programs going strong at community colleges nationwide. Community College Review Blog. Retrieved from: www. communitycollegereview. com/blog/2-2-programs-goingstrong-at-community-colleges-nationwide

Dickler, J. (2021, Jan 18). Free college could become a reality under a Biden administration. *CNBC news*. https://www.cnbc.com/2021/01/18/biden-administration-free-college.html

Fisher, K. (2021, Jan 25). What next edition. Latitude(s): What matters in global education and why? https://www.getrevue.co/profile/latitudes/issues/what-next-edition-308885?utm_campaign=Issue&utm_content=view_in_browser&utm_medium=email&utm_source=latitude%28s%29

FSU Immigration Updates. (2021, Jan 21). Florida State University Center for Global Engagement. https://cge.fsu.edu/immigration-updates-for-fsu-international-students

Gobel, R. (2012, October 4). Why international students should consider community colleges. https://www.usnews.com/education/best-colleges/articles/2012/10/04/why-international-students-should-consider-community-colleges

Inside Higher Ed. (2021, Jan 22). Latest news on Coronavirus and higher education. https://www.insidehighered.com/news/2021/01/22/live-updates-latest-news-coronavirus-and-higher-education

Malveaux, G. (2019). How to survive and thrive as a community college consortium. In G. Malveaux & L. R. Raby (Eds.), *Study abroad opportunities for community college students and strategies for global learning* (pp. 265–283). IGI-Global.

Marcus, J. (2021, Jan 10). What the Capitol riot means for US foreign policy. *BBC*. https://www.bbc.com/news/world-us-canada-55585546

Maxouris, C., & Hanna, J. (2021, Jan 20). US surpasses 400,000 deaths from Covid-19. *CNN*. https://www.cnn.com/2021/01/19/health/us-coronavirus-tuesday/index.html

NAFSA. (2021, Jan 22). Biden administration immigration portal. https://www.nafsa.org/regulatory-information/biden-administration-immigration-portal

Open Doors. (2020). Home—annual release. *Institute of International Education.* http://opendoorsiie.wpengine.com/annual-release/

Redden, E. (2021, January 13). Foreign students allege forced labor, trafficking at college. *Inside Higher Ed.* https://www.insidehighered.com/news/2021/01/13/international-students-accuse-western-iowa-tech-community-college-forced-labor

Raby, R. (2019). Changing the conversation: measures that contribute to community college education abroad success. In G. Malveaux & L. R. Raby (Eds.), *Study abroad opportunities for community college students and strategies for global learning* (pp. 1–21). IGI-Global.

Redden, E. (2020a, Nov 16). New international enrollments fall 43%. https://www.insidehighered.com/admissions/article/2020/11/16/international-enrollments-drop-16-percent

Redden, E. (2020b, Nov 18). U.S. visa data show 21% decline in international students. https://www.insidehighered.com/quicktakes/2020/11/18/us-visa-data-show-21-decline-international-students

Redden, E. (2021, Jan 5). Mourning Erasmus. *Inside Higher Ed.* https://www.insidehighered.com/news/2021/01/05/uk-exits-student-exchange-program-brexit-deal-will-continue-participate-eu-wide

UNESCO. (2020, March). COVID-19 educational disruption and response. *UNESCO Institute for Statistics data.* https://en.unesco.org/covid19/educationresponse

Weissman, S. (2020, Dec 16). What a Biden administration could mean for community colleges. *Diverse.* https://diverseeducation.com/article/198654/

Author Bios

Gregory F. Malveaux, PhD, is a Professor in the Department of English and Literature and has been the College-wide Coordinator of Study Abroad and International Education at Montgomery College, Maryland. His previous books include: *Study Abroad Opportunities for Community College Students and Strategies for Global Learning,* w/Raby (IGI Global, 2019); and *Look Before Leaping: Risks, Liabilities, and Repair of Study Abroad in Higher Education* (Rowman & Littlefield, 2016).

Krishna Bista, EdD, is a Professor of Higher Education in the Department of Advanced Studies, Leadership and Policy at Morgan State University, Maryland. Dr. Bista is the founding editor of the Journal of International Students, a quarterly publication in international education. He is also the founding chair of the Study Abroad and International Students SIG at the Comparative and International Education Society. His latest books are *The Experiences of International Faculty in Institutions of Higher Education,* w/Glass and Xi Lin (Rutledge, 2022), *Online Teaching and Learning in Higher Education during COVID-19,* w/Chan and Allen (Rutledge, 2022), *Inequalities in Study Abroad and Student Mobility,* w/Kommers (Rutledge, 2021), *Higher Education in Nepal,* w/Sharma and Raby (Rutledge, 2020), and *Global Perspectives on International Experiences in Higher Education* (Rutledge, 2019).

Index

academic backgrounds, 91
academic environment, 106, 136, 159, 161
academic programs, 3, 5, 9, 136, 218
acculturative process, 95, 120, 128
acculturative stress, 12, 118, 119, 121, 123, 125, 127, 129, 131, 234, 235
adjustment, 24, 92, 102, 120, 129, 130, 158, 171, 172
administrators, 1–3, 6, 7, 10, 36, 118, 121, 136, 137, 141, 144–146, 148, 193, 210, 228
advising, 12, 133–135, 137, 139, 141, 143, 145, 147, 149, 151, 170, 171, 234, 235
advocacy, 24, 26, 53, 146, 148, 171
African American, 6, 216
Altbach, 55, 66, 68
American Association of Community Colleges, 6, 12, 21, 76, 82, 178, 238
American Community Colleges, 3, 11, 12, 133, 232, 234, 235
American higher education, 5, 67, 90, 99, 151, 216
Anderson, 134, 148
anxiety, 117, 119, 141, 158, 198
Asian, 8, 92, 97, 101, 103, 120, 124, 126, 130, 161, 162, 180, 198, 201, 209
associate degree, 17, 42, 91, 159, 224
Ayers, 20, 28, 32

Baccalaureate, 12, 155, 235
Bégin-Caouette, 63, 66, 203, 212
belonging, 34, 100, 101, 160, 169
Bishop State Community, 4, 215–217, 219, 231

Bista, 3–10, 12–14, 17, 18, 20, 198, 201, 215, 216, 218–220, 222, 224, 226–228, 230, 232, 234, 236, 238, 239
Black, 4, 7, 13, 16, 161, 162, 215–219, 224–227, 231, 236
Black community colleges, 215, 216, 218, 219, 224, 226, 231, 236
Blackboard, 4, 190
Brandom, 98, 100
Broward College, 3, 6, 41
Bunker Hill Community, 41
Burnett, 29, 33

California, 4, 5, 9, 11, 23, 33–36, 40, 73, 78, 82, 90, 91, 95, 102, 136, 137, 141, 155, 156, 161, 172, 184, 186, 191, 226, 231, 237
campus resources, 148
Canadian Community Colleges, 11, 12, 55, 56, 57, 59, 61, 63, 65, 67, 69, 203, 207, 232, 233
Cantwell, 72, 74, 78, 83
career counseling, 94, 95, 98, 100
career decisions, 93, 95, 98, 101
career development, 18, 89, 90, 91, 92, 95, 96, 97, 98, 99, 100, 101, 102, 103
career development professionals, 98
career developmental stages, 96
career outcomes, 89, 96, 97
career preparations, 99, 234
career services, 94
cartography, 16, 17, 18, 20, 24, 26
cartography themes, 26
challenges, 2–5, 9, 12, 18, 20, 87, 91, 94, 133, 139, 189, 193, 232, 234, 235

Index 241

Chen, 22, 29, 33, 58, 66, 158, 172, 231, 238
Cheng-Levine, 3, 21, 135, 136, 139, 140, 141, 143, 144, 146, 147, 148
China, 5, 11, 29, 43, 44, 45, 49, 61, 62, 63, 90, 103, 119, 141, 156, 159, 180, 189, 190, 191, 194, 205, 207, 237
Chinese international student, 96
City College of San, 21, 41
Coahoma Community College, 4, 215, 217
cognitive changes, 158
college policies and practices, 89
college support 3, 25, 27
communication, 111, 132, 172, 193
Community College Journal, 13, 20, 21, 32, 34, 35, 66, 67, 68, 83, 84, 100, 101, 171, 183, 212, 227
community college publications, 30
Community College Review, 21, 36, 69, 85, 103, 117, 238
community college students, 5, 31–33, 37, 38, 44, 47, 48, 55, 56, 67, 76, 96, 101, 104, 115–117, 126, 131, 142, 143, 149, 159, 160, 172, 198, 238, 239
comparative 25, 27
Comparative Education, 17, 31, 35, 103, 172, 185, 214
Consumer Price Index, 77
Copeland, 22, 28, 33
coronavirus, 7, 12, 98, 101, 102, 149, 150, 185, 191, 195, 200, 201, 228, 238
Coronavirus Aid, Relief, & Economical Security (CARES), 142
COVID-19, 2, 4, 7, 8, 10, 12, 19, 30, 50, 51, 53, 58, 64, 65, 67, 82, 97, 101, 104, 133, 135–151, 178, 179, 181, 185, 187–189, 191, 195, 197, 200–202, 205, 210, 213, 219, 222, 225, 228–230, 233–236, 239
COVID-19 restrictions, 137, 141, 148
Creswell, 17, 33, 106, 109, 116
cultural norms, 99
culturally relevant activities, 98
culture, 29, 34, 64, 69, 92, 95, 118–122, 126–128, 136, 149, 158, 171, 173, 175, 181, 182, 184, 185, 197, 200, 221, 225, 226, 235, 236
culture barriers, 92
Curricular Practical Training, 93, 194

DACA, 7, 8, 133, 136–138, 142, 148–150, 235
data collection, 17, 54, 109
De Anza College, 41, 231
Deferred Action for Childhood Arrivals, 7, 74, 143
Delta Cost Project, 74, 83
Denmark Technical College, 4, 215, 217
Department of Homeland Security, 93, 100, 144
digital divide, 140
discourse, 19, 16, 31, 32, 33, 35, 36, 155, 173, 174, 225, 233
discrimination, 29, 84, 99, 158, 169, 174, 179, 180
dissertations, 15, 17, 20, 30, 31
diversity, 3, 8, 10, 11, 12, 19, 57, 63, 67, 69, 84, 92, 95, 96, 134, 136, 157, 161, 167, 170, 174, 212, 225, 232, 233, 237
domestic applicants, 94
Durrani, 91, 93, 100, 159, 170

Egyptian student, 138
Elsner, 22, 26, 30, 33
emerging market countries, 156
employer biases, 91, 94, 99
employment authorization, 157
English, 3, 4, 6, 7, 10, 12, 13, 17, 39, 42, 49, 54, 55, 62, 63, 90–92, 102, 104–117, 119, 123–128, 130, 145, 151, 159, 170, 186, 209, 234, 235, 239
enrollment, 3–7, 9–13, 19, 33, 37, 38, 52, 71, 72, 74–79, 81, 82, 84, 85, 104, 107, 117, 121, 133, 135–138, 147, 148, 156, 161, 171, 174, 203, 206, 221–224, 227, 230, 233–237
entrepreneurial ambitions, 90
ESL students, 12, 104, 105, 107, 109, 111, 113, 115, 117, 234
Everett Community College, 140, 141, 189
exchange programs, 3, 7–9, 11, 219, 220, 223, 228, 229, 231, 237

F-1 students, 137, 144, 145, 172
faculty members, 2, 9, 160, 193, 219, 223–226
federal financial aid, 143, 157
female international students, 96
film industry, 90

242 *Index*

financial influence, 5
first- generation college students, 169
Fischer, 7, 8, 12
Fisher, 55, 66, 229, 238
food insecurity, 225
foreign travel bans, 134
Frost, 20, 22, 28, 33
funding for community colleges, 73

Garcia, 22, 55, 67, 101
Ghazzawi, 30, 34, 91, 100
Giammarella, 29, 34
global, 3, 8, 10, 12–15, 17, 19, 21,
    34, 35, 137, 139, 141, 143, 144,
    149–151, 173, 175, 177, 179, 181,
    183, 185, 187, 189, 191, 193, 195,
    197, 199, 201, 205, 213, 215, 217,
    219, 221, 223–227, 235, 236, 238,
    239
global chaos, 7
global economy, 19, 99, 233
global expansion, 8
González Canché, 71, 72, 74–76, 78,
    80, 82–84, 86, 233
Government of Canada, 64, 66, 67
graduate students, 5, 20, 48, 93, 101,
    102, 180, 186, 228
Green River College, 41, 231
Green River Community College, 6

Hagedorn, 3, 4, 9, 11, 12, 19, 20, 22,
    32, 36, 55, 67, 72, 82, 84, 85, 91,
    101, 157, 159, 168, 170
Hanover Research, 64, 67
Hausman tests, 77
HBCU, 4, 215, 218
heterogeneity, 30, 31, 76, 80, 81, 82,
    96, 101
higher education, 3–5, 7, 8, 10, 13,
    15, 16, 31, 35, 36, 38–40, 45,
    50–52, 54, 55, 57, 58, 66, 70–75,
    81, 83–86, 96, 116, 119, 121, 129,
    130, 133, 135, 138, 142, 143, 148,
    150, 151, 155, 156, 158, 159, 168,
    170, 171, 172, 175, 176, 177, 179,
    181, 184, 185, 186, 188, 189, 192,
    196, 197, 198, 201, 203, 204, 205,
    206, 210, 212–216, 225–230, 232,
    233, 235
Hispanic, 6, 19, 84, 107, 130, 151,
    218, 234
Historically Black Community
    Colleges, 215, 236

homesickness, 158
host institutions, 157, 167
Houston Community College in
    Texas, 3
Houston Community College System,
    40, 231

identities, 107, 116, 169, 170, 182,
    183, 197, 224, 236
Illegal Immigration Reform and
    Immigrant Responsibility Act, 144
immigration, 2, 7, 8, 12, 13, 55, 58,
    61, 65, 67, 91, 93, 94, 96–100,
    102,103, 144, 147, 150, 151, 170,
    172, 194, 205, 206, 212, 213, 217,
    218, 229, 230, 233, 238
immigration policies, 2, 7, 8, 55, 91,
    93, 96–99, 233
in-person classes, 145
indigenous values, 225, 236
Indira Gandhi's National Open
    University, 9
institutionalization, 24, 26
intergroup expectations, 158
international education, 5, 9, 11–14,
    16–18, 20, 21, 23, 31–37, 53–58,
    60, 67, 68, 71, 84, 85, 89, 95,
    101, 103, 116, 121, 129, 133–137,
    148–151, 170–172, 185, 187–197,
    199–202, 205, 209, 212–215, 219,
    223–232, 235–237, 239
international enrollment, 8, 133, 148,
    159
*International Journal of Higher
    Education*, 31, 35
international student enrollment, 5,
    9, 10, 19, 32, 50, 51, 53, 72, 73,
    74, 78, 82, 83, 100, 134, 135, 147,
    159, 183, 231, 238
international students, 1–5, 7–9,
    11–18, 20, 21, 34, 37, 38–51, 53,
    55–57, 61, 67, 83, 87, 89–91, 98,
    100, 118, 121, 128–130, 133,
    135–137, 139, 141, 143, 145, 147,
    149, 151, 155, 156, 158, 162–164,
    167, 173, 174, 184, 185, 196, 201,
    207–209, 215, 217–219, 223, 224,
    226, 227, 232–237, 239
international transfer students, 155,
    160–163, 166, 168–170
internationalization, 4, 3, 7, 10, 12,
    17, 19, 23, 28, 31–34, 36, 38, 51,
    52, 55, 59, 70, 72, 74, 82, 84,

86, 156, 173, 174, 176, 177, 180, 185, 186, 209, 212, 214, 219, 220, 224–227, 233, 238
intersectionality, 96, 97, 169
isolation, 119, 168

job opportunities, 48, 60, 90, 95, 97, 143, 157
Journal of Comparative and International Higher Education, 31

Kidder, 29, 34
Kirkwood Community College, 138–141, 143
Knight, 57, 68, 72, 84
Koyama, 29, 34
Kuh, 137, 149

language, 4, 9, 10, 16, 19, 29, 57, 62–64, 69, 90–92, 95, 97, 99, 104–106, 109–116, 118, 120, 122–126, 128, 136, 139, 145, 158, 159, 170, 186, 197, 219, 221, 234
language learning, 109, 114, 234
Latin America, 6, 29, 34
Latinx college, 104
Lee, 6, 55, 67, 72, 84, 173, 184
Legusov, 18, 55, 56, 58, 60, 62, 63, 64, 65, 66, 67, 68, 69, 70, 233
Levin, 4, 12, 20, 22, 28, 34, 36, 85, 101, 174, 184, 185, 205, 213
local government, 147
lockdown, 142
logistical issues, 142
Lone Star College System, 41, 231
loneliness, 158
Los Angeles Community College District, 91
Lynch, 30, 34, 100

Madison Area Technical College, 6
Malveaux, 3, 4, 6–10, 12–14, 17, 18, 20, 133–138, 140, 142, 144, 146, 148, 149–151, 225, 227, 228, 230–232, 234–236, 238, 239
Mamiseishvili, 9, 13, 58, 68, 71, 84
Mango content, 5
Manhattan Community, 41, 121, 129, 131, 132
marginalized field of study, 31
mentorship, 93
Miami-Dade College, 40, 41, 231

Ministry of Colleges and Universities, 68
Montgomery College, 7, 13, 17, 20, 41, 134, 135, 137, 150, 151, 188, 190, 194, 231, 239
Moodle, 4
Mullin, 72, 73, 84
multilingual ability, 92
Murakami, 142, 143, 150
Muslim, 7, 138, 178
Mwangi, 16, 35, 176–178, 183, 184

NAFSA, 4, 8, 13, 19, 21, 35, 47, 53, 145, 146, 150, 151, 157, 171, 193, 229, 238
National Association of Colleges and Employers, 94, 101
non-academic skills, 90
Northern Virginia Community College, 3, 40, 231

Open Doors, 5, 11, 13, 14, 18, 20, 23, 30, 37, 38, 40, 44–48, 50–54, 84, 89, 101, 129, 135, 149, 150, 155–157, 159, 171, 188, 231–233, 239
Optional Practical Training, 8, 42, 93, 102, 157, 172, 194
Orange Coast College, 41, 137, 141, 144, 231
orientation sessions, 168
Out-State Tuition & Fees, 77, 79
overgeneralization, 96

pandemic, 7, 12, 19, 68, 133, 139, 179, 182, 187, 189, 191–193, 195–199, 201, 235, 236
peer-reviewed studies, 91
Perez-Encinas, 58, 68
Pfeffer, 73, 85
Pima Community College, 6
policy implications, 98
policy issues, 12, 133, 234, 235
political climate, 4, 146
post-COVID predictions, 133

Raby, 3, 8, 12–20, 22, 24, 26, 28, 30, 32–36, 149, 181, 182, 185, 216, 225–227, 232, 233, 238, 239
Redden, 63, 68, 133, 150, 229, 239
research method, 16, 74, 106, 121, 188
research university, 161
revenue via student, 73

244 Index

Richland College, 41
Riley, 29, 35

safety and well-being, 145
Salancik, 73, 85
San Mateo County, 41, 231
Santa Monica College, 9, 40, 41, 91, 231
Seattle Central College, 41, 231
Seneca College, 61, 68, 69
SEVP, 102, 137, 144, 145, 150
Shorter College, 4, 215, 218
Simon Fraser University, 61, 69
Sinophobic slurs, 8
Social Capital, 92
Social Cognitive Career Trajectory Theory, 97
Social Justice, 12, 173, 175, 177, 179, 181, 183, 185, 235, 236
Stein, 16, 35, 176, 177, 185
STEM, 6, 48, 49, 103, 135, 157, 159, 171, 172, 231
stress, 2, 18, 29, 34, 92, 96, 97, 100, 102, 117–122, 124, 126–131, 140, 144, 158, 160, 178, 182, 184, 194, 235
struggles with online learning, 140
Student Engagement, 94, 110, 198, 201, 226
Student Financial Aid survey, 75
student success, 12, 29, 104, 105, 117, 171, 172, 196, 199, 200
student-issued visas, 134
study abroad, 2–4, 6–8, 11, 52, 63, 89, 135–138, 150, 151, 174, 215, 216, 219, 223, 228, 230, 232, 237, 238
subpopulation, 161
SUNY COIL, 5, 13
support services, 12, 26, 33, 104, 126, 155, 167, 170, 189, 193, 198, 199, 200, 211, 214, 236, 238
systematic data, 95

the future, 2, 3, 35, 52, 72, 131, 137, 148, 226, 227
Time Series Analysis, 11, 15, 232, 233
time zone differences, 140–142
time-series, 20
TOEFL, 119, 159, 162
Tompkins-Cortland Community College, 5
traditional international students, 161–163, 166, 167, 169, 170

transfer experience, 160
transfer students, 161, 167
transition, 10, 19, 36, 60, 61, 91, 92, 105, 106, 109–112, 114, 115, 158, 160, 161, 170, 171, 195, 211, 213, 231, 234
travel bans, 138, 173, 178, 179, 181, 182
Trenholm State Community College, 4, 215
Trump administration, 8, 136, 137, 148, 149, 173
tuition, 4–6, 18, 56–58, 60, 61, 63, 64, 72–76, 78–80, 82, 83, 91, 157, 159, 174, 192, 200, 206, 210, 212, 222, 225

undergraduate student, 161
UNESCO, 36, 55, 69, 85, 133, 151, 228, 239
United States, 3, 5, 7, 8, 10–12, 15, 17, 19, 32–34, 37–40, 45–48, 50, 51, 55, 58, 65, 71, 72, 80, 82, 89–95, 97, 99, 101–104, 106–109, 112, 116, 117, 119, 120–127,129, 131, 133–135, 138–142, 144–148, 150, 155–157, 163, 170, 172, 174, 175, 177, 178, 180, 182, 184, 185–189, 191, 194–196, 200, 207, 215, 218, 221, 228, 229, 231, 233, 234, 236, 237
US Bureau of Labor Statistics, 74, 85
US Census Bureau, 90, 104
US counterparts, 48, 95
US Department of Education, 13, 14, 53, 83, 85, 227
US economy, 4, 5, 13, 134, 135, 149, 158

Viggiano, 19, 29, 30, 36, 71, 72, 85, 173–176, 178–180, 182, 184–186, 236
virtual communication, 7

West, 5, 8, 13, 23, 114, 193, 201, 218
White students, 7
Wodak, 16, 33, 36

Zhang, 4, 16, 17, 20, 22, 28–30, 35, 36, 55, 69, 71, 72, 76, 85, 92, 103, 119, 126, 130, 212
Zhou, 29, 36

Printed in the United States
by Baker & Taylor Publisher Services